The Making of *Slap Shot*
Behind the Scenes of the Greatest Hockey Movie

Jonathon Jackson

John Wiley & Sons Canada, Ltd.

Library and Archives Canada Cataloguing in Publication

Jackson, Jonathon
   The making of Slap shot : behind the scenes of the greatest hockey movie ever made / Jonathon Jackson.

Includes index.
ISBN 978-1-118-09649-9

   1. Slap shot (Motion picture).   I. Title.

PN1997.S555J32 2011   791.43'72   C2011-901853-5

ISBN 978-1-118-09649-9 (Paper); 978-0-470-15941-5 (Cloth); 978-0-470-16015-2 (ePDF); 978-0-470-67800-8 (ePub); 978-0-470-54210-1 (Mobi)

Production Credits
Cover design: Ian Koo
Interior design: Adrian So
Typesetter: Thomson Digital
Printer: Kingsport Books
Cover image credit: Photodisc/Thinkstock

Editorial Credits
Executive Editor: Karen Milner
Production Editor: Pauline Ricablanca

John Wiley & Sons Canada, Ltd.
6045 Freemont Blvd.
Mississauga, Ontario
L5R 4J3

Printed in the United States

1 2 3 4 5 STG 15 14 13 12 11

This book is dedicated to my parents, Barry and Marlene Jackson, and to my sons, Tayler, Pake and Bobby.

It is also dedicated to the memories of Strother Martin, George Roy Hill, Brad Sullivan, Ned Tanen, Paul Newman and Dede Allen.

Table of Contents

Table of Contents

Foreword

If rock 'n' roll were a sport . . . . it would have to be hockey. Volatile, lyrical, relentlessly aggressive. This connection took hold upon seeing The Rolling Stones completely rip up Maurice Richard Arena. Hard-hitting, feisty and fearless in their first ever concert in Canada, end of April 1965, two weeks after my team got knocked out early in the Memorial Cup playoffs.

The Beatles at the Forum, Dylan at Back Bay, The Doors at the Whisky, Hendrix in Central Park with the Rascals, Led Zeppelin at the Casino, The Who at the Rock Pile, Pink Floyd at Le Centre Sportif, Black Sabbath at Winterland, Aerosmith at Wolman Rink . . . . And later, right while we're shooting *Slap Shot* who should roll into town? Springsteen and the E Street Band to play a one-night stand at our Johnstown War Memorial, the Chiefs home arena.

One Saturday night I coaxed my teammate Reg Dunlop (51 years young) into Lower Manhattan and CBGB's to see and hear some brand new music. While the Ramones rattled the walls Reggie grinned from ear to ear and gleefully shouted "This is what we're doing every day on the ice."

Newman. Ultimate Punk with a heart of rowdy, unbounded generosity. Lead singer and gang leader with giving hands of perpetual cool, Paul never wavered in his delight with *Slap Shot*, maintaining his experience was "the most fun I ever had making a movie — absolutely!"

Foreword

Braden's striptease is pure rapture. Inspired by the very early Elvis, it launched a vividly delicious riff that continues to come in handy every day of my life.

Mischief, magic, monkey-business, mayhem. Thank you George, Nancy, Ned, the Hansons, all the original Chiefs.

Jonathon Jackson has provided a timeless back beat. Rock steady bass coupled with a mighty set of drums. Jackson has doggedly assembled the boards, fastened the glass, skated some extra miles to flood hard ice in his kick-ass rink. Let's put on the foil. Drop the friggin' puck.

Michael Ontkean

Prologue

From "Slap Shot," the aptly titled hockey blog of the *New York Times*, September 27, 2008:

Hockey mourns the passing of Reggie Dunlop
By Stu Hackel

The Charlestown Chiefs announced today the passing of former coach Reginald (Reggie) Dunlop, who famously coached the Chiefs to the Federal League championship in 1977.

Dunlop died Friday at his home in Westport, Conn. He was 83.

As player-coach of the Chiefs in the mid-70s, Dunlop presided over a rag-tag group of players who were floundering near the basement of the Federal League when he engineered a remarkable turnaround that catapulted the club into the playoffs and, eventually, the league championship.

"This is a sad day for Chiefs fans around the world," said former Chiefs general manager Joe McGrath. "Reggie symbolized the never-say-die underdog spirit of our club that so many people around the world have come to identify with. Our hearts are broken today, but we are all better for having Reg in our lives."

"Reggie was one of a kind," said former Charlestown Times-Herald sports editor Dickie Dunn. "He was a wise veteran with a young attitude. We were good friends away from the rink and he

always would give me inside information and scoops. I'll miss him terribly."

The exploits of the Chiefs have become widely known within hockey circles, both professional and amateur, through the film "Slap Shot," which was based on the team's miraculous reversal of fortune. Untold numbers of hockey fans, players, coaches and executives have memorized lines of dialogue from the film and it is considered one of the best sports movies of all time.

Rarely has there been such a penetrating portrait of any sport's culture and the depiction of this controversial era of hockey, the tumultuous 70s, remains a touchstone of hockey humor three decades later.

Tributes like the above mock obituary speak volumes about the film *Slap Shot*, about Reggie Dunlop and about the man who portrayed him.

The death of Paul Newman on September 26, 2008, was not unexpected. The beloved actor, director, race-car driver, political activist and philanthropist had been suffering from lung cancer. But the news that he was gone was still met by sorrow and grief all around the world.

His many screen performances were reviewed, discussed and dissected by writers, commentators and fans. Highlighted were the roles for which he had received Academy Award nominations — Brick Pollitt, Fast Eddie Felson, Hud Bannon, Lucas Jackson, Michael Gallagher, Frank Galvin, Donald "Sully" Sullivan and John Rooney. Also cited were other popular characters he had brought to the big screen — Ben Quick, Ari Ben Canaan, Lew Harper, Butch Cassidy and Henry Gondorff.

Prologue

The role of Reggie Dunlop also got particular attention. Newman never received any official film industry recognition for his convincing portrayal of the irascible hockey player-coach. In fact, many people believed he had made a terrible mistake in accepting a part that transformed the screen legend into a disreputable low-life. Let's be honest here — Reggie was vulgar, childish, dishonest, manipulative, conniving, opportunistic, abusive and abrasive.

But what a character! Newman delivered a performance in *Slap Shot* that completely transcended all of the character's negative attributes. In spite of everything, Reggie was undoubtedly the hero, the glue that held everyone and everything together . . . and so he would remain until the very end, accountable to no one, not even to himself. That is, had Reggie been the kind of man who searched within himself for things like accountability. It's no wonder that the brilliant film critic Pauline Kael saw right through the shocking (for its time) language and the cartoonish brutality and recognized Newman's work for what it truly was: "the performance of his life — to date."

Newman knew it too. Part of the reason for his superb performance was that he was, in effect, portraying a slightly exaggerated version of himself.

"That character is a lot closer to me than I would care to admit — vulgar, on the skids," he said in a 1982 interview, although he also acknowledged that *Slap Shot* remained "one of my favorite movies."

He wasn't the only one who had a special place in his heart for a film that has been cited numerous times over the years as one of the greatest sports movies ever made. *Slap Shot* and the quasi-fictional Charlestown Chiefs are so revered that the tributes that followed Newman's death included many from the world of hockey and sports:

During a break in their first pre-season game after he died, the Anaheim Ducks showed a clip from the film on their scoreboard. The clip was followed by the words "Paul Newman (a.k.a. Reggie Dunlop) 1925–2008."

Frank Deford, who had penned a scathing review of *Slap Shot* for *Sports Illustrated* in 1977, wrote in the magazine the film had been "a boon to hockey."

The Johnstown Chiefs, who play in the Pennsylvania city where *Slap Shot* was inspired and filmed, and who are named after the Charlestown Chiefs, announced they would wear commemorative patches with Dunlop's No. 7 on their uniforms during the 2008–09 hockey season.

Recognizing that part of the movie was filmed in their home city, depicting a quasi-fictional Syracuse team as Charlestown's rival for the league championship, the Syracuse Crunch retired the No. 7 in Newman's honor prior to their 2008–09 home opener. The number remained out of circulation for the entire campaign.

Surrounding all of this was the release of a new *Slap Shot* movie sequel in November 2008, as well as the memoirs of Dave Hanson, a real-life pro hockey player who has portrayed Jack Hanson in all three *Slap Shot* films to date. Appropriately, Newman provided a promotional blurb for Hanson's book.

As his health began to decline in 2007, prompting Newman to announce his retirement from the film industry, he very kindly also contributed to the book you hold in your hands. Although he was never fond of being interviewed, he graciously answered via fax and email a number of questions about *Slap Shot* and Reggie Dunlop.

Prologue

It has been the author's intention to create a comprehensive work that is worthy of its associations with *Slap Shot* and with Paul Newman and his legacy. Although Newman is no longer with us in body, his spirit will live on, as will the timeless and unforgettable characters he brought to life in an entertainment career that spanned more than 55 years.

Nancy Dowd, who wrote *Slap Shot* and created the template of the character of Reggie Dunlop, said as much on September 29, 2008, when she commented on the *New York Times* blog about Stu Hackel's mock obituary:

I am pleased to inform you and Coach Dunlop's devoted fans on the New York Times' Slap Shot site that reports of his demise are, happily, like those of Mark Twain: premature. Even "Slap Shot 2" couldn't kill him. He skates eternally in our memories, in our hearts and, most important, our DVD's. In fact, I ran into him recently at The Palm Isle. He looked fabulous. The fur collar on his signature leather coat was impeccable and his platforms stood tall. However, in these sad days, he insisted I pass along his immortal advice to one all: don't ever play Lady of Spain again.

Old time hockey. Du hockey comme dans le temps.

Love and kisses to the grieving Tri-State area,

Nancy

Chapter 1

Entertainment for the Whole Family!

—— ● ——

You have to wonder if Michael McCambridge ever got to watch a hockey game before he ended up with somebody's, well, you know.

His mother, Charlestown Chiefs owner Anita McCambridge, wasn't above violence in hockey as long as she could make a profit from it, but she'd be damned if she would ever allow her children to watch the sport. Kids are impressionable, you see. They might stick up a bank. Heroin. You name it.

Imagine Anita's horror at learning that the members of her former hockey team, the scourge of the Federal League, over time had evolved but not necessarily changed; they're still the face of goon hockey at its peak. But, strangely, they've also become the epitome of family-friendly entertainment.

The Hanson Brothers were initially shunned and mocked by their disapproving teammates. Their intellect, or lack thereof, was called into question by their coach who found them so frightfully bizarre that he vowed they would not play for his club. Today, however, they are idolized by millions of fans around the world, from 82-year-old legend Gordie Howe to children whose parents weren't even born when the Hansons stepped onto the War Memorial ice to commence what fans have dubbed "the greatest shift in hockey history."

Go ahead, Google it. You'll see.

It's difficult to explain the transformation of the Hansons from "retards" and "criminals" to icons who still tour North American arenas every year, dispensing their special brand of tough, in-your-face hockey, without having changed a whole lot about their style. These three men, all in their mid-50s, are also still making movies, the latest of which was subtitled "The Junior League," earned a PG rating and was aimed at audiences of all ages.

Then again, sometimes you just have to appreciate the irony, rather than try to explain or justify it.

Anyway, let's give Anita McCambridge the benefit of the doubt. She seemed like a smart woman — maybe she too eventually came to see the Hansons and the Chiefs as more than just cash cows. After all, she wouldn't have been the first person to come to a particular judgment about these people and then change their mind later.

For example, Frank Deford, in a review of *Slap Shot* that was published in the March 7, 1977, edition of *Sports Illustrated*, called Paul Newman "aimlessly vile" in reference to his scene with Kathryn Walker, McCambridge's portrayer. He also said Newman was simply out of his element.

Chapter 1

"*Slap Shot's* player-coach should properly be a lost, fey figure, desperate at the end of the road. That's the way these fellows are. Instead, Newman plays him with the cocky insouciance of a Butch Cassidy, and that is simply not the character."

In a tribute to Newman that appeared in *SI* on September 30, 2008, Deford sang a different tune: " . . . hockey people adored him for his performance in *Slap Shot*. That movie was such a boon to hockey, just as he made pool more glamorous, playing Fast Eddie Felsen in *The Hustler* and then in *The Color of Money*. If Paul Newman was connected, it must be good."

But the magazine had long since atoned for Deford's scathing initial thoughts. This process actually began with a backhanded compliment only two weeks after that review was published, in the March 21, 1977, Scorecard column, edited by Robert W. Creamer. Creamer wrote that people in hockey had been criticizing the film for what they claimed was its focus on violence, calling it unrealistic that the on-ice shenanigans would be even tacitly encouraged, as was depicted in the film. But Creamer also detailed a recent real-life incident in which John Ferguson, then the coach of the New York Rangers, had become so incensed during a game that he flew into a rage, using foul language, making rude gestures and hitting a linesman with a thrown water bottle. He was fined $500 for the tirade, a punishment Creamer seemed to think was ridiculous.

"Ted Williams was once fined $5,000 for spitting in the general direction of the crowd. And that was before inflation. Maybe we'd better take another look at *Slap Shot*," Creamer wrote.

Well, it was a start.

In August 1999, *SI* columnist Steve Rushin wrote about the top sports films of all time and included a reference to Charlestown's heroes. "Every movie ever made about a team of profane outcasts — Mean Machine in *The Longest Yard,* the Chiefs in *Slap Shot,* Chico's Bail Bonds in *The Bad News Bears* — has been, without exception, brilliant."

The magazine produced its first Top 20 Sports Movies list in February 2001, and *Slap Shot* made the list at No. 9. The film's profile grew starting in 2002 when its first sequel was released and so was a 25th anniversary DVD that included not only commentary by the Hanson Brothers but also the film's original soundtrack. The music had been replaced by generic sound-alike songs for TV airings of the movie and on its VHS releases, but viewers could now once again thrill to the authentic 70s sounds of Maxine Nightingale, Leo Sayer, Elton John and Sonny James while, equally true to the 70s, Newman broke one fashion law after another.

In late March 2003, the magazine's staff placed Newman at No. 3 on its list of actors who had turned in the most believable athletic performances, citing his ability to lie, cheat and play dirty "like a pro." At the same time, the staff named *Slap Shot* as the top hockey film of all time. "When you talk about hilariously foul-mouthed movies, this comedy about a hapless minor league hockey team is the gold standard."

The staff compiled a new list in August 2003, the all-encompassing Top 50 Greatest Sports Movies. *Slap Shot* was slotted in at No. 5. A little more than a year later, Mark Bechtel commemorated the Academy Award nominations by awarding fictional "sports flick Oscars." He chose Lindsay Crouse as best supporting actress for *Slap Shot.* Brad Sullivan fell just shy of a nomination for best supporting actor, but Newman was chosen best actor for playing Reggie Dunlop. He beat out himself in *The Hustler*, Kevin Costner for *Bull Durham*, Gene Hackman for *Hoosiers* and Robert De Niro for *Raging Bull*.

"He was absolutely perfect for the role. He was at the film's center and was surrounded by an oddball, hilarious cast, but he never let the movie descend to the level of farce," Bechtel wrote, also praising Newman for allowing his co-stars to deliver most of the film's memorable lines, "while he gave it all a realistic edge, keeping the film grounded — funny without being stupid."

When *Sports Illustrated* chose the Hanson Brothers for the cover of its summer double issue in 2007 and included a major feature story on the Hansons by Austin Murphy, it was official — the film's rehabilitation in the eyes of *SI* was finally complete.

Famed movie reviewer Gene Siskel acknowledged his own first impression of *Slap Shot* had been wrong. He appeared with reviewing partner Roger Ebert on *Late Show with David Letterman* on September 10, 1993, and Letterman asked the pair if they had ever had occasion to rethink an initial review.

"*Slap Shot* was an example," Siskel said.

"Oh, I like that movie, great movie," Letterman interjected, jokingly referring to the Hansons as "the Ramone Brothers."

"I agree," Siskel continued. "My initial review was mixed and then I saw it, like, two weeks later, thankfully, and I knew it was a terrific film, a great working-class story. A wonderful risky performance from Paul Newman . . . just a terrific film."

Newman's performance was indeed risky. He had played ne'er do wells before, characters you weren't supposed to like but did anyway. But the role of Chiefs player-coach Reggie Dunlop took Newman to a level that was arguably lower than that occupied by, say, Hud Bannon. *Sports Illustrated* was right — Dunlop did lie, cheat and play dirty like a pro. He refused to grow up. He duped, betrayed and threatened friends and blackmailed his boss to get what he wanted. He expressed his frustration and anger with the vilest of words. He seemed at times to bask in his own sleaziness. His attempt to go straight near the end, sincere though it might have been, lasts only until he realizes that the path he has followed throughout the story could actually lead him to a pot of gold after all. "I could make a goddamned fortune," he exults.

Of course, in real life, Newman had already made a fortune as well as a legend, having enjoyed one of the most successful and prolific careers in film history. Although he was known for his handsome features, particularly his striking blue eyes, he was a talented actor who didn't like to take the easy route. He refused to rely on his looks. He consistently tackled projects that he found interesting and challenging. One such film was 1964's *The Outrage*, in which Newman disguised himself with a fake wig and mustache and brown contact lenses to play a Mexican bandit and rapist.

Yet, for all the times Newman had pushed the envelope throughout his career, in *Slap Shot* he took a chance that few others of his stature would have dared. This was because he agreed to play not only Dunlop but also the character exactly as intended, with no softening of his persona or language, no winking at the camera. It must be remembered that the use of profanity, gratuitous or otherwise, in mainstream films was still very new. When John Schuck, as Painless Pole Waldowski, told another character in *M*A*S*H* that his "fucking head (was) coming right off," it was the first time the word "fuck" had ever been used in the dialogue of a major motion picture. The year was 1970.

The criticism Newman received for *Slap Shot* was probably to have been expected. Despite that, he never shied away from his performance; on the contrary — he took pride in it and went to great lengths to defend it and the film. For the rest of his life, he remained very proud of *Slap Shot* and his participation in it, repeatedly telling people that he had never had so much fun making a movie.

"*Slap Shot* is one of my favorite films and Reggie Dunlop is one of my favorite characters," he said in a June 2007 interview. "They are both classics."

His opinion is now widely recognized, and his performance is now seen as proof of his immense talent as an actor. Who else could have made Reggie a likable character without changing any of his defining characteristics? The noted *Chicago Sun-Times* film critic Richard Roeper (*Ebert & Roeper*) suggests no one else could have straddled that line between playing Reggie as an absolute bastard with few redeeming qualities and turning him into an obvious clown, winking at the camera.

"With Newman, you didn't get that sense. He's that guy (on the screen)," Roeper says, suggesting Burt Reynolds and Robert Redford as two actors of the time who wouldn't have been able to resist mugging. "You just never get the sense that he's giving us a hint, 'Oh, come on, you know I'm just putting it on — I'm a good guy!'"

That's not to say Newman didn't acknowledge the audience at certain points, but his work in these scenes is very subtle. He acted them out in a way that took for granted the viewers' intelligence; Newman believed we would understand, without being told, exactly why Reggie is doing what he is doing — the sudden stop after walking past the Hansons' hotel room where they are playing with their race cars, the last look back at the pay phone after being hung up on while trying to call Francine, the quick glance we get right before he opens the locker room door to greet the Hyannisport police officers. "He's bringing us into the performance without overdoing it," Roeper says.

Howard Baldwin recognized the brilliance of Newman and the film right away. He lived through hockey's 1970s goon age as the owner of the World Hockey Association's New England Whalers. He moved with the Whalers to the National Hockey League and eventually owned two other teams in the league before moving into motion picture development and production. As such, he can offer a unique perspective on the success and continuing relevance of *Slap Shot*.

"It was a very smart, entertaining movie that reflected that era," says Baldwin, whose film projects include the hockey movies *Sudden Death*, with Jean-Claude Van Damme, and *Mystery, Alaska*, with Russell Crowe, as well as the Academy Award-nominated *Ray*, about legendary musician Ray Charles. "If it's a good movie, it doesn't matter whether it's a sports movie or a love story or a war movie or whatever — it's a good movie. And these guys made a good movie. The characters were a lot of fun. You got vested in the characters. That's what it takes to make a good movie."

Chapter 1

Hockey players, naturally enough, were the first people to get it, especially those who have lived in spartan conditions on rickety buses and in shabby dressing rooms.

"I think every hockey player has definitely seen it at least a couple of times and knows all the lines," says Cincinnati Cyclones captain Barret Ehgoetz, who has watched it many times while having ridden his fair share of buses around his home province of Ontario and across the United States.

"I've only seen *Slap Shot* probably 50 to 100 times," Jeff Jackson, head coach of the Notre Dame men's hockey team, told Allison Hayes for the ND athletics news site www.blueandgold.com in December 2007. "It's always one of the favorites on the bus trips."

"When I coached juniors, that movie was playing on the bus every year," Mike Babcock, Stanley Cup-winning coach of the Detroit Red Wings, told the *San Jose Mercury News* in January 2008.

A year earlier, in February 2007, Babcock told John Niyo of the *Detroit News* that during his coaching career he has used clips and lines from the movie to motivate his players or just to get some laughs. "There's just so many unbelievable lines in that movie."

"In juniors," Red Wings veteran Kirk Maltby said to Niyo, "I think it was probably on the TV on every bus trip we ever took."

"I think the first time I saw it was when I was a major junior player on the buses," NHL goalie turned TV analyst Darren Pang said in a September 2008 interview with Bob Young of the *Arizona Republic*. "It was the No. 1 VHS on the bus. You always had guys on the team who could recite every line."

They not only love *Slap Shot*, they take pride in it, just as Newman and his co-stars did. It was an attitude that engendered itself early on in the production.

"It was a blessed venture from the very beginning," says Jennifer Warren, who played Dunlop's estranged wife Francine. "The script was golden; we all fell in love with the script, and we came together for the joy of doing wonderful material. That's why everybody was so happy on that set."

Paul D'Amato, who played Chiefs nemesis Tim "Dr. Hook" McCracken, says the movie has lasted and still resonates because it was real and it came across that way.

"This movie has the things in it that I think Aristotle and the classics would be proud of. When you think about Aristotle's *Poetics* — plot, character, thought, language, music and spectacle — this is what he wrote out, saying these things are important. If you look at *Slap Shot*, it meets all of those criteria, number one. Number two, there wasn't a special effect in it. There were guys and girls doing things in their character via this dialogue to accomplish this task and make people laugh. And people laugh 30 years later because the same things are funny."

The late Ned Tanen, who was the president of Universal Pictures when *Slap Shot* was produced, had the final say in the approval process that saw it brought to the big screen. He said that while he felt it was hilarious, he also recognized it as social commentary — screenwriter Nancy Dowd's depiction of contemporary America, particularly Rust Belt America. It's a viewpoint that has become more apparent with time.

"It was a brilliant movie. It's defined this country and not necessarily with a lot of attractive qualities," Tanen said in

Chapter 1

February 2007. "Unfortunately, they were true then and they've become more true now, much more."

When you think of a cult classic film, *Slap Shot* should immediately come to mind. *USA Today* film reporter Susan Wloszczyna explains her personal criteria for a cult classic and how *Slap Shot* fits the description.

"It's one that didn't start off maybe being appreciated in its time, but a few people took to it. It touched a chord in them that doesn't get touched normally by more mainstream, normal films. What it needs is the sense of space between then and now," she says. "I think people were so hung up by the sex and the language and the violence and the fact that Paul Newman was in the middle of it all that they didn't quite understand that (*Slap Shot*) got at something that was very unique to a sports film, and very real and honest. I do think cult films tend to have exaggeration, which this does, but also at the core there is some kind of honest emotion, a rawness that doesn't get exposed enough in mainstream movies because they want to appeal to the broadest audience possible.

"And there are not a lot of good hockey films. There are just not. This is one that really gets at something about the sport that people appreciate."

"It's literally my favorite sports movie," says Barbara Morgan, executive director and co-founder of the Austin Film Festival, in the capital city of Texas. "I love that movie. I like comedies, but that's a special movie. It's not just the inappropriateness of it; you could see it happening. It seemed not so much ridiculous as more accurate, life on a minor league hockey team. And the casting was great. It's a film, honestly, that you could never make today. That's, I guess, a little bit of what I love about it. It really is a film you could never make today."

While many critics have reconsidered their initial opinions of *Slap Shot*, legendary journalist and author Dan Jenkins has never needed to do so. He wrote in *GQ* in November 2007 that it was "the best sports film of the past 50 years." He goes even further today.

"As a lifelong sportswriter I am the first to proclaim *Slap Shot* the best sports movie ever made," he says. "Why? Because it was not only falling-down hilarious and captured the good-natured profanity of sports, but at the same time circled all the edges of truth, and even underlined many of them. Most sports movies are embarrassingly stupid and naive because they're made by Hollywood nitwits who fall into two categories: jock-sniffing hero worshippers and naïve punks.

"I have worked in Hollywood and even got three films on the screen but never had any control, thus I marveled at the accident that became *Slap Shot*. It's what my novel *Semi-Tough* should have been on the screen, but wasn't, and *Slap Shot* remains one of those movies I wish I'd written. How it got to the screen as well as it did remains a modern miracle, like *Casablanca*."

With apologies to the 1980 U.S. Olympic hockey team, let's see how the first "miracle on ice" came to be.

Chapter 2

The Toughest Team in the Federal League

———— ● ————

The Johnstown Jets ended up as world-beaters, but they were a struggling club in the North American Hockey League when Nancy Dowd came into their lives, and they into hers, in late 1974.

Even now, it seems a curious match. The NAHL was a gritty minor league circuit that ranked low on the pro hockey food chain, at least two steps below the elite National Hockey League. Dowd, meanwhile, was significantly more up-market. A native of Framingham, Massachusetts, she was a graduate of prestigious Smith College, where she had majored in French, and where she was embarrassed by her roommate's liberal use of profanity. She also earned a masters degree from UCLA.

Nancy's only sibling was a brother, Ned, six years younger. He had also aspired to higher education, graduating from

Bowdoin College in Brunswick, Maine, and studying for a year at McGill University in Montreal. But while Nancy had chosen a career in the arts, working as a "putative writer" in Los Angeles, Ned had taken a different tack.

"I was a liberal arts major, but I had great designs on being a professional hockey player," Ned says. "That's all I wanted to do at that time in my life."

He had played hockey since childhood, and he was good enough to land a place on the roster of Bowdoin, a Division II team in the NCAA. He scored 43 goals in three seasons of varsity at Bowdoin and then played a year at McGill, registering 15 goals and 46 points while playing for coach Herb Madill.

"Ned was a phenomenal hockey player," says Bob O'Reilly, who played with Dowd at McGill and against him in the NAHL. "He was by far the best player on our team and probably top five in the league."

Madill says Dowd "had the body of a Greek god," an assessment O'Reilly agrees with. They remember his powerful skating stride and an incredible wrist shot, comparable to that of latter-day Toronto Maple Leafs captain Wendel Clark. But they also recall that despite his size — 6'3", 210 pounds — Dowd wanted little to do with physical play on the ice.

"He was naturally strong but it just wasn't in his makeup," O'Reilly says, noting that this was a problem for a pro hockey player in the early and mid 1970s. "In today's world, he'd be in the NHL — not even a doubt in my mind."

Dowd's play at McGill earned him a free agent contract with the NHL's St. Louis Blues, who had an affiliation agreement with the Johnstown Jets, and he scored 32 goals as a rookie in Johnstown. That got him a look with the Kalamazoo Wings of the International Hockey League in the fall of 1974, but it didn't work out and he soon returned to the Jets. Trouble was afoot when he got there.

The Jets got off to a terrible start, losing game after game. Attendance had plummeted in the previous season and the on-ice product wasn't luring fans back. There seemed to be a question of whether the Jets had a future in Johnstown, or anywhere for that matter. The players knew things were getting desperate. They commiserated about their situation and, very late one night, or very early one morning, a drunken Dowd phoned his older sister Nancy.

Nancy, in an online letter to *Slap Shot* fans on the website www.madbrothers.com, recalled that Ned told her what was happening. She asked him who owned the team. He replied that he didn't know. "And at that moment I knew I was going to write the screenplay that would become *Slap Shot*."

The question of who owned her brother's hockey team so intrigued Nancy that within a short time she had written an outline for a story about "a loser team in a loser town" and about "a man desperate to stay free as the Chrysler plant moves ever nearer." She knew the story could not progress beyond that simple outline unless she immersed herself in Ned's surroundings. She needed to be in Johnstown, to see the Jets, to see how they lived and worked, what they were up against. So she packed up and flew back east. No one could possibly have known it at the time, but it was a move that would result in cinematic history beyond anyone's wildest dreams.

—— ● ——

The NAHL's roots, and those of the Jets, were in the Eastern Hockey League, which had begun in 1933 as an amateur loop that grew out of an intramural league at Madison Square Garden in New York City. Its founder was Thomas Lockhart, who served as its one and only commissioner until it ceased operations in 1973.

For much of its existence after it became a fully professional league in 1954, the EHL was looked upon as the wild west of hockey. There was very little job security in the sport, with only six teams in the NHL until 1967. Hundreds of players vied every year for 100 or so available NHL jobs. Most of those who made it were never able to feel comfortable — they knew there were scores of players one and two levels below them who would literally do anything for their roster spot.

Hockey had always been a tough, rugged sport — a "combination of ballet and murder," as celebrated Canadian poet Al Purdy termed it. Hall of Fame players such as Eddie Shore and Ted Lindsay made their names and reputations with equal amounts of talent and truculence. Even the game's foremost superstars, Maurice (Rocket) Richard and Gordie Howe, could and did handle themselves impressively against all comers.

"Everyone was tough enough to take care of themselves," Marcel Pronovost, another Hall of Famer, told Dave Waddell of the *Montreal Gazette* in a December 2007 interview. "We had to be because if we didn't take care of ourselves, we knew we'd get sent to the minors. That's the place you really wanted to avoid because that's where the real enforcers were."

"There were a lot of good players who were sent (to the EHL) that wouldn't play there just because of the reputation of the league," says Reg Kent, who played for the Johnstown Jets from 1965 to 1974.

The EHL featured some of the toughest and most vicious characters who ever laced up skates — John Brophy of the Long Island Ducks, Norm Ryder of the Nashville Dixie Flyers and Blake Ball of the New Haven Blades, to name a few. The top NHL bad men rarely approached 200 penalty minutes per season and only two men ever hit that plateau prior to 1969. By contrast, the numbers in the EHL were often mind-boggling — "Indian" Joe Nolan set the tone in 1955–56 with 352 minutes, 20 years before he became Clarence "Screaming Buffalo" Swamptown in *Slap Shot*. Ball, who would play Gilmore Tuttle in the film, racked up at least 287 minutes for seven years in a row.

"The league was really, truly run from the standpoint of 'anything went,'" Kent says. "If you got in a stick fight with a guy, they'd throw you out of the game and that was the end of that. Try a stick fight today and see what happens — you're banned for life."

That's not to say you had to be a thug or even a fighter to last in the EHL, because that wasn't necessarily true. But you had to be mentally tough. Only the strong-willed survived in a league where teams carried only 14 men on their rosters — one goalie, nine forwards and four defencemen.

"If you could play in that league, you could play any-where in the world," says Ted McCaskill, who was an extra in *Slap Shot*.

McCaskill played pro hockey for 13 years, five of them in the EHL with Nashville. He was 26 when he came into the loop out of senior hockey in his hometown, Kapuskasing, Ontario. By the time he left the EHL, he was one of its most feared fighters and stickmen. His proficiency with his stick was such that he was the inspiration for the *Slap Shot* character

"Dr. Hook." Really, it's not much of a stretch from Ted McCaskill to Tim McCracken.

"The first year I played in that league, I thought I was going to get killed. I was just a hockey player trying to make a living," McCaskill says. "But you go into places like Johnstown and Philadelphia and Long Island and New Haven, man, they were tough. They'd kick your ass just to try to beat you. So I figured after that first year, boy, I'd better get tough. And I did. And if I was going to be tough, I was going to be the toughest."

Howard Baldwin came into this environment in 1966 eager to start a career in professional hockey management. The Philadelphia Flyers were going to enter the NHL as an expansion team the following year and they hired Baldwin to help run the Jersey Devils, their farm team in the Philadelphia suburb of Cherry Hill, N.J. His title was business manager, although he also drove the team bus on occasion and even coached the Devils for a week during that first season. Three other people staffed the front office — a secretary, coach Vic Stasiuk and public relations consultant Stu Nahan, a former minor-league goalie and future broadcasting legend whose main job was doing play-by-play for the Philadelphia Eagles football team.

Baldwin had played hockey in school and was the son of the late Ian Baldwin, who played three years of varsity at Harvard and was named the Crimson's most valuable player in 1932. But Baldwin had never seen hockey like it was played in the EHL. He remembers being "horrified" by what he saw in the first games of the 1966–67 season. It wasn't long, though, before he was hooked.

"Every game was three or four hours because there were so many fights," Baldwin says. "Yet there was a character and a charm and an appeal to it that made it very much like what *Slap Shot* captured. I don't know how to put it. It was almost romantic, in a way. It was a pretty fun era."

In years to come, Baldwin would help get the World Hockey Association off the ground, spearhead that league's merger with the NHL, own or co-own three NHL clubs and win a Stanley Cup with the Pittsburgh Penguins in 1992. But nothing ever quite matched up to his single season in the EHL, when the Devils went all the way to the league final against Nashville. "That year was my favorite of all the years I had in professional hockey," he says.

———— ● ————

In 1973, the EHL split along geographic lines into two new entities, the NAHL and the Southern Hockey League. The Jets, who had been founded in 1950 and who were consistently part of the EHL after 1955, became charter members of the NAHL. But they didn't get off to a good start; after compiling the fourth-best record in the final season of the 12-team EHL, the Jets slumped to fifth place out of seven clubs in the new league. They finished 44 points behind the first-place Syracuse Blazers, who went on to win the first Lockhart Cup as playoff champions.

The prospects for Johnstown's second NAHL season took a big hit when veteran Reg Kent, who had led the team in scoring in 1973–74 with 86 points, was traded to the rival Binghamton Broome Dusters. The deal fell apart and Kent headed west to play in Spokane. He had scored 274 goals and 818 points in his nine seasons in Johnstown, and his offensive skills would be missed.

Dave Johnson had scored a team-high 41 goals but was also gone, bound for Denver. As it turned out, only seven men who had worn a Jets uniform in 1973–74 would return the following season. Only four of them had finished among the team's top 10 scorers; Ned Dowd was one of them. But there was reason to be optimistic. Jets legend Dick Roberge, the all-time minor league scoring champion, agreed to serve as coach and general manager. Veteran Galen Head had been player-coach the previous year, but he was happy to give up the bench responsibilities, and he assumed the on-ice captaincy.

Returning to the Jets after an absence of several seasons was John Gofton, who had once registered a 63-goal campaign in Johnstown, although his lasting fame would eventually come from being cast in *Slap Shot* as the drunken Nick Brophy of the Hyannisport Presidents.

The Jets also had a significant Minnesota flavor. Team architect John Mitchell, whose title at the time was "executive director," had long held a soft spot in his heart for the North Star State, having spent several years there as a player with the old minor-pro Duluth Hornets.

Mike Crupi was the first Minnesota player recruited by Mitchell to play in Johnstown, debuting with the Jets in 1967. He was followed by Jack Dale and Dick Paradise and all three performed very well, with Dale scoring 100 points in 1968–69 and Paradise and Crupi both registering more than 200 minutes in penalties in their only full seasons with the Jets.

Crupi was a defenceman who liked to play it rough. Many people believe he would eventually have made it to the NHL if he hadn't been killed in a car crash at age 22 in January 1969, an incident that is thought to have inspired the late, unseen *Slap Shot* character of Jacky St. Pierre — "he could have been great."

Chapter 2

"He was real popular," Ron Docken says of Crupi's reputation in Johnstown. "After him, the Minnesota kids were held in high regard. I happened to be one of the people who went out there and a couple of other people followed me."

Docken, a Bloomington-born goaltender who was destined to play Yvon Lebrun in *Slap Shot*, was turning 26 at the start of the 1974–75 season. It would be his third campaign in Johnstown and he had established himself as the team's No. 1 netminder. Docken had played at the University of Minnesota, where his coach was a former NHLer named Glen Sonmor, who happened to be John Mitchell's son-in-law.

Sonmor had left the university in 1972 and was now running the Minnesota Fighting Saints of the upstart World Hockey Association, a rival to the established NHL. The Fighting Saints, who played in the state capital of St. Paul, were formed to go head-to-head with the NHL's Bloomington-based Minnesota North Stars. The wily Mitchell decided to firm up the Johnstown–Minnesota connection through an affiliation agreement with the Fighting Saints — a deal which ostensibly meant the Jets would develop prospects for the big club. But Sonmor and his staff had to be careful; it was just as likely that Mitchell would pull strings to land better players for his own operation.

"He wanted to win. He was looking after his own interests," Sonmor says. "And he was a great judge of talent."

The new affiliation brought 20-year-old Dave Hanson to Johnstown — driven there by Docken, in fact, after the Jets training camp in Niagara Falls, Ontario. Never having been to Johnstown before, he was completely unprepared for his first look at the steel town. It was getting dark when he and Docken arrived, and the sky was filled with smoke and the occasional burst of fire from the stacks at the steel mill. He wrote in his 2008 autobiography, *Slap Shot Original*, that it felt like he was falling into "the bowels of hell."

Hanson was born in Cumberland, Wisconsin, about 85 miles northeast of St. Paul, but his family moved to the Minnesota capital when he was a toddler. He was an All-City athlete in hockey, baseball and football in high school and received a hockey scholarship to the University of Minnesota, but he left in his second year without ever having played for the varsity team because he felt junior hockey would be a more direct route to the pros.

Two years of junior in St. Paul both ended with league championships. Hanson also earned the nickname "Killer" for his take-no-prisoners style, and the Fighting Saints didn't need much convincing of his potential. They made him their fifth choice in the 1974 WHA draft. But he needed seasoning before he could step into the big league, and the man who ran the Jets was more than happy to add the youngster to his roster.

"Johnny Mitchell knew talent and he knew how to put a team together," Hanson says. "He knew the kind of team that Johnstown liked and that's what he put together that year."

Dave Hanson reconnected with two old foes at training camp, Jeff and Jack Carlson, and he met their younger brother Steve there for the first time. The Carlsons, who hailed from a Minnesota town called Virginia, were also in Johnstown courtesy of the Fighting Saints, but really it was like they had been destined for the steel town from the very beginning.

Virginia is located in the Mesabi Iron Range, the largest of four distinct iron deposits in northeastern Minnesota. The

region was unpopulated until iron ore was discovered there
in the late 1880s, and the resource-based industries of mining and timber have dominated the local economy ever since.
Places such as Virginia grew in prominence as the iron ore
fueled the development of a booming American steel industry, the mineral sent from the Range to Duluth and shipped
from there to steel mills in cities such as Detroit, Cleveland,
Pittsburgh and Johnstown.

Hockey was a prominent sport on the Range from the very
beginning. Although Canada is acknowledged as the sport's
birthplace, it was introduced to the United States in the 1890s
and immediately become popular in places there even as it
was still spreading across its home and native land.

Ice polo, played on skates, was for many years a popular winter game in Minnesota and many other parts of the
northern US, but Minnesotans took to hockey eagerly. The
first covered ice rink in the state opened in Minneapolis
in 1900, and one year later four teams joined together to
form the Twin Cities Senior Amateur League. Players in the
northern parts of the state also quickly became proficient,
leading to the creation of elite teams in places like Duluth
and Two Harbors, both on the shore of Lake Superior, and
Eveleth, a few miles south of Virginia on what is now US
Route 53.

Eveleth's clubs were consistent winners of state championships at the high school and men's amateur levels, and its
steady output of players to the college and professional ranks
led to it being chosen as the home of the United States Hockey
Hall of Fame when it was established in 1973. But there was
good hockey also being played in neighboring communities
such as Virginia.

"Basically, it's a lifestyle. The kids still go out on the ponds and skate, play pick-up games. It's part of the whole aura of hockey," says Bill Hanna, executive editor of the Virginia-based newspaper, the *Mesabi Daily News*.

Virginia is the hometown of Olympic hockey players Steve Sertich and John "Bah" Harrington, the latter a member of the 1980 Miracle on Ice gold medal winners. But its most famous hockey products are the Carlson brothers, Jeff, Jack and Steve, who exemplified a rugged style of hockey that Hanna says is emblematic of Virginia — of the Range as a whole, in fact.

"It's a tough area. It's very resilient, and part of that is because of the mining economy. People know they have to fight and scratch for a living, and that plays out on the rinks too. Not dirty, but tough. It's tied to the heritage of the whole area."

"Iron Range hockey, in some ways, is probably similar to Canadian hockey. There's skill involved, but it's hard-nosed hockey," agrees Keith Hendrickson. "Tough, in your face, 'see you in the corner' kind of stuff."

Another Virginia native, Hendrickson is the longtime head coach of the city's high school hockey team, the Blue Devils. He played for the team when his father, Dave Hendrickson, was the coach, and the Carlson boys were his teammates.

"I'm a few years younger, but I played with Jeff, Jack and Steve when I was a ninth grader. They were good guys, good teammates," he recalls. "There were three of us ninth graders on that team and there were a lot of seniors who were Jack and Jeff's age, and there were a lot of tough guys, not just Jack and Jeff. It was kind of intimidating to go to practice every day, just hoping it wasn't your day when you were going to get picked on by one of those guys. But it never really happened; they were good. It was a great era, really, for Iron Range hockey. It was a really high caliber back then."

Steve Carlson describes growing up in Virginia as a Mystery, Alaska-type town where, in the winters, everything recreational revolved around hockey. There was one indoor arena and four outdoor rinks, all equipped with lights, all available for play most any time of the day or night.

"It was cold, so you would put your skates on at home and skate up the street, jump on the ice and play," he says. "We had a warming shack there, so you'd play for 15 or 20 minutes, go in and thaw yourself, then go again. It was all day. There was nothing like it."

The Carlsons lived in a part of town known as Ridgewood. Jack Carlson Sr. and some other men built the outdoor rink in Ridgewood with donated lumber and other materials. The elder Carlson worked for a local mining company which provided whatever was needed — lights, nets, paint for the red and blue lines on the ice, and more.

The handy father also built a makeshift Zamboni to flood the ice. Every Saturday night, he would hook up the tank to the family car and drive it to the city's utility department, where he would fill the tank with hot water. Ten or 15 kids with shovels and whisk brooms would be at the rink, sweeping away the snow that had accumulated on the ice. Jack Sr. would tow the tank around the ice, the water emerging from a pipe and flooding the ice as he drove. A cloth attached to the pipe would smooth the surface as it was freshened with the hot water. The result, after sitting overnight, was a pristine rink that Steve still cherishes today in his memories.

"We would have perfect ice for the Sunday afternoon games. The rule was, no one could skate on it until game time. It would be as flat as could be, like a lake with no wind."

The hockey played there, however, was rarely pristine. Steve Sertich remembers Ridgewood as a tough area of Virginia, and he says the games played there were generally more physical than on the city's other outdoor rinks. But the Carlson boys thrived in that environment. They were all big, strong and athletic, and they excelled at various sports.

"I played baseball with all of them too. Jeff was our pitcher when we went to the Little League Regionals. We lost in Rapid City, South Dakota, but Jeff was our big pitcher. He could throw the ball," says Sertich, the head coach of the women's hockey team at Bemidji State University in Minnesota.

Mike is the oldest Carlson boy and, according to youngest brother Steve, was the best hockey player in the family. Mike was a defenceman with size and power — he was 6'5" and weighed 220 pounds while still in high school — but he soured on the game as a teenager and instead turned to basketball.

Jeff and Jack Jr., three and four years younger than Mike, stayed with hockey through high school. Many Virginia High School graduates were given opportunities to play hockey in college — Steve Sertich starred at Colorado College while his older brother Mike Sertich, Bah Harrington and Keith Hendrickson were all standouts at the University of Minnesota-Duluth. Those opportunities, however, weren't made available to the Carlsons. They had to find another route. In 1972, they found it in Minneapolis, where the Junior Bruins were entered in the new Can-Am Junior Hockey League.

That's where they met Dave Hanson for the first time. Hanson was with another Can-Am team, the Minnesota Junior Stars, and the two squads quickly became rivals. It wasn't long before Hanson was dropping the gloves and chucking the knuckles with the Bruins' tough guys. He remembers those bouts well and still considers Jack Carlson the toughest man he ever encountered.

"Jack would hit you with a hundred punches that felt like sledgehammers. Jeff would hit you with one that felt like a Mack truck," Hanson says. "They're tough boys."

Steve Carlson, one year younger than Jack and two years younger than Jeff, had been left behind to finish high school in Virginia while his brothers went off to Minneapolis. A more skilled player than his brothers, he was drafted by the Flin Flon Bombers of the Western Canada Hockey League, one of the top junior leagues in the world. But Steve wanted to play with his brothers, and Jeff was now too old to play junior. The three decided to turn pro, and they set their sights on the Minnesota Fighting Saints.

The Fighting Saints were looking for ways to stand out in their struggle for acceptance alongside the established NHL North Stars. One stunt was an open tryout camp in the fall of 1973, a camp that attracted the attention of the Carlson brothers. "We did it just as a gimmick to get some interest. We didn't expect to find anybody," says Glen Sonmor. "And, to our discredit, we didn't realize fully what we had when we discovered these three guys."

The Carlsons impressed the club and earned an invitation to the main training camp. They played together as a line, with Steve at center between Jack on the left side and Jeff on the right, and, by one account, they recorded 36 goals in

54 shifts on the ice. Eager to prove their toughness, they also terrorized anyone who came near them. Sonmor and his head coach, Harry Neale, were interested in the brothers but they felt the kids just didn't have enough experience to be able to step right into the WHA. They suggested the Carlsons try the semi-pro United States Hockey League, which offered a level of hockey comparable to Senior A in Canada.

Before they left to try their luck in the USHL, the Carlsons contacted the North Stars and asked them for a tryout as well. They spoke with the late John Mariucci, an Eveleth native who is regarded as the godfather of Minnesota hockey. He was the North Stars' assistant general manager at the time, but he had been the longtime coach of the University of Minnesota Golden Gophers and he was an ex-NHLer who, in true Iron Range fashion, was known as much for his fists as his talent.

"We told them, 'We're Minnesota boys. We'll pay for our hotel, we'll pay for our meals, you don't have to give us nothing. Just let us on the ice for a couple of days to show you what we have,'" Steve says. "And I'll never forget this statement — John Mariucci said to us, 'If you guys want to play hockey together, you might as well go home and join the circus.'

"That bothered us."

———— ● ————

But Mariucci's dismissal didn't keep the brothers down, and neither did a false start in the USHL. They first approached the Waterloo Black Hawks, who wanted to sign only Steve. The Marquette Iron Rangers offered to take all three Carlsons, so off they went to Michigan's Upper Peninsula.

Chapter 2

Playing together on a line like they had wanted, Steve led the Rangers in scoring and finished sixth in the league with 79 points while Jack had a team-best 42 goals and was chosen the league's most valuable player. Jeff chipped in 25 goals and 64 points, as well as 170 penalty minutes in 55 games. Jack had 175 minutes.

Jack might have picked up those extra five minutes early in a game against the Green Bay Bobcats that was later adapted and found its way into *Slap Shot* lore. According to the Carlsons, Marquette coach Leonard "Oakie" Brumm targeted Bobcats tough guy Ernie DuPont before the game in question, offering a $50 bounty to the first Iron Ranger to knock the opponent down. The Carlson line started the contest and Jack beat Jeff to the punch, going right after DuPont on the first shift and belting him to the ice. That incident, it is said, inspired the movie bounty on Tim "Dr. Hook" McCracken.

Another Iron Rangers game in 1973–74 saw the team play against a squad of inmates in the maximum-security prison in Marquette. Brumm had worked as the prison's athletic director two decades earlier and, after supervising the construction of an outdoor rink at the facility — inside the walls, mind you — he brought the Detroit Red Wings in for a 1954 contest against the prisoners.

"It was pretty scary but it was fun," Steve remembers of the prison game in which he played. "The guys were great."

The Fighting Saints, meanwhile, were living up to their name and had become the toughest team in the WHA. Obviously, they were still very interested in the Carlsons. Their next draft pick after Dave Hanson was used to select Steve, then Jack was chosen two rounds later. The Detroit Red Wings also took Jack in that year's NHL draft. But NHL teams didn't draft players under age 20, and Steve was only 19. The brothers were determined to stay together if at all possible, and the Saints were willing to sign all three — Jeff, who had not been drafted by any team in either league, was inked as a free agent.

The club believed the Carlsons still weren't ready for the WHA, though. They were sent to Johnstown, where they attacked a pop machine upon their arrival, another episode that eventually became part of *Slap Shot*. John James, who covered the Jets for the *Johnstown Tribune-Democrat* newspaper, didn't see it happen but he was told about it by his boss, the late Fred Yost, who met the brothers when they hit town and witnessed the bizarre scene.

Jets president Don Hall remembers that Dick Roberge was up in St. Paul watching the Saints. He phoned back home and told Hall the Carlsons could play for the Jets, but the team had to put them on the payroll immediately. The Jets camp hadn't started yet and Hall wondered where he would find the money in the team's budget for the expense.

"He said, 'If we don't, they're going to knock everybody out of camp and make *this* team,'" Hall remembers, laughing. "I said, okay, put 'em on a bus and send 'em to Johnstown."

Sonmor has had 35 years to second-guess his decision to send the Carlsons to Johnstown, and he admits now he may have been wrong. "Looking back," he says, "we would have been much better off if we had just put the three of them in with us and let them play all the time."

———— ● ————

Other newcomers to the Jets in 1974–75 included two future *Slap Shot* cast members. Guido (Billy Charlebois) Tenesi, a rugged

Chapter 2

21-year-old defenceman from Ontario who had split the previous season between Tulsa of the Central Hockey League and Hershey of the AHL. Jean (Andre Bergeron) Tetreault, also 21, was a Quebec-born forward who had spent most of 1973–74 with Roanoke Valley of the SHL, where his teammates included a young Mike Keenan.

Tetreault couldn't speak English very well but apparently he knew all about the NAHL. Steve Carlson remembers Tetreault lining up for a face-off in the first game of the season.

"The other guy said, 'Hey, how you doing?' He thought the guy wanted to fight him so he dropped his gloves and started fighting him. He didn't know what the guy had said. He thought the guy had challenged him by saying, 'How you doing?'"

"That was the league," Tetreault says, shrugging.

Docken was joined in net by Jean-Louis "Louie" Levasseur, a 25-year-old rookie with little pro experience. The native of Rouyn-Noranda, Quebec, came out of Senior A in Ontario, where he won an Allan Cup national championship with the Orillia Terriers in 1973. Some of the Terriers were offered professional contracts — Claire Alexander, who had played briefly for Johnstown in 1966–67, gave up his job as a milkman and within two years was playing regularly with the Toronto Maple Leafs — and Levasseur signed with the Fighting Saints. Veterans John Garrett and Mike Curran were ahead of him on the goaltending depth chart, though, and the Saints dispatched Levasseur to the Jets.

Many goalies are known for oddball behavior and Levasseur was no exception, engaging in some truly strange acts. According to one story, he once dressed up in fishing gear at a Jets team party and spent a couple of hours with a rod and a lure, trying to catch a bar of soap in a fishbowl.

"Goalies are flaky, I guess, but Louie was perhaps a little bit different," Sonmor acknowledges, diplomatically.

"Louie was about as flaky as you can get," says Docken, who was comparatively well-grounded, having majored in sociology and physical education in university. "Louie did so many things that I didn't understand. You just look around and say, okay."

Levasseur actually had to carry the load early on in 1974–75 because Docken had suffered a broken wrist playing ball. Captain Galen Head also missed a number of games because of a knee injury and the Jets got off to a terrible start. There were eight teams in the league and Johnstown fell into the lower half of the standings very early. Christmas and New Year's came and went and the team had still not righted itself.

"I didn't think they were going to make the playoffs. They just didn't have it," says John James.

Things would change, though, suddenly and dramatically.

Chapter 3

Folk Heroes

———— ● ————

On January 16, 1975, the seventh-place Johnstown Jets took a 15–22–4 record into Utica, NY, for a game against the Mohawk Valley Comets.

Brian Conacher, a former NHL forward, was the Comets' coach and general manager. He recounted, in his 2007 autobiography, *As the Puck Turns*, his impression of Johnstown's three Carlson brothers. "They were a bespectacled and bizarre-looking trio," Conacher wrote. "All over six feet tall and weighing more than two hundred pounds, they were big, raw-boned and gangly, scary to watch and worse to play against. Look at one of them the wrong way, and you stood a good chance of getting jumped by all three of them."

All three were troubled by poor eyesight. Contact lenses weren't the option then that they are now, so the Carlsons wore glasses while they played. While it wasn't unheard of for hockey players to wear glasses while on the ice — the most prominent example was Al Arbour, a defenceman with Detroit, Chicago, Toronto and St. Louis — never before had all three members of a forward line worn Buddy Holly-style black horn-rimmed glasses.

That wasn't all that was odd about the Carlsons, who sported consecutive uniform numbers — 16 (Jack), 17 (Steve) and 18 (Jeff). Along with Dave Hanson, they taped up their hands like boxers and also wore leather golf gloves under their regular hockey gloves. They would scuff up the knuckles of the golf gloves, soak them in water and leave them overnight on a radiator to dry and harden. The gloves were devastating weapons because the players would slip them on right before a game, making sure to fight on the first shift before their sweaty hands softened the leather again.

They deny they wore tinfoil on their hands, but that claim is disputed by Conacher and even by their own coach, Dick Roberge. Philadelphia Flyers broadcaster Steve Coates had a seven-year career in the minors between 1973 and 1980 and told Sam Carchidi of the *Philadelphia Inquirer* they weren't the only ones doing it. "It truly was *Slap Shot*," Coates said of the NAHL. "They could make another movie with stuff I could tell you."

Conacher contends the Carlsons, frightening as they may have been, "weren't bad hockey players." But he would have few kind thoughts for them on this particular January night. It was a volatile game — the Comets wound up thumping the Jets 7–1 — and it turned downright ugly late in the third period. Someone in the stands, incensed at Jeff Carlson joining a fight that involved Jack, threw something and hit Jeff in the face. It's been said the object was a cup of ice. Roberge says it was ball bearings, nuts and bolts. Maybe it really was the keys to the camper. Whatever it was, Jeff reacted as one would expect.

"In a reflex rage," Conacher wrote, "he hurled his hockey stick like a spear in the direction of the culprit. Then all hell broke loose on the ice and in the stands. Jets players scrambled over the glass barrier behind the benches and into the stands. Sparks flew as skate blades hit concrete and the seats. Patrons scrambled to get away from the enraged players."

Order was eventually restored, but Jeff and Jack Carlson and Guido Tenesi were arrested, taken to jail and charged with third-degree assault. They eventually paid fines, $250 for Tenesi, who pleaded guilty to the lesser charge of disorderly conduct, and $500 for each of the Carlsons. Like the Marquette bounty of the previous season, this incident would eventually be adapted and immortalized on celluloid. For the time being, though, the Jets had found a sense of purpose.

———— ● ————

The era was dominated by the likes of the Philadelphia Flyers, who had been dubbed the "Broad Street Bullies" for a punishing brand of hockey that featured — or, depending on your opinion, was marred by — countless fights and bench-clearing brawls. Intimidation was the name of the game and it worked wonders. By 1973, the Flyers had become serious contenders for the Stanley Cup, and a year later they became the first expansion team to win the cherished trophy.

Philadelphia didn't pioneer the concept of intimidation as a tactic; that philosophy dates from the game's very origins. Also not new were the crowds who ate up that kind of behavior. Toronto Maple Leafs founder Conn Smythe recognized this. His expression, "if you can't beat 'em in the alley, you can't beat 'em on the ice," was a Leafs mantra for decades and served as the title of his posthumously published memoirs. Once, after a wild fight between Bob Bailey of the Leafs and Montreal's Maurice Richard, Smythe told the press that he and other hockey executives should take steps to "stamp out that kind of thing, or people are going to keep on buying tickets."

The Flyers gooned their way to another Stanley Cup in 1975 and other teams at all levels of hockey were stocking their rosters with players whose strength, if not their sole purpose, was fighting. Violence and penalty totals quickly increased as more and more teams began to learn that they too could win with a mix of talent and thuggish behavior.

The Johnstown Jets were no exception. They continued to brawl and they began to win, starting with an 8-5 thrashing of the Cape Codders on January 19. It was the first of seven straight victories for the Jets, a streak that pushed them back up the NAHL standings. It also helped them to establish a special bond that Dave Hanson, among others, says was vital in the club's resurgence.

He and fellow defenceman Tenesi occupied the third floor of a home in Johnstown. The three Carlsons were on the second floor. On off days, generally Sunday afternoons, the quintet gathered upstairs and set up slot car courses all over the apartment — they had brought their toys with them, as Reggie Dunlop would say. It was a source of amusement to the other Jets at first. Eventually, some of the other players started coming over. Before long, team keg parties at the Carlson-Hanson-Tenesi residence were the norm.

"We had a colorful group of guys," says Ron Docken. "It was a fun team to play for. The camaraderie was fabulous and everybody got along so well. We enjoyed going into other

Chapter 3

people's places, and they didn't enjoy us coming. Believe me, nobody wanted to play us."

"Their physicality wore teams down and made it so they didn't want to come into the War Memorial to play," agrees John James. "We've had better teams (in Johnstown), but this team just kept coming and coming and coming."

The Jets played in the Cambria County War Memorial on Napoleon Street, at the edge of the downtown core. The building opened in 1950 and immediately became a focal point of the community. "The building can only seat 4,000 people, but you always had your regular 2,700, your season-ticket holders, and they were great fans, they really were," Roberge says. "You knew you were going to have a building fairly full most of the time. It was just a good place to play."

Johnstown is actually one of a collection of municipalities — the city and a number of surrounding boroughs and townships — with a total population of about 150,000. A significant portion of that population worked at the steel mill in Franklin Borough or in the area coal mines. They were blue-collar workers and they liked their hockey rough and tumble. More often than not, the Jets gave them what they wanted, and that was certainly the case as the 1974–75 campaign wore on.

This was the environment that Nancy Dowd happened into after deciding to visit her brother Ned. She was appalled but totally fascinated. She soaked in as much detail as she could, including some gems that unfortunately didn't make it into *Slap Shot*. One centered on a "wall of shame," a rogues' gallery the team established for its opponents, using photos from newspapers and game programs. It was like a hit list for the Jets; men on the wall of shame were disparaged with a variety of vulgar epithets. Their transgressions, however minute, were listed under their pictures.

Nancy hung out with the Jets for a month or so, at the arena and at their homes, inside their dressing room, on their bus. She wanted to experience them in their natural habitats and to use their banter to create characters and situations that were as real as possible. She bought a subscription to the periodical *Hockey Digest* and devoured a book about the Philadelphia Flyers called *The Broad Street Bullies*, given to her by her father. "I promise you, that book to me was right up there with *Anna Karenina*," Dowd told Philadelphia morning radio host Michael Smerconish of WPHT 1210 AM in a July 2007 interview.

When Dowd left Johnstown, she left behind a tape recorder and asked her brother Ned to continue to try to capture the atmosphere surrounding the team. Most of the Jets were aware of the recorder, but it was easily ignored as they went about their business. "He carried it everywhere and he just recorded all of this shit that went on," says John Gofton. "He would send the tapes to Nancy, and Nancy in turn would write."

The season and the brawls continued unabated. On February 2, Johnstown visited the Broome Dusters of Binghamton, NY. The Dusters had been founded one season earlier by entrepreneur Jim Matthews, a native of Parry Sound, Ontario. When he formed the club, he brought a number of fellow Parry Sounders to the organization. Among them was Ron Orr, who became the first general manager. Searching for players, Orr contacted a childhood friend who at the time was trying out for the Toronto Toros of the WHA. The friend, Rod Bloomfield, immediately left the tryout camp and joined Orr in Binghamton.

The men had grown up and played hockey together along with their respective younger brothers, Rodger Bloomfield and

Bobby Orr, all of them only about a year apart in age. "We were the four musketeers," Bloomfield says. "We were together all the time."

Bloomfield was a newcomer to pro hockey at age 25 and had never even played Junior A. He stood only 5'6" and weighed about 160 pounds. But Orr knew Bloomfield would be all right in the NAHL, and he was — he led the Dusters in scoring in each of his first four seasons with the club, winning the league's most valuable player award in 1975 and the scoring championship in 1977 with an astounding 124 assists and 173 points.

"He's our spark," teammate Frank Hamill said of Bloomfield in a February 1974 interview with Bill Higdon of the *Utica Observer-Dispatch*. "What he can't do with a hockey stick is not worth doing . . . We have players on this team making $50,000 under big-league contracts, and they can't carry Bloomfield's skates, by comparison."

"Roddy could handle himself. He wasn't a big guy, but he could fight," Orr says. "He could skate, score, he did everything. And he had more fans than you would believe."

Those fans, on the night of February 2, were wearing fake horn-rimmed glasses attached to oversized noses. More than a few Dusters, for reasons known only to them, were wearing them during their warm-up. The Carlson brothers took it for the insult that it was. "We came in after our warm-up," says Dick Roberge, "and I think it was Steve Carlson that said, 'Coach, as soon as that puck is dropped, we're pairing up.'"

Binghamton's Ted McCaskill well remembers the ensuing brawl, because he lined up against the Carlsons to start the game. His teammate, defenceman Gary Jaquith, says it was the greatest fight he ever saw.

"It was a hell of a fight," agrees McCaskill. "I was the centerman. I looked up and here are the three guys. I figured, oh, shit. I'm in trouble now. I knew what was going to happen. But they made a mistake."

McCaskill heard the Carlsons talking as they huddled briefly before lining up. He watched as they further signaled their intentions through quick glances at each other while waiting for the puck to drop. "I knew they were after me," McCaskill says. "I had been around a long time."

He had done it all, scoring 100 or more points on three different occasions in the EHL. He also topped 100 penalty minutes eight times during a career that included stints with the Minnesota North Stars and the WHA's Los Angeles Sharks. He knew how to take care of himself on the ice. On this particular occasion, McCaskill was aware he was giving up a couple of inches, some pounds and more than a few years to his opponents. But the hockey stick, as Ted Lindsay used to say, is the great equalizer. And McCaskill, the real-life "Dr. Hook," knew how to use it to his advantage.

"I said, the left-winger is going to come at me first. So I just chopped him with the stick, then I cross-checked the center. By that time, the right-winger (Jack) had me. We fought for probably 30 minutes. It was great."

Thirty minutes is not an exaggeration. It began with the sticks but the two men wound up using everything at their disposal to punish each other while their teammates paired off and hammered away. The Dusters fans, still decked out in the fake glasses, went bananas. When it was finally over, an out-of-control McCaskill was screaming that he would cut the heads off each and every one of the Carlsons.

"That was one of the best fights I have ever seen in the history of hockey. One of the greatest fights," Steve Carlson says. "It went from one end to the other end. In the players' boxes, out of the players' boxes, just throwing. What a fight. Ted McCaskill was a tough boy."

The Jets won the game that eventually followed. It was one of 23 wins over the team's final 31 regular season games, a stretch that boosted Johnstown from seventh to fourth place in the standings. The Jets were 15 points in arrears of first-place Syracuse but they were also only three points out of second place. They were hot, and they entered the playoffs believing anything was possible.

Steve led the club in scoring, collecting 30 goals and 88 points and finishing sixth in the league scoring race. His brothers also did well, although Jack probably did too well as far as Johnstown was concerned. He accounted for 27 goals and 246 penalty minutes in only 50 games and was promoted to the Fighting Saints in February. His career with the Jets was over; in fact, Jack played until 1986–87 and never again suited up in the minors.

Jeff registered 14 goals and 250 penalty minutes while Dave Hanson added 10 goals and 249 penalty minutes. Jerry Welsh, another newcomer, added 30 goals in his only season as a Jet before starting his two-decade-long career as coach of the Ohio State University Buckeyes. Jean Tetreault was third in team scoring with 54 points and Tenesi led all rearguards with 12 goals and 42 points.

Francois Ouimet, another defenceman, netted 12 goals of his own but may have been credited for far more than that number. He had a fan in a budding young broadcaster named

Bob Costas who, while attending Syracuse University, called the radio play-by-play for the Blazers.

"He loved the name Francois Ouimet," Steve says of Costas, laughing at the memory. "Anyone that touched the puck, Francois was the hero of everything that happened on the ice, because he loved the name. 'Ouimet gets the puck, he shoots, he scores!' It wasn't even Francois scoring."

The Jets first eliminated the fifth-place Cape Codders, a series marked by a bench-clearing brawl in Game 2 that was cited by *Johnstown Tribune-Democrat* sportswriter Joe Gorden as "one of the worst" in the NAHL's short two-year history.

It started with a single fight between Jeff Carlson and Codders defenceman Mike Penasse, his team's penalty minute leader. Steve happened upon the scene, everybody on the ice paired off and the Codders cleared their bench. "Dave Hanson followed for Johnstown and a bitter free-for-all broke out," Gorden wrote, "with Hanson doing considerable damage to various players at random."

Jeff kept up a relentless attack on Penasse, repeatedly pushing his way through on-ice officials as well as Codders who tried in vain to protect their teammate. Penasse finally climbed into the stands and made his way from there to the safety of his team's dressing room. Jeff eventually wound up among the paying customers as well.

"After every player from Cape Cod was beaten up, Jeff went after their bus driver in the stands. The bus driver had been yapping at him," says Ron Docken, laughing.

One-game suspensions were handed out to Jeff and to Dave Hanson. Steve was banned for the rest of the season for abusing an official. Jets president Don Hall remembers that the league had also wanted to suspend the Carlsons after the Utica brouhaha. Hall and John Mitchell countered with a proposal to keep the brothers in Johnstown and allow them to play only in home games, a plan at which the league bosses looked askance — after all, the Carlsons had been a primary factor in the Jets becoming the biggest draw in the league. Eventually, Jeff was kept out of Utica for the rest of that season and Steve was reinstated to the playoff roster after the Jets appealed his suspension.

"We were terrorizing the league," Hall says. "That was good because, for the first time in a long time, we were filling the building and things were really going great."

It was just as Reggie Dunlop later explained it to Anita McCambridge — attendance had quadrupled. Her accountant, you'll remember, was certainly pleased.

Eliminating the Codders put the Jets up against Syracuse in the semifinal round. Syracuse, as it would be in *Slap Shot*, was the team to beat; the Blazers were vying for their third consecutive championship. They had compiled the best record in the league and were coming off a first-round playoff bye.

The Jets had played the Blazers even during the regular season, splitting five of the 10 games they played against each other. But they hadn't won in Syracuse in more than four years, a 38-game stretch that dated back to March 1971. And because Syracuse had home-ice advantage in a seven-game series by virtue of its higher finish in the standings, Johnstown would have to snap that dubious streak if it was to win the series.

Louie Levasseur, flaky though he may have been, had taken over the No. 1 job in net and his superb goaltending gave his mates a fighting chance. "Louie got a hot hand, and I was all for it," Docken says. "Believe me, I was cheering for him every step of the way."

The team as a whole was playing with a great deal of confidence. The Blazers had a tough club, too, but nobody in Johnstown thought they were any tougher or better than the Jets. It boiled down to respect, and Docken says the Jets had none at all for any member of any other team. Roberge told the *Tribune-Democrat* before the series started that he doubted the Blazers were happy to be playing Johnstown. Unfortunately, if he ever encouraged fans to come to the War Memorial and watch the Jets "cream them pucks from Syracuse," it appears to have gone unrecorded.

Syracuse won the first game at home, but the next two games were played in Johnstown and the Jets won them both to take the series lead. The series shifted back and forth, each club winning all of its home games before returning to Syracuse for the seventh and final game on April 14. The Blazers led 1–0 after the first period but goals by Jean Tetreault, Steve Carlson, Vern Campigotto and Mike Chernoff gave the Jets a 4–4 tie after 40 minutes of play.

Both clubs tightened up, not wanting to give up a goal that could decide the series. Steve finally settled matters with just over three minutes left in regulation time, beating Syracuse goalie Joe Junkin with a 15-foot wrist shot. The Jets won 5–4 and were off to the final against the Binghamton Broome Dusters.

"That last game in Syracuse, Louie Levasseur just played his heart out in the nets, and he beat them," Roberge says of his netminder who made 39 saves that night. "He actually was the one that won that seventh game for us. He was just fantastic.

"That was one year I'll never forget."

The final series took more than a week to get going, as the arenas in Johnstown and Binghamton were unavailable due to other events. By the time it started, Johnstown had a serious case of hockey fever. It didn't matter that the series itself was fairly anti-climactic — the Jets won the first three games 5–1, 7–4 and 2–1. Game 4 was set for May 1, 1975, at the War Memorial. The official capacity at the time was 4,040 seats, but the championship-starved crowd that packed the building that night far surpassed that number. Apparently they stopped counting at about 4,300.

"It was unbelievable. You couldn't buy a ticket to get in there. People were just everywhere," Galen Head says.

The Jets didn't disappoint, jumping out to a 3–0 first-period lead. The outcome was now a foregone conclusion to all concerned, including the Dusters. The visitors had never liked driving to Johnstown, calling it "the valley of death." Knowing they were beaten, they wanted nothing more than to get it all over with. And the Jets weren't about to push their luck. Word went up and down their bench to play out the contest as peacefully as possible; it was the last game for Binghamton veteran Ted McCaskill and no one wanted to risk him losing his fearsome temper and ending some Jets' careers along with his own.

With four minutes left in the third period and Johnstown leading 6–2, fans in the stands started a "we're number one" chant that continued until the final buzzer. Scores of people poured over the boards to join the Jets in their on-ice celebration. It had been 13 years since Johnstown's last championship, and the city was determined to share in it.

"The presentation of the Lockhart Cup was made at centre ice," wrote *Tribune-Democrat* reporter Sandra K. Reabuck. "But with all the players, fans and Jets Hockey Club and league officials packed in the centre, all that the crowd could see was the three-foot high silver cup held overhead. Veteran Jets Galen Head and Vern Campigotto attempted to make a triumphal, traditional skate around the ice with the trophy, but they were hampered by the happy fans. The two Jets scurried off the ice at an exit with only a half-sweep of the arena floor."

"It's something I'll never forget as long as I live. It was just such a great feeling," Head says.

John James had been covering the Jets since the late 1960s. The Johnstown native had been watching them since 1955 and had seen the clubs that won three consecutive EHL titles between 1960 and 1962. "But this team was no doubt one that sticks out in my mind," he says of the 1975 squad. "They were a wonderful bunch of guys to be around."

The fans were not forgotten as the team celebrated in its dressing room. A bottle of champagne was delivered to the crowded concourse, and the victory parties went on for several more hours. But nobody was too tired or hung-over for a parade the very next day, one that would later be re-enacted in the final scenes of *Slap Shot*. Several thousand people lined the streets and watched proudly as the hockey players were named honorary citizens of Johnstown.

Nancy Dowd wasn't there, but she was also a beneficiary of the championship. She might have initially thought of the Jets and Johnstown as "a loser team in a loser town," but now she had a Cinderella ending for her story.

Little did she know that the story had only just begun.

Chapter 4

Finding a Buyer

——— ● ———

Nancy Dowd wasted no time in trying to sell her idea for a movie about the Johnstown Jets. She outlined the concept to her literary agent, the late Stu Robinson, who contacted a friend, another agent he knew was trying to make the jump into the world of film production. The friend agreed to meet Dowd.

"I had been a literary agent for years and before that I had been in publishing," says Bob Wunsch. "I had been in the theater and stories interested me. I was a producer looking for good stories that were original and different. When Nancy came into my office with this story, I thought, this is original, different and incredibly smart. I just flipped for the idea.

"Nancy told me that she had visited her brother a great deal when he was playing in Johnstown and had gotten to know a lot of the players. She had this clutch of stories about the players and she started telling me her outline for a story, and I thought it was sensationally good, an absolutely wonderful idea for a movie."

It has been written that Dowd originally envisioned a documentary but was convinced to write a screenplay instead. If that's true, it happened before Dowd met Wunsch, because the outline she showed him was for a feature film. The outline has been preserved in George Roy Hill's papers, which he donated to the Margaret Herrick Library, a film research facility in Beverly Hills, owned and operated by the Academy of Motion Picture Arts and Sciences. The first part of the outline reads as follows:

"The Johnstown Jets are a minor league team in the North American Hockey League, a bus league. The life is tough and the teams are composed of young guys (age 17 to 25) trying to make it to the big apple, the NHL, and older guys (25 to 35) who know they are too old to make it and are just trying to hang on for another season. For six months every year they travel long, miserable hours over icy roads to play in such cultural centers as Utica, NY, Lewisboro [sic], Maine, Hyannisport, Massachusetts. In their off hours they watch *Days of Our Lives*. None of the Jets knows who owns the team."

Dowd's scenario then introduced Reggie Dunlop, the team's player-coach. In an attempt to prevent the pending disbandment of the club, he turns the Jets "into a goon squad." He spreads a rumor that the Jets will be sold and relocated to a Florida retirement community if they win the league championship. She described it as "a catch-22 situation — to win, they have to think they've been bought. To be bought, they have to win."

Chapter 4

A high-scoring young forward named Ned Braden is the only member of the Jets who refuses to fight. Despite his resistance, the Jets soon become the scourge of their league. "Opponents are afraid to cross the Jets' blue line for fear of losing teeth, eyes, minds, etc.," Dowd wrote. "Jets' violence, outlandish, premeditated tactics of harassment and intimidation scare the shit out of everybody.

"Johnstown loves their gladiators. In other towns, Jets become fashionably notorious. Attendance quadruples."

Reggie is summoned to meet the team's female owner, who is on to his game. She tells him the team will not be sold. Later, the rumor does become fact as the Jets sail to the championship in an "orgy of villainy, violence and transgression of decency." But Reggie, despite having saved the club, will not accompany it to its new Florida home; he is dismissed because he is deemed an "unsavory symbol of extravagant violence — not a good image for retirement community."

There is a chance, at the end, for Reggie to land on his feet. He is invited to join the Minnesota franchise in the WHA. "His dream of the big apple has come true. But he determines that they want him to become resident goon. Sick of the violence and harassment, he turns down offer."

It was the quality of this story rather than an attraction to hockey that elicited Wunsch's interest, but he knew that quality alone would not sell the story. He had no track record in Hollywood as a producer and Dowd had none as a writer. Sports movies at the time were generally unpopular and so was the thought that a woman could possibly write one. Furthermore, the movie as Dowd saw it was as real as real could be, which meant violent and profane, even vulgar. There was little chance that anyone in Hollywood with the power to green-light such a film would actually agree to do so. Wunsch knew all this, because he was far from naïve. But he was idealistic, and so he leapt at the chance to bring Dowd's film to the big screen.

He and Dowd visited several studio executives — among them Jere Henshaw of Universal Pictures — to pitch the idea, and they were turned down flat every time. Wunsch decided to approach someone else he knew, a man who was not only a sports buff but who had made the kind of successful career transition Wunsch was trying to pull off. That man was Stephen Friedman.

The Brooklyn native, a graduate of the Wharton School of Business at the University of Pennsylvania and Harvard Law School, worked in the legal departments of Columbia Pictures, the Ashley Famous talent agency and Paramount Pictures before deciding to go out on his own as a producer. Friedman's first step after forming his own company, Kings Road Entertainment, was the acquisition of the film rights to a Larry McMurtry novel called *The Last Picture Show*. The film adaptation, directed by Peter Bogdanovich and released in 1971, was nominated for eight Academy Awards and won two.

"Stephen had been my friend for years and years and years — we went way back. He was running a small, success-ful company, with tremendous self-confidence," Wunsch says. "He was a very talented and interesting man and he had balls and taste. When I brought him this idea, he said, abso-lutely, and he funded it."

That meant Wunsch and Friedman commissioned a screen-play from Dowd. They would pay her $25,000 for it. Once they had a script, rather than just a vague idea about a hockey team, the pitches would resume. Dowd worked quickly and, when she presented the script to her benefactors, they realized their money had been well spent; the script met all of their expectations. Dowd called it *Hat Trick* but Wunsch, feeling the title was "a little Fred-Astaire-ish," took it upon himself to rename it. He decided on *Slap Shot*.

"I knew immediately that there was a movie to be made in it. I was extremely excited," Wunsch says. "I thought the job she had done on the first draft of *Slap Shot* was one of the great first drafts I've ever read, and I've read a lot of first drafts in my many years as an agent, producer and studio exec."

The first draft came very close to what ended up in the final cut. Dowd turned the Jets into the Charlestown Chiefs, a minor league team based in a steel town. The resemblance of the Chiefs to the Jets and of Charlestown to Johnstown was immediately apparent to anyone familiar with the city and its hockey club. Almost everything in the film depicted something that happened in real life. The Chiefs, like the Jets, featured a kooky French-Canadian goalie, three bespectacled brothers who terrorized the opposition and became local folk heroes, a somewhat dotty but well-meaning general manager, and an American-born, college-educated, goal-scoring non-fighter whose first name was Ned.

Ned Dowd acknowledges that he shied away from fighting when he played hockey, but says it was due more to necessity than any deep-seated opposition to violence. He notes he was at a disadvantage from the time he entered the NAHL — his Canadian peers learned how to use their fists in junior hockey, but he spent his career to that point in environments such as high school and college, where fighting wasn't tolerated.

"It's not like (Nancy) said, 'Okay, this is going to be Ned.' She just gave him the name," he says of the character of Ned

Braden. "I had no moral issues with fighting. I just wish I was a little tougher. If I was tougher, I would have been a better fighter and I would have jumped in there more. I just wasn't a very good fighter."

The script was loaded with irony. Nancy Dowd depicted the players as grown men who, due as much to their environment as their attitudes, are unable to emotionally mature. They act like boys on and off the ice and have a difficult time being acknowledged as adults by the world outside of hockey. Consequently, they are unable to form or sustain meaningful relationships with women. The subtext would be hidden from the viewing public by the humor, violence and vulgar language, but it certainly would have been noted by people in the film industry.

As fast as the screenplay had come together, word began to spread about it. The project that no one else wanted just a short time earlier became a prominent conversation piece in Hollywood. The first serious interest came from Al Pacino, one of the hottest film actors of the day. As Wunsch puts it, "Al went crazy for it."

Pacino had shot to fame with acclaimed performances in *The Godfather, Serpico, The Godfather Part II* and *Dog Day Afternoon* and had received Academy Award nominations for each of the latter three films. Like Wunsch, he was represented at the time by lawyer Barry Hirsch, and that's how *Slap Shot* came to his attention. He decided he wanted to play Reggie Dunlop.

In a 1976 interview with Nancy Coleman of the *Johnstown Tribune-Democrat*, Nancy Dowd described Dunlop as "a lively kind of guy, alert and clever, rather manipulative, very complex." She saw the character as younger than how he was eventually portrayed by Paul Newman, although that must not have been much of a stretch since she obviously wouldn't have expected Dunlop to be played by a 51-year-old actor.

Wunsch believes Pacino, who turned 36 in 1976, could easily have played Reggie. "He would have been phenomenal. I actually think he might have been better than Paul. He would be very different, because of course he's dark, he doesn't have a twinkle, but he has an incredible violent, sort of passionate underside. I think he would have been absolutely brilliant."

But talks with Pacino did not go smoothly. According to Wunsch, Pacino started talking about changes he might have in mind for the script and about the director he thought would be best for the project. He wanted Sidney Lumet, with whom he worked on *Serpico* and *Dog Day Afternoon*. Although Lumet had fine credentials and although Friedman had collaborated with him on the 1974 film *Lovin' Molly*, another adaptation of a Larry McMurtry novel, Wunsch was concerned the movie as he and Dowd had envisioned it would perhaps not come to pass if he gave in to Pacino. He had also come to know Dowd quite well by this time and he guessed, correctly as it turned out, that she would be "recalcitrant" about rewrites to the script. "That's when I decided I ought to go to somebody else," Wunsch says. "That's when I went to Pat Kelley."

Kelley was an associate of George Roy Hill, another acclaimed director who had helmed such classics as *Butch Cassidy and the Sundance Kid* and *The Sting*, for which he had won the Academy Award as best director in 1973. Hill, through a company he called Pan Arts, had a development deal with Universal Pictures and was actively looking for a new project. Wunsch and Kelley were friends, and the neophyte producer

suspected that Hill's point man — and, subsequently, Hill himself — would be intrigued by the nature of the script. "It's macho and vulgar. George was macho and vulgar, although extremely educated. He was a very educated, cultured man, but with a real macho, vulgar, all-male kind of streak to him."

The script was read by Kelley and passed on to Bob Crawford, another of Hill's longtime associates. Like his younger brother Johnny Crawford, he was a child actor who achieved fame in a '50s TV western — Johnny starred in *The Rifleman* on ABC while Bob was in NBC's *Laramie*. He had also been directed by Hill in a 1959 TV play called "Child of Our Time," which aired on the CBS anthology series *Playhouse 90*. Both Crawford and Hill were nominated for Emmy Awards for their work on "Child of Our Time."

Crawford stayed in touch with Hill and eventually moved behind the scenes at the older man's request, shooting a documentary about the making of *Butch Cassidy and the Sundance Kid* while the production was taking place. The finished product, narrated by Hill, was well received and won an Emmy. Crawford would be involved in every one of the director's films from then on, working as a line producer in charge of everyday matters. One of his duties between projects was to help screen the scripts that came in, and he still remembers the day he read *Slap Shot*.

"I was agog at the language but also at the violence and the kind of eclectic storytelling that was going on," he says of his initial reaction. "I read it quickly and took it into George and threw it on his desk and said, 'I don't know what to make of that, but it's wild. You should read that.'"

They went to lunch later and found themselves chuckling about the antics of the characters, especially "the three

Chapter 4

brothers, those guys with the Coke-bottle glasses." Crawford says Hill initially wasn't sure what he could do with such a film, if anything, but neither of them could stop laughing or pointing out particular bits in the screenplay that caught their attention. Hill was also surprised that a woman had written it, and he decided he wanted to meet Nancy Dowd.

"So Nancy came in and talked about it — 'You were in the *locker room* with these guys?!' — and she was just riveting about the life and the atmosphere and the reality of it. George was captivated by her personally and her enthusiasm for it. Then he began reading the script again and began having fun with the hockey and the characters and coming to terms with how he could portray it, what the tones would be, how outrageous he could be, how comic. He had a natural comic flair; George loved slapstick but he always wanted to have something real going on. He always grounded himself with, 'If I can believe this . . .' and he believed what was going on with Nancy and Ned and the team. Then he could be totally passionate and committed and jump into a world he knew nothing about and let them show him what it was."

Hill later told Nancy Coleman of the *Johnstown Tribune-Democrat* that he had been attracted to the "rawness" of the screenplay. He saw it as "a cross-section of an aspect of American life that I haven't seen done on film: minor-league hockey . . . sports stories are usually biographical, taking the life of a great athlete and putting that on the screen in somewhat heroic form. This is not that. This is a whole culture, a whole atmosphere that I don't think has been done — at least, honestly — on film before."

He said he was not repulsed by the language. Rather, he welcomed it because he knew it represented an honest portrayal of the hockey culture. "People who make movies don't like to have obscenities because it gives you a worse rating, and people won't go to see it. Therefore, they present a picture they think the people would like to say life is like, rather than what it actually is like . . . but if you're going to set out to do something that's real and has some basis in fact and in our own culture, then I think you've been dishonest if you don't do it fully and really.

"It's not going to shock hockey people, people who know about sports. It may shock people who think no baseball player or hockey player or football player ever uses a four-letter word. These people are living in never-never land."

—————— ● ——————

No one could ever have accused Hill of living in never-never land. He had been far afield in his life and had many varied interests, illustrated by his unwillingness to stick to one particular genre in his films. That, along with his desire to avoid publicity, earned him respect from some circles but also caused his work to be dismissed by others who couldn't put him in a box.

"(Martin) Scorsese kind of has a lock on what he does well," says John Hill, the director's son and a film editor who worked with his father on several movies, beginning with *Slap Shot*. "But George Roy Hill, he did whatever a good story was. It's almost like a detriment. He was a great storyteller but his films are so diverse, people don't really get a handle on him."

Diverse as Hill was, he apparently knew very little about hockey despite an upbringing in Minneapolis, Minnesota, where he was born on December 20, 1922. He developed youthful interests in acting, music and flying, and had earned his pilot's licence by the time he entered Yale University to study music. While at Yale, he continued to act, joining the university's dramatic society — later becoming its president — and taking roles in various musical productions.

Hill graduated in 1942 and joined the US Navy 10 days later. He trained as a pilot and transferred to the Marine Corps before being sent to the Solomon Islands, where he was mainly responsible for delivering supplies and transporting the wounded, usually without the benefit of protection from enemy ground fire. He began writing while in the service and, after the war's end, he studied literature and began acting again at Trinity College in Dublin, Ireland. His acting career blossomed after he returned to the United States, and he met and began seeing an actress named Louisa Horton. They married in 1951.

His career was interrupted by a recall to active Marine duty during the Korean War, but it also allowed Hill to reconsider his options. Acting had become too emotionally distressing for him. More distress, though, was to come before he even got overseas. One foggy evening, with his military plane's instruments not working, Hill had to rely on the directions of an operator in the control tower in order to safely land at the airport in Atlanta. "That guy talked so calmly," he said to Nancy Coleman in 1976. "I was so taken with the capacity of the man to do this that I transposed that incident into a night fighter's in Korea and sold the play to television."

It was called "My Brother's Keeper," and it was one of three scripts Hill sold to NBC's *Kraft Television Theatre* before he left the Marines. Writing had proven to be a catharsis, as well as a smart artistic and financial move. The play was broadcast in 1953 and Hill was even given a role in the production as a newspaper correspondent. This is noteworthy because the casting director who selected him was Marion Dougherty, who would later work with Hill on most of his movies, including *Slap Shot*.

Hill soon began directing for live television. He helped to adapt the book *A Night to Remember*, about the Titanic disaster, and directed the production for *Kraft Television Theatre* in 1956. It was one of many projects on which he collaborated with other writers, and in the future he would always work with his films' writers in order to more fully realize his vision, although in most cases he would not take any credit for his contributions. "He had a very good sense of storytelling," says Andrew Horton, a film scholar, screenwriter and author who wrote the book *The Films of George Roy Hill* about his uncle by marriage — Horton's father was Louisa Horton Hill's brother.

The live production of "A Night to Remember" was a landmark. According to Horton's book, Hill employed a whopping 106 actors, six different cameras and as many as 25 sets. That Hill managed to bring it all off without a hitch, shifting quickly between the various sets which were "sinking" at different angles, was nothing short of amazing. The play was nominated for two Emmy Awards, one for writing and one for directing, and it was turned into a film two years later. The same thing happened with "Judgment at Nuremberg," which Hill directed for *Playhouse 90* in 1959. Maximilian Schell played the defence attorney in the televised play and reprised the role on film in 1961, winning the Academy Award for best actor.

Hill also directed on Broadway before making the move to films in 1962. The work he had done on the small screen, which always meant looming deadlines and coping with precious little preparation time, was invaluable training, which he freely acknowledged. "When I went out to Hollywood," he told Horton, "I was probably more expert at editing than many who had been in Hollywood for years. My whole thought process of seeing a film before I ever got on the set developed from working for television."

"Coming from that so-called golden era of television, you were cranking out hour-long dramas on a pretty tight schedule," says film critic Richard Roeper. "A lot of script, a lot of blocking, and the story and the actors had to take over. His directing style, a lot of the directing was done before he ever said 'action,' and then it was pretty much going to go the way it was going to go, as opposed to a director who spends six hours on a set fiddling with the lighting and changing his mind about the angles and trying to re-invent the wheel.

"My guess is that's one of the reasons (Paul) Newman probably liked working with him, because I don't think he had a lot of patience for that either."

Hill's Broadway career began in 1957 and led directly to films when he was offered a chance to direct the movie version of the Tennessee Williams play *Period of Adjustment*, which Hill had already staged in New York. He immediately set the tone for his future career by establishing in the film what he told Horton was "an ironic point of view," something that dominated his life and which would frequently be present in his later films. In *Period of Adjustment*, the example was a main character's use of a hearse to drive to — and from — his wedding.

"I think it's just my nature. I'm not interested in doing very heavy dramatic material," Hill said. "Whenever I find something that is serious . . . I will find some way of defusing the seriousness with irony or comedy or a slightly cynical point of view."

And so the irony in Dowd's screenplay would have been as enticing to Hill as was its "rawness." *Slap Shot* would also be consistent with Hill's pattern of films in which the protagonist was either a con artist (*The World of Henry Orient*, *The Sting*) or living a fantasy (*Slaughterhouse-Five*) or both (*The Great Waldo Pepper*). Dowd and producers Bob Wunsch and Stephen Friedman, meanwhile, were attracted to Hill's commercial and critical track record.

Wunsch had been right, though, about Dowd's reticence to permit changes to the script. But she was won over by Hill's commitment to personally work with her, both prior to and during the production. "My father really took her under his wing, and I think she was there for most of the shoot," says John Hill, who took a year off from college in order to work on *Slap Shot* as an apprentice film editor.

With Hill on board, thoughts again turned to who would play the key role of Reggie Dunlop. Al Pacino was not out of the running, and he made an overture to Hill about signing on. To this day, it's not clear whether Hill rejected Pacino out of hand or whether the actor may have over-reacted to an innocent question and pulled himself out of contention.

"I should have made that movie. That was my kind of character — the hockey player," Pacino said in a 1983 interview with author Lawrence Grobel for a *Rolling Stone* magazine feature, later reproduced in the book *Al Pacino — In Conversation with Lawrence Grobel*. "I wanted to talk to (Hill) about it, and all he said was, 'Can he ice skate?' That's all he was interested in, whether I could ice skate or not. That was a certain kind of comment. He didn't want to talk about anything else. It was like he was saying, 'What the hell, it could work with anybody.' The way in which he responded said to me that he wasn't interested."

Horton says Hill briefly considered Jack Nicholson for the role. Nicholson, having scorched the ears of filmgoers who saw and heard him in the highly profane 1973 movie *The Last Detail*, could have plausibly delivered the harsh dialogue expected of Reggie Dunlop. But Hill soon settled on a favorite colleague after learning Paul Newman was both interested and available.

———— ● ————

Like Hill, Newman's interest in hockey was peripheral at best, despite growing up in an environment where the game had thrived. He was born on January 26, 1925 in Cleveland Heights, Ohio, a suburb of Cleveland, where hockey was embraced as much as in any other industrial city in the US Northeast.

The first professional hockey team there was the Indians, who were established in 1929 and played in the 2,000-seat Elysium Arena. The franchise was also briefly known as the Falcons before becoming the Barons in 1937. That same year, the Barons moved into the new Cleveland Arena on Euclid Avenue, about eight miles away from Shaker Heights, another suburb where the Newman family settled in 1927.

Newman's arrival came a year after that of his brother Arthur and completed the family. The boys' father, Arthur Newman Sr., was the son of Jewish immigrants from Europe. He and his brother Joseph were partners in a successful sporting goods store in Cleveland, which ensured the Newman boys would have some kind of involvement in athletics.

"We were in elementary school when we got our first skates and hockey sticks," says Arthur Newman Jr. "The Elysium was one of the first rinks in the United States with artificial ice, and that's where we learned to skate, all during the '30s. The suburb that we lived in had ponds at various places around the city and they would freeze. We had a pond directly across the street from the elementary school that we went to and we had a pond at our junior high school."

Arthur Jr. developed a love for the ice and laced up the blades every chance he got, a passion that would last until he was in his sixties. His brother shared in the winter fun throughout their childhoods and cheered for the Barons, but he also found himself drawn to acting and performing. Paul was seven years old when he first appeared on stage, playing a court jester in a school production of "Robin Hood." He continued to perform in plays through his years at Shaker Heights High School, but didn't take acting particularly seriously at that time.

Newman worked part-time in his father's store and dreamed of joining the US Navy after graduation. Hoping to become a pilot, he enlisted in January 1943, four days before his 18th birthday. He briefly attended Ohio University in Athens before starting his training in the summer of 1943. Unfortunately, his dreams of becoming a pilot were dashed when it was discovered that he had been betrayed by his later-to-be-famous steel blue eyes — Newman was color-blind. But his eyes worked well enough for him to be able to operate a radio and a gun on torpedo bombers, and Aviation Radioman Third Class Newman served in the Pacific theater.

After the war, Newman resumed his studies with the help of the GI Bill. He enrolled at Kenyon College in Gambier,

Ohio, graduating in 1949 with a BA in English. He also rekindled his interest in acting while at Kenyon, joining the student dramatic society and performing at every possible opportunity. Later, Newman studied drama at Yale prior to launching a successful acting career in television, on Broadway and in films.

His iconic status had been secured by the time Newman signed on to play Butch in *Butch Cassidy and the Sundance Kid* in 1969. Initially, he had been slated to play Sundance opposite Steve McQueen but, when George Roy Hill was brought in to direct the film, he insisted the two swap roles. According to Andrew Horton, who interviewed Newman for his book about Hill, Newman was not confident about his ability to handle the part, as his previous comedic films had not done well. Hill convinced him by telling him to simply play it like he would play anything else. Newman followed Hill's advice and turned in a solid performance.

"Newman gave credit to Hill for helping him develop that kind of sense of humor," Horton says. "Obviously, *Slap Shot* just let him turn loose."

Newman immediately demonstrated his loyalty to the director after McQueen left the project. Hill thought a young actor named Robert Redford could play Sundance, but a studio boss who felt Redford lacked the sufficient star quality tried to force Hill to accept first Marlon Brando and then Warren Beatty. The dispute wasn't resolved until Newman threatened to follow McQueen off the picture. Hill got Redford, and the movie was made the way he wanted to make it.

Hill also gained two lifelong friends. Redford has frequently referred to *Butch Cassidy* as the film that made his career and changed his life. His Utah resort is named Sundance after his character, and the resort eventually lent its name to what would become one of the world's pre-eminent annual film festivals. Hill's bond with Newman went even deeper. "I would have to say that Paul Newman was his closest friend," says John Hill. "It wasn't just a working relationship. They were very close."

The three men teamed up again four years later in *The Sting*. Both Newman-Redford-Hill films wound up in the all-time box office Top 10 and were also major critical successes. *Butch Cassidy* was nominated for seven Academy Awards and won four. *The Sting* did even better, earning 10 nominations and winning seven, including best picture and best director.

Newman, for whatever reason, did not receive a nomination for either film. But the pictures did enhance what had become his most familiar screen persona, that of the charming manipulator. It seems only natural, then, for Hill to have recognized what Newman could bring to the character of Reggie Dunlop in *Slap Shot*. The actor seems to have quickly grasped this as well. Admittedly bored with acting because of what he felt were a lack of original, challenging projects, Newman was dazzled by Nancy Dowd's script, calling it the most original thing he had seen in years — "just delicious" was how he described it in a 2003 interview with Lawrence Donegan of *The Observer*, a British newspaper.

Bob Crawford says Hill initially hadn't thought at all about Newman for *Slap Shot*, but indulged his friend when he heard about the project and asked if he could read the script. Newman came back to Hill after looking it over, expressing wonder that Hill would be involved with such a film. What follows is Crawford's account of the ensuing discussion:

Newman: "What are you *doing?*"

Hill: "Well, I know this isn't for you. You're too old, and you can't skate anyway."

Newman: "Actually, I *can* skate."

Hill: "You *can*?!"

"He went out and looked at Newman skate, and Newman could skate backwards," Crawford remembers, laughing. "It was a great thrill."

Much to the director's relief, Newman had no qualms with the harsh language, agreeing it was true to the lifestyle. Nor did he have reservations about his ability to convincingly play a professional hockey player despite having turned 50 (it certainly helped that, with the exception of his greying hair, he looked far younger than that). He did realize he had work to do before he would be ready to start filming, but he knew how he could prepare. He called his brother Arthur, who had worked on a number of Newman's movies as a production manager. More importantly, he was still an avid skater and hockey player, activities Paul had left behind decades earlier. Arthur agreed to help Paul train for the role, and the brothers hit the ice together for the first time since their childhoods.

"I hadn't been on skates for 40 years but skated every day for two months before we started rehearsal," Newman said in June 2007.

And now the film's producers, with an Oscar-winning director and a superstar actor committed to *Slap Shot*, were able to go back to the studios with significantly more to offer than before. Universal Pictures was approached again, a smart move for three reasons. First, Universal and its parent company, MCA, utterly dominated film and TV production and distribution at the time, churning out hit feature films as well as TV movies and series. Second, Hill and Universal had a strong working relationship — the studio had released his four most recent pictures, and five of his last six.

The third reason had to do with the man who would make the decision on behalf of Universal. The company's executive suites were and are located in a dark 15-storey building known as the Black Tower. Studio president Ned Tanen occupied an office on the tower's top floor, right next to that of his boss, MCA chairman Lew Wasserman. But Tanen enjoyed a great deal of autonomy in the films Universal produced, a freedom enhanced by the fact that blockbusters such as *American Graffiti*, *The Sting* and *Jaws* were all realized early in his tenure as a production executive.

Tanen had been in the entertainment business since the mid 1950s and was the type of executive who still had enough of the fan in him that his interests leaned toward the creative rather than the business side of things. "He believed in you, and he would put his money where his mouth was," filmmaker Joel Schumacher told Pat Saperstein of *Variety* after Tanen's death in January 2009.

He had not been part of the earlier process in which Universal rejected the project, but he alone would make the call this time. Wunsch and Friedman probably couldn't have found a better person to be in that position, given that Tanen's sense of humor, which was described by Schumacher as "wry, dark and ironic," would have been right up the alleys of Hill and Dowd.

Tanen said in February 2007 that his mind was made up as soon as he read Nancy Dowd's "brilliant, brilliant" script, which had him convulsed with laughter. "I've never read a screenplay where I kept falling out of my chair. But when I read that script, I fell on the floor. I just fell on the floor and I said, 'I'm making this goddamned movie.' Both Newman and Hill were committed, they both said they wanted to do it. I said, 'Well, here we go.'"

Universal, Wunsch and Friedman, through Kings Road, signed an agreement on November 17, 1975 to make *Slap Shot*. Less than seven months had elapsed since the Johnstown Jets had copped the Lockhart Cup and they were steaming toward a repeat, using their sticks, skates and fists to cut another wide swath through the NAHL. But they were doing it without the services of winger Ned Dowd, who by this time had agreed, at his sister's request, to serve as the film's technical advisor and stunt coordinator.

He had left Johnstown and signed with the NAHL's Lewiston Nordiques. Dowd was only 24 years old and still hoped to make it to the big leagues. But a phone call from Nancy convinced him to put his plans on hold; as it turned out, he would never return to pro hockey.

"She called me to say she had written a script and there was a possibility it would get made," Dowd says. "I had never worked on a movie before, so I said, okay, I'll give it a shot. And the rest is history."

Chapter 5

——— ● ———

Many a film project remains in development limbo for years, if it ever gets made at all. Not *Slap Shot*. Less than four months after the paperwork was signed to make the movie, principal photography began in Johnstown, Pennsylvania.

It was of immense help that the script was ready and the director and star were both available and willing to get started right away. It was also hockey season, meaning there were plenty of players on hand who would be able to fill out the cast and work as extras.

Of course, it wasn't quite that simple.

First of all, director George Roy Hill needed to be brought back on board. At one point before the contracts were all signed, sealed and delivered, Hill abandoned the whole idea and took off. Paul Newman enlisted a private detective to track him down in Palm Springs and then talked him into returning to the project. His enthusiasm in the film restored, Hill began to search for actors who could skate and play hockey.

Mike Fenton was the original casting director. Fenton was responsible for casting some of the film industry's biggest hits of the 1970s, such as *American Graffiti*, *The Godfather Part II* and *One Flew Over the Cuckoo's Nest*. He arranged casting sessions at the Pickwick Ice Center in Burbank, California, near Universal Studios. There was no shortage of actors who wanted a role in *Slap Shot*, so quantity was not a problem for Fenton and Hill and technical advisor Ned Dowd. Quality, however, was an issue.

Among the prospects were two young men on the brink of fame. Peter Strauss and Nick Nolte had played brothers Rudy and Tom Jordache in the 12-part TV miniseries *Rich Man, Poor Man*, a Universal production which was being readied for broadcast on the ABC network starting in February 1976. Strauss and Nolte were both being considered for the pivotal role of Ned Braden. Unfortunately, neither of them could skate.

"Every actor wanted to be in the film," Strauss says, speaking publicly about his *Slap Shot* experience for the first time since 1976, "and every actor lied and said, of course we skate. Then we all ended up at the only rink in Burbank bribing anyone for lessons.

"I had no knowledge. Zip. I had never even seen a hockey game."

John Barbour, a Toronto-born actor, comedian and TV host — remember *Real People* on NBC? — was at the rink trying to help the novices learn how to skate. They had two or three days to try to absorb as much as they could before the casting session would begin in earnest. In spite of the brevity of his lessons, Strauss' audition went well and he almost succeeded in convincing Hill he could do the job. Paul Newman's competitive nature, however, changed everything.

Newman suggested a relay race to conclude the day and Strauss agreed. They would each anchor a team of five skaters, from one end of the ice to the other, and the prize for the winning quintet would be a case of beer. The first four legs of the contest went off without incident. Newman and Strauss took off to decide the race.

"Only when we were about even, and approaching the end of the rink, did I remember my class in fast stops was scheduled for the following day," Strauss says ruefully. "It wasn't pretty when I hit the boards. Everyone heard the leg break!"

The broken leg spelled the end of Strauss' participation in *Slap Shot*. It also somewhat hindered his promotional efforts for the miniseries that would make him a star. "I had to do a publicity tour for *Rich Man, Poor Man* the following week and was in cast up to and including the knee. But Newman and director George Roy Hill sent a case of wine to my house. Class," Strauss says.

———— ● ————

One actor who made the grade in Burbank was Jerry Houser, a 23-year-old Los Angeles native who made his acting debut in the 1971 film *Summer of '42*. Houser had become a fan of the Los Angeles Kings while in high school and started playing hockey around the same time.

"Nobody knew about hockey out here at all. We started playing on cement out here because no one knew how to skate," says Houser, who won a role in *Slap Shot* as Dave "Killer" Carlson. "One of my friends went away and learned how to skate and came back saying, you know, there's a whole other side to this game. So we all went out and bought skates. The only place you could buy a hockey stick out here then was in the Sears catalogue."

Houser learned to skate well enough that, when word began to spread about this new hockey movie, other actors started calling him up and asking if they could go skating together, hoping to pick up some pointers. One actor who didn't need the help was Allan Nicholls, who made it into the film as team captain Johnny Upton.

Nicholls brought everything to the plate — a solid background in performing as well as ample skating and hockey knowledge. He also boasted a Hockey Hall of Fame pedigree as the grandson of Riley Hern, a goaltender who won four Stanley Cups with the pre-NHL Montreal Wanderers. Nicholls had begun playing hockey at age four in his native Montreal and, following in the footsteps of his mother's father, started off in net. The first time he played hockey out of the nets, he didn't have the proper equipment and was forced to improvise.

"I took two *Life* magazines and wrapped them around my shins. I balled up a couple or three pairs of socks and put them over my kneecaps. I pulled hockey socks over them and they looked exactly like shin pads," he says.

Nicholls turned to music as he grew up, singing with a popular Montreal rock band called JB and the Playboys. Roles in the Broadway production of *Hair* followed before Nicholls was cast in *Nashville* in 1975, establishing a working relationship with director Robert Altman that would last for the rest of Altman's life. It was while hanging out at Altman's Los Angeles office that he heard about a new hockey movie from a friend. Scott Glenn had auditioned for *Slap Shot* and, knowing Nicholls was from Canada, assumed he must know how to play hockey and encouraged him to try out as well.

Once again, Nicholls was *sans* equipment, specifically skates. But he met and befriended Ned Dowd, who of course had gone to university in Nicholls' hometown, and Dowd told a wardrobe person to buy Nicholls a good pair of skates. "I got these Bauer Supremes. They were the most expensive skates I had ever owned in my life," Nicholls laughs.

More casting sessions took place in New York, at the original Sky Rink on West 33rd Street at 10th Avenue in Manhattan. They went better than had the Burbank experience, as there were more actors based in or near New York who were comfortable on skates. Unfortunately for Nick Nolte, it increased the competition to play Ned Braden. Hill finally decided that Nolte, although he tried hard to literally get up to speed on the blades — Jerry Houser still remembers the blisters on Nolte's ankles from his skates — just couldn't skate well enough to pull off a realistic performance.

Nolte and Strauss were in good company, though; they were far from the only notable or soon-to-be-famous actors who tried but failed to earn a place in *Slap Shot*. The list includes John Travolta, David Soul, Tim Matheson, Tommy Lee Jones, Kurt Russell, Kevin Tighe, Kevin Dobson, Donny Most, Robby Benson, Harrison Ford, Paul Michael Glaser, Rick Nelson, Richard Gere, Gil Gerard, Tom Berenger and John Lithgow, among many, many others.

Art Hindle was already famous in his homeland for having starred as hot Toronto Maple Leafs rookie Billy Duke in 1971's *Face-Off*. But Hindle wasn't a hockey player and in *Face-Off* he was doubled on the ice by actual Leafs defenceman Jim

McKenny (Billy Duke was even given McKenny's uniform number, 18). Hindle was out of the running fairly early.

Henry Winkler — yes, The Fonz — was seriously considered for a number of different roles. Among them were the characters of Dave "Killer" Carlson and one of the Hanson Brothers. The four characters had been inspired, respectively, by Johnstown Jets defenceman Dave "Killer" Hanson and the forward line of Jeff, Jack and Steve Carlson; Nancy Dowd merely transposed the surnames when she wrote the screenplay.

Many characters had the traits and/or names of actual men who were current or former players in the North American Hockey League. Charlestown Chiefs players Billy Charlebois and Jim Ahern shared surnames with Bob Charlebois of the Cape Codders and Kevin Ahearn of the Long Island Cougars. Morris Wanchuk, originally Morris Saginaw, was named for one-time Jet Morris Stefaniw. The character was renamed for Mike Wanchuk, briefly Ned Dowd's teammate with the Kalamazoo Wings of the IHL.

Hyannisport Presidents center Nick Brophy was originally named Nick Fotiu, who had begun his pro hockey career with Cape Cod. The character was renamed after legendary minor league player-coach John Brophy. Because of the presence of the Brophy name in *Slap Shot*, and because Reggie Dunlop is a player-coach, it has long been assumed that Dunlop was based on the real Brophy, who, interestingly, is on record as both loathing and loving the film.

Player-coaches were common throughout the history of the EHL and NAHL. For example, Dick Roberge, Tom McVie, Galen Head and Jim Cardiff all worked as player-coaches with the Jets in the 1970s, and this was also during a time when assistant coaches were unheard of. The idea of one man simultaneously playing and coaching may or may not have had anything to do with the man's coaching capabilities; as often as not, it was to help a team to save money.

Ned Dowd says Reggie Dunlop was named after former teammate Reggie Kent. The character would wear the same No. 7 on his uniform that Kent had sported throughout his career in Johnstown. Dowd allows that Dunlop was based in part on Jets legend Roberge.

"Maybe a little bit of Roberge, because he was the coach, although he wasn't the player-coach when we were there. He was an amalgam," Dowd says. "People want to read more into who was who and all that, but basically it was like a little postcard to that team and to what kind of went on, the lifestyle. It's a comedy, and there's no great moral tale there."

Others see it differently, although Roberge himself won't say what he thinks about the character's inspiration. Former Jets captain Don Hall, who by this time was the team's president, says it was well known locally that Dunlop was based almost entirely on Roberge.

"The whole movie was an inside joke. The people in Johnstown knew the inside and outside of the whole thing," Hall says. "First of all, there was no question that the movie was the history of Dick Roberge. No question about that. It was about Dick Roberge, his life, his divorce, the whole bit. It was his life."

Jets goalie Louie Levasseur was the inspiration for a character first known as Denis Lafleur. His surname was later changed to Lemieux, which must have been confusing for the real-life Cape Codder forward whose name was also Denis Lemieux. Ron Docken, Johnstown's other netminder, should have been immortalized when his nickname, Doc, was given to a Chiefs player who was later written out of the script. The same fate befell the character of Jerry Marsh, named after Jets sniper Jerry Welsh.

Charlestown TV-radio broadcaster Jim Carr originally had the surname Yost, the name borrowed from *Johnstown Tribune-Democrat* sports editor Fred Yost. However, the character of Jim Carr was based not on Yost but on real-life Johnstown sportscaster Bill Wilson, who wore a toupee that was, allegedly, "sensationally ugly." It never fell or was pulled off his head during a broadcast, although Dave Hanson threatened during the Jets' championship run that he would yank it if they did in fact win the title. Wilson kept his distance after the final game.

———— ● ————

Another character had an obvious antecedent. Uber-goon Oggie Oglethorpe was clearly inspired by Bill "Goldie" Goldthorpe, described in a November 1975 *Utica Daily Press* article as "easily the most notorious player in the history of the young NAHL."

"I am the king," Goldthorpe, then 22, told reporter John Pitarresi. "I may not get the best of every fight, but I'll come back and get him so he won't be able to come back."

Goldthorpe hailed from Hornepayne, Ontario, a small community about 100 miles north of Wawa. A tough kid with an aptitude for hockey, his parents sent him to live and play in Thunder Bay, a hotbed where he could hone his skills. Albert Cava brought Goldthorpe up to his junior club in 1970–71 and the teenager fit right in, afraid of nobody on or off the ice. Cava told Allan Maki of the *Globe and Mail* in July 2002 that Goldthorpe was the best penalty killer he had ever seen.

But there were stumbles along the way. After a game in Green Bay, a delayed flight led to a team drinking session in the airport bar, which led to a brawl on the tarmac, which led to the police being called. Goldthorpe either couldn't or wouldn't leave well enough alone and was hauled off to jail. The next day he was escorted to the border — "his subsequent deportation to Canada."

Another run-in with the law further bolstered his infamy. Jailed after another fight during a visit home to Hornepayne, it was arranged for Goldthorpe to serve his sentence in Thunder Bay. He was released for practices and games only. Combined with the fact that he had worked in the summer as a grave-digger, word got around that Goldthorpe had been jailed for robbing graves. Anything seemed possible, given his reputation and his appearance, described by Dave Hanson in his autobiography as "a guy who had a big blond Afro hairdo, a leather face with several missing teeth, and eyes as black as coal that sunk into his head."

In 1973, Goldthorpe came out of junior and joined the Syracuse Blazers, registering 20 goals, 46 points and 285 minutes in penalties in only 55 games. He added five goals and 13 points in 15 playoff contests as Syracuse cruised to the championship. He also developed a dislike for Blazers play-by-play broadcaster Bob Costas, leading to a frightening incident on the team bus. As Costas recalls it, he was reading the *New York Times* when Goldthorpe grabbed the newspaper, tore it to shreds and showered Costas with the pieces. Costas, youthfully stupid, responded by telling the player he would teach him how to read. Goldthorpe had to be restrained by teammates from doing to Costas what he had already done to the newspaper.

Goldthorpe earned a playoff call-up to the Minnesota Fighting Saints. The Saints tried to demote him to Johnstown the next season but he refused to report to the Jets, playing instead with the Blazers, with Syracuse's AHL team and with the Baltimore Blades of the WHA. He was a spectator for an NAHL contest in January 1975 between the Blazers and the Broome Dusters in Binghamton, where he came out of the stands during the pre-game warm-up, challenged Dusters defenceman Gary Jaquith and sparked an epic brawl. Jaquith remembers that at the height of the melee, Dusters manager Ron Orr raced across the ice and suckered Goldthorpe while he was tangled up with someone else.

The 1975–76 season was equally eventful. Goldthorpe wore the uniforms of four different NAHL and WHA clubs that year. Naturally, he ended up in Binghamton and played more games with the Dusters than with anyone else. And it was as a member of the Dusters that Goldthorpe blew any chance he might have had to play the character he inspired.

The Dusters visited the Jets for a game and several Dusters got into a brawl with the Johnstown fans; Binghamton captain Rod Bloomfield recalls that the team eventually needed a police-and-dogs escort out of the arena and to the city limits. Emotions in the team's dressing room were still running high after the game, particularly between dueling Dusters enforcers Goldthorpe and Paul Stewart. They had never gotten along from the time Goldthorpe joined the club — Goldthorpe suckerpunched Stewart at a team party and bit him in the ensuing fight, sending the future NHL referee to hospital for a tetanus shot — and now they were jawing at each other as a visitor was set to walk through the door. The visitor was Art Newman, and he was looking for extras for his brother's movie.

Chapter 5

Just as Newman came in, Goldthorpe, having had enough of Stewart, threw a bottle of pop at his teammate. It missed him, shattering on the wall above him and spraying glass and pop all over the shocked Stewart and the even more shocked Newman.

"That was it," Goldthorpe told Maki. "They thought I was an undesirable."

———— ● ————

Stephen Mendillo never saw Goldthorpe play, but he was familiar with the type. He had seen all the goons of the old EHL while growing up in New Haven, Connecticut, in the 1950s and 1960s.

He learned to play the game there under the tutelage of Murray Murdoch, the original iron man of the NHL who never missed a game during an 11-year career with the New York Rangers. Murdoch was coaching the Yale University hockey team when he and some other men, including Mendillo's father, Dr. John C. Mendillo, helped found the New Haven peewee program.

Dr. Mendillo was a surgeon who both practised and taught at Yale. His love of sports led him to serve as the doctor for the university's hockey and football teams and for the New Haven Blades of the EHL. Stephen cheered for the Blades and remembers their thugs as well as, if not better than, their skill players.

"I was really familiar with the goings on. I had seen the Johnstown Jets come to New Haven, I saw all those teams. I used to watch them fight, and they really had some doozies," he says. "Don Perry was a great fighter and a lot of fun to watch. He was the king of the ice. Blake Ball came along and he was a big guy, a big bruiser, and he could just slap people around, no problem. And there was Moose Lallo. He's an obscure figure in a way, but he was Mr. Bad in New Haven, worse than any of them."

Mendillo played hockey through high school and college but also pursued a love of acting, receiving a master of fine arts degree from Yale in 1971. He appeared in a number of plays in his hometown and on Broadway and made his first film appearance in 1972's *Across 110th Street*, starring Anthony Quinn. Cast as Jim Ahern in *Slap Shot*, Mendillo was eager to tackle the role when he realized the inspiration had been, more or less, the same brand of hockey he had grown up watching.

"When this came along I thought, they're going to make a movie about these guys? That's a good idea. It had a good story behind it, a great script. To George Roy Hill, it was Greek. George was amazed at it all, because he didn't know any of it. But to me it was, I know this stuff, and worse. They went pretty easy on it if you ask me," he says, laughing.

Brad Sullivan was another New England product, having moved from his Chicago birthplace to Cape Cod with his family when he was a teenager. He earned a degree in agriculture from the University of Maine, an education briefly interrupted in 1952 by the Korean War.

The GI Bill paid for Sullivan to complete his degree as well as for two years of studies at the American Theatre Wing in New York. Sullivan had started taking acting classes upon his return to Maine, and he was interested to see where show business might take him. "It took me better than 30 years before I had any idea I was going to have a career," he said good-naturedly.

Chapter 5

He worked steadily on stage before making his first film in 1972. One year later, he was hired to play a killer in *The Sting*. His next project with Hill and Newman would be in *Slap Shot* — he was cast as the hilariously lecherous Mo Wanchuk — although it was entirely coincidental that the project came to his attention.

Sullivan had played club hockey at university and stayed involved with the sport after moving to New York. "I played quite extensively, summer and winter, an average of maybe twice a week," he said. It was at one of those sessions, late one night at the Sky Rink, that he realized Hill had booked ice time right after a group with which Sullivan was playing. Hill didn't know that Sullivan played hockey, and the director asked him to stick around.

Paul D'Amato was there that same night. Like Ned Dowd, he grew up in Massachusetts and actually graduated from high school in the Dowds' hometown, Framingham. By then, he had been on skates for years. "I always wanted to be a hockey player, but I never thought that I would in actuality be," he says. "I knew I was only, in my era, Division II-caliber, small college. I knew that I didn't have that talent level."

He concentrated on acting and enrolled at Emerson College in Boston, a performing arts and communications institution, and graduated with a major in theater and minors in speech, English and history. While acting in a play in New York, he attracted an agent who wondered how to promote D'Amato.

"He said, 'How can I sell you? What can I do to get you going further in your career? What can you do that other actors can't do?' I said, 'Well, I ski very well, but I can skate like the wind.' He laughed and he said, 'The next time there's a hockey film, I'll let you know.' About three weeks later, I get a call and he says, 'You have to go to the Sky Rink in New York at 1 o'clock in the morning and audition for a hockey film with Paul Newman.'"

D'Amato remembers being so excited he could barely tie his skates. When he got on the ice, someone slid a puck to him. He rifled a shot from the blue line that sailed over the net and crashed against the glass behind the goal. The noise got people's attention. Mendillo and Sullivan skated over and the three of them worked together for a little while, passing a puck back and forth and rushing it up the ice.

"The whistle blew," D'Amato says. "The next thing I knew, George Roy Hill was calling us over. 'Can you act?' 'Yes.' 'Can you be in my office in the morning?' 'Yes.' 'Okay, you're done.' I thought, I'm done? The audition's over? All right!"

The next day, he was given a bit to read. It was Johnny Upton's part in the fashion show. Hill told him he would be in the film but he didn't know yet what role D'Amato would play. Go home and start skating regularly, he told the actor. D'Amato was living in Vermont at the time and was able to secure some ice time from a friend who coached a local high school team. Eventually he was cast as the villainous Tim "Dr. Hook" McCracken, "the coach and chief punk on that Syracuse team."

Yvon Barrette has Allan Nicholls to thank for getting cast as goalie Denis Lemieux in *Slap Shot*. Nicholls read for the part first; having grown up in Montreal, he can do a passable French-Canadian accent. But he also suggested that Hill and Mike Fenton try to find some actual French-Canadian actors, and for that they should go to Quebec.

TV actor Yvan Ponton was chosen to play Jean-Guy Drouin, a forward who apparently couldn't speak very much

English. That didn't stop the Charlestown Chiefs from putting an "A" on his sweater and making him an alternate captain, but anyway. They also located Barrette, an actor with a sports background from a town called Alma, 100 or so miles north of Quebec City.

"They had already auditioned something like 500 French-Canadian actors for the part, but they didn't find the one they were looking for," says Barrette, who was contacted by Fenton and asked to meet with Hill at the Sky Rink.

Barrette had played hockey as a child, but he was also an avid runner and his favorite sport was actually basketball. He could have been a sports coach for a living, but instead he followed a dream to be a professional actor, studying at the National Theatre School of Canada. He then appeared in a couple of films before Fenton tracked him down.

———— ● ————

The real gem found in casting was a young man who was an exceptional hockey player as well as a gifted actor with name recognition in the business.

Thirty-year-old Michael Ontkean made his acting debut at age five, following in the footsteps of his performer parents. Born in Vancouver and raised mainly in Montreal, he also loved hockey and started playing at around the same time. In a 1990 interview for the press kit for his TV series, *Twin Peaks*, he remembered his youthful attraction to hockey as "like an early call to some sort of sub-zero priesthood. I rarely spoke. I was in a state of constant motion with perpetually frozen toes."

Ontkean played at St. Mike's in Toronto, Junior B in Montreal and Junior A in New Westminster, B.C. He won a scholarship to the University of New Hampshire and, wearing No. 8, spent three years with the Wildcats varsity team in NCAA Division I, the top level of US college hockey. Ontkean is a member of the university's Athletics Hall of Fame and of the Wildcats' Century Club, having compiled 111 points, including 63 goals, in 85 career games.

In the 1967–68 regular season, Ontkean led the nation with 30 goals, but Clarkson's John "Jocko" McLennan, later a Canadian corporate director whose posts included president of Bell Canada, emerged from the playoffs with 32, making him tops in the NCAA. Despite his scoring prowess, Ontkean, unlike Ned Braden, was never all-Eastern. But he was a flashy, left-shooting right-winger on the Wildcats' top line, playing alongside centre Rich David and left-winger Bobby Brandt. During their three years together, they combined for 189 goals and 397 points.

"It was wonderful to watch them," says Gary Jaquith, a Wildcats teammate and later an extra in *Slap Shot*. "Mike was a very good hockey player. He could have done pretty well (in pro). He definitely had some tools."

After Ontkean's NCAA eligibility ran out, he stayed at the university to complete his degree in English literature while playing semi-pro hockey in the nearby city of Nashua. "I paid him 20 bucks a game, win or lose, and nothing for practices," says Ron Peters, who founded, managed and coached the Nashua Maple Leafs of the New England Hockey League.

"Mike was a good team player. He was very quick, very fast, soft hands, had a nice shot. I don't think I ever saw him throw a punch. He was a tough, hard-nosed guy. He took his checks and he gave them, but I don't think I ever saw him fight."

Chapter 5

Ontkean's best trait, according to those who knew him then, was his personality. Jaquith looked up to his older teammate and remembers him as a genuinely nice person with many friends. Peters recalls trying to recruit Ontkean and several other former Wildcats, and telling them league rules prevented him from offering more than $20 per game. It was an explanation that was largely falling on deaf ears.

"These other six or seven guys were saying, 'No, no, screw that, we're not playing for that.' Mike Ontkean was the sole voice of reason in the room. He said, 'Hey, guys, 40 bucks a week, two games a week, for doing something you love — how can you beat it?' He turned them right around."

Ontkean could have been earning much more than $40 a week playing hockey, but he turned down offers to play pro. He had gotten involved in the theater at UNH, and he decided to return to acting. He moved to Los Angeles, where he continued to play semi-pro with that city's Blades, and in 1972 he was cast in *The Rookies*, an ABC TV movie about young police officers. The movie was turned into a weekly drama series, which became a hit. Ontkean became a star.

Stardom, however, didn't interest him very much. He walked away from *The Rookies* after two seasons — walked away from show business, in fact. He moved to a small town in Maine, where he worked at repairing motorcycles, played music in local bars and played pick-up hockey for fun. It was another two years before he learned of a project that would allow him to combine his two loves — acting and hockey. He flew to California to try out.

Ontkean was probably the most accomplished hockey player of all the actors who tried out for *Slap Shot*. The role of

Ned Braden, a college-educated natural on the ice who wanted nothing to do with fighting in the sport, seemed tailor-made for him. But there were two other serious candidates, both very well known in the New York theatre community. One was Billy Carden and the other was Paul Rudd. Carden, for whatever reason, didn't make the grade and went on with his career as a respected actor, director and teacher. Rudd, no relation to the Frat Pack actor of the same name (*Anchorman, The 40-Year-Old Virgin*), took himself out of contention.

He decided instead to act in a play for Joe Papp, a legendary New York director, producer and impresario who had helped to launch the stage careers of Rudd, George C. Scott, Meryl Streep, Brad Sullivan and others. As much as he would like to have had a chance to act in *Slap Shot*, Rudd believes he made the right choice. "People told me afterward, you made a mistake. I heard that for years," he says. "We all have regrets, but that one didn't bother me very much."

And so Ontkean won the part. Given his exceptional hockey ability, he may well have been George Roy Hill's first choice all along. He feels he had won the director's confidence during the weeks of skating that went on as casting decisions were being made. Ontkean also became especially close to star Paul Newman during this time, and he remembers how "invaluable" Ned Dowd was as an on-ice coordinator. "He intuitively knew what needed to be done," he says.

He also recalls that it wasn't Hill who shared with him the news that he had been chosen to play Ned Braden. "It was actually Paul Newman himself who told me that I got the part, which was enormous. He told me on the ice one morning when we were there for our workout. He said, 'Congratulations.' I said, 'Why, what happened?' He said, 'We're officially team-mates.' And he could tell by my face that I was in shock; he thought I'd already been told.

"It was a mind-blowing moment. Definitely one of the greatest days of my life," Ontkean says, laughing. "He took me out afterward to celebrate. George Roy Hill was probably going to tell me at the end of the workout that day, but Paul and I were there early and it couldn't have worked out better for me. That was the ideal way to find out."

———— ● ————

After a self-imposed hiatus of almost two years, Michael Ontkean was once again a professional actor. Another pivotal role, that of Ned Braden's wife, Lily, was given to Lindsay Crouse, a relative newcomer to acting, although hardly a stranger to show business.

When she was born in 1948, she was named Lindsay Ann Crouse in homage to a Pulitzer Prize- and Tony Award-winning writing duo, Lindsay *and* Crouse. Russel Crouse was her father and, with Howard Lindsay, he enjoyed a very prolific writing career that lasted nearly 30 years and brought such classics as *Life with Father*, *State of the Union* and *The Sound of Music* to the stage.

Lindsay graduated from Radcliffe College in 1970 and worked as a dancer before turning to acting. Like Rudd, Crouse's stage debut was in a Joe Papp-produced play in Central Park. The production of "Much Ado About Nothing" later moved to Broadway and Crouse went with it. When she auditioned for *Slap Shot*, she had just wrapped her first film, *All the President's Men*.

Jennifer Warren, another actress with one major film under her belt, was cast as Francine Dunlop, Reggie's estranged wife. Warren had ample stage experience but her first major movie role was in 1975's *Night Moves*, with Gene Hackman.

The Greenwich Village native had worked off-Broadway while in high school, but didn't study acting in college, majoring in art history at the University of Wisconsin-Madison. She got her BA in 1963 and, by some fluke, was then able to study drama under Sir Tyrone Guthrie, a Tony Award-winning director who helped to found the Stratford Festival in Ontario before establishing a resident theater in Minneapolis.

"The theater department at Wisconsin was nice enough to nominate me for a McKnight Fellowship at the Tyrone Guthrie Theater even though I had never taken one course," she says, laughing, "for which I will forever be in their debt."

After returning to New York, Warren furthered her studies with another acting legend, two-time Tony recipient Uta Hagen. She starred alongside Robert De Niro in an all-but-forgotten 1969 film called *Sam's Song* and made her Broadway debut in 1972. Warren still remembers getting the script for *Slap Shot* and her reaction to it. "I read it and I thought, whoa, this is wonderful. I met George Roy Hill, I had one reading and that was it. I was Francine, of Gilda's Cut 'n Curl."

Slap Shot would be the film debut for Swoosie Kurtz, who was chosen to play Shirley, the wife of Chiefs captain Johnny Upton. But you could say she was already somewhat accustomed to the spotlight. The press was on hand when she was born in 1944, in Omaha, Nebraska, the daughter of United States Army Air Force Col. Frank Kurtz, the most decorated American pilot of the Second World War.

Chapter 5

Col. Kurtz was best known for his connection with the Swoose. The Boeing B-17 Flying Fortress bomber was in the Philippines when Pearl Harbor was attacked, and it conducted the first combat mission after America entered the war. Subsequent damage to the plane was repaired with spare parts from other B-17s, creating a patchwork aircraft that reminded its pilot of a Kay Kyser song about a bird that was half-swan, half-goose. The song was called "Alexander the Swoose." Soon the plane was also being called the Swoose and Kurtz became publicly identified with it while breaking various speed records over and around the Pacific Ocean.

And so it was completely natural that the birth of Frank Kurtz's first child — his only child, as it turned out — should receive the media's attention. "I was a press hog from the very beginning," jokes Swoosie, who was to have been named Margo after her mother. But someone in the press suggested Swoosie in honor of the plane, and Swoosie she became. It rhymes with Lucy but pronouncing and spelling it has been problematic for many people over the years. Many others simply don't understand the name. "They think my parents were drunk when they named me, or my sister couldn't pronounce Susie. I've heard them all," she says.

Swoosie majored in drama at the University of Southern California and studied for two years at the London Academy of Music and Dramatic Art before returning to America and launching a stage career. Her first Broadway role was in the 1975 revival of "Ah, Wilderness!"; her castmates included Steve Mendillo and Paul Rudd. She was appearing in another play in New Haven when *Slap Shot* came along, but it was a minor role and she had no problem extricating herself in order to do the film.

She was chosen by Marion Dougherty, who took over the casting process from Mike Fenton at some point for reasons that remain unclear (Fenton and partner Jane Feinberg were listed in the credits of *Slap Shot* as the casting directors, while Dougherty was listed as the "talent coordinator"). That she had become involved would have been no surprise to anyone who was familiar with George Roy Hill. They had been working together for more than 20 years and she had handled the casting on the majority of his films, starting with *The World of Henry Orient* in 1964.

When Dougherty began working on NBC's *Kraft Television Theatre* in 1949, it was a time when choosing a performer for a project was still fairly simple — producers and directors would generally pick someone who was under contract to the studio in question and just slot them into the role without a great deal of thought. That changed with Dougherty. She began to develop a process that would determine the best person for each job.

"I invented casting," she says without a hint of braggadocio. "I gave first jobs to people like James Dean, Robert De Niro, Warren Beatty, Jack Lemmon. I gave Paul Newman a one-line part in a *Kraft* cast."

Dougherty established a strong working relationship and friendship with Hill on *Kraft* and other TV dramas, and their work together often yielded fantastic results. When Hill was directing *Hawaii* in 1966, he needed an actress to portray a queen, but a suitable pro could not be found. Dougherty hired a Tahitian woman named Jocelyne LaGarde, even though LaGarde had never acted before and could not even speak English, as the character was required to do. LaGarde learned the necessary dialogue, won a Golden Globe Award for best supporting actress and was nominated for an Oscar in the same category. And then she "retired" from acting after her first and only role!

Despite Dougherty's successes in the business — she cast *Midnight Cowboy*, which won the Oscar as best picture of 1969 — she found it tough to get recognition for her achievements. It wasn't due to her gender, it was the job title that rankled some in the industry. "They would never allow me to have the title 'casting director.' The Directors Guild decided that they owned the word 'director,' which is ridiculous," she says. She was not credited on screen for casting until *Slaughterhouse-Five* in 1972, when Hill insisted on it.

——— ● ———

One of Dougherty's favorite people was film veteran Strother Martin, who was also a close friend of Hill and of Paul Newman. Dougherty chose Martin to play Chiefs general manager Joe McGrath. Martin tagged along with Jets boss John Mitchell to research the role and everyone who knew Mitchell agreed that Martin absolutely nailed the part.

"Strother Martin did a beautiful job with Johnny Mitchell. It was so perfect," says newspaper reporter John James.

It was a typically thorough performance by Martin, who completely inhabited every character he played. He generally portrayed less-than-savory individuals; even when they were on the right side of the law, they were often unseemly. A perfect example is the prison captain he played in 1967's *Cool Hand Luke*, where he violently assaults Newman's title character and then calmly asserts that "what we've got here is failure to communicate."

That was his third of six appearances in Newman films. He appeared six times with John Wayne and twice in the films of

James Stewart, also co-starring in Stewart's TV mystery series *Hawkins* in 1973–74. Martin was equally adept at comedy and delivered memorable performances in guest spots on sitcoms such as *I Love Lucy*, *The Dick Van Dyke Show* and *Gilligan's Island*.

Martin was a genial, cultured and thoughtful man who, by the time he was cast in *Slap Shot*, had been in show business for more than 25 years. The native of Kokomo, Indiana, attended the University of Michigan on a diving scholarship and was a swimming instructor in the navy during the Second World War. After moving to Los Angeles, he worked again as a swimming instructor and began to get movie work as an extra.

"He was a wonderful man," Dougherty says of Martin. "He had such a wonderful sense of humor. He was just a great guy."

Two other acting veterans were chosen to portray members of the Charlestown media. Although M. Emmet Walsh didn't make his first professional acting appearances until 1969, hitting the Broadway stage and the big and small screens that year, he more than made up for lost time and racked up more than 35 credits before winning the role of *Times-Herald* newspaperman Dickie Dunn.

"Marion Dougherty brought me in. She was one of my early champions," says the Vermont native, a 1958 graduate of Clarkson University, where he was known as Mike Walsh — now you know what the M stands for.

Walsh received a bachelor of business administration degree at Clarkson, with a major in marketing. From there he went to New York and began an acting career that has impressed, among others, film critic Roger Ebert. Over the years, Ebert has compiled a tongue-in-cheek glossary of film "rules" that

Chapter 5

generally pokes fun at clichéd dialogue and scenes — such gems include the "Law of Relative Walking Speeds: No matter how fast the would-be victim runs, the slasher can always keep up just by walking steadily." At some point, Ebert also devised the "Stanton-Walsh Rule: No movie featuring either Harry Dean Stanton or M. Emmet Walsh in a supporting role can be altogether bad. Exceptions are *Chattahoochee*, starring Walsh, and *Wild at Heart*, starring Stanton."

John James was at the time nearing the middle of his 20-plus-year tenure as the hockey writer for the *Johnstown Tribune-Democrat* and believes he was likely the inspiration for Dickie Dunn. He enjoyed Walsh's portrayal of the character. "No one will confirm that, but I get the impression that I was," James says, laughing. "And if people relate to me as Dickie Dunn, that's fine. That's a compliment to be among those guys, to be able to have been part of that team and that era. It was an exciting time."

Andrew Duncan was cast as sportscaster Jim Carr. Duncan hails from Trenton, Michigan, one of the "downriver" communities of Wayne County, south of Detroit. He was a hockey fan from childhood and remembers listening to the radio into the early hours of the morning on March 25, 1936, as the Detroit Red Wings and the Montreal Maroons battled into the sixth sudden-death overtime period of their NHL semifinal playoff game. It would become the longest game in NHL history and Charlie Harwood was calling the play-by-play from the Montreal Forum, the broadcast originating from CRCM in Montreal and relayed to Detroit-area listeners via CKLW in Windsor, Ontario, across the river from the Motor City.

It was a Tuesday night/Wednesday morning, which meant school the next day, but eight-year-old Andy hung in until the very end and was rewarded for his patience. "I was listening under my covers," he says, chuckling. With three minutes and 30 seconds left in the ninth period of play — after more than 176 minutes of action — Mud Bruneteau finally scored to give Detroit a 1–0 victory. The Red Wings went on to win their first Stanley Cup that year.

Duncan earned two degrees at the University of Michigan, a BA in English literature and an MA in art history. He furthered his graduate studies at the University of Chicago but never completed his doctorate as intended. He was drawn instead to comedy and performing, and in 1955 he and several other students and alumni formed an improvisational theater group called The Compass Players. This group, which included future stars such as Alan Alda, Alan Arkin, Ed Asner, Valerie Harper, Barbara Harris, Linda Lavin, Anne Meara and Jerry Stiller, evolved into a new troupe called The Second City; Duncan was part of its first performance in Chicago in December 1959.

A natural and unselfish straight man, Duncan received a wonderful compliment from castmate Arkin, who in 1978 said Duncan "was in a lot of ways the glue that held it all together" as The Second City, performing at home and in Los Angeles, Toronto, London and on Broadway, achieved international fame.

"There is a reason that successful talk-show hosts command such high salaries. The ability to speak to an audience about everyday things in one's own person seems easy but is difficult, and rare," founding producer Bernard Sahlins wrote in his 2001 memoir *Days and Nights at The Second City*. "In all my years at The Second City, there have been only three or

Chapter 5

four actors who could master this feat. Andrew was the first and perhaps the best."

Duncan left The Second City in 1963 and worked steadily in television and in writing and recording copy for commercials before making his film debut in 1968. He was a late addition to *Slap Shot* after the original actor playing Jim Carr balked upon learning the sportscaster would have to wear a gaudy toupee and have it come off during the filming. Dougherty recommended to George Roy Hill that Duncan take over.

"He was afraid to be seen bald," Duncan says of the unidentified original actor, adding with a laugh, "I was going bald but I didn't give a damn."

Hill trusted Dougherty's judgment and hired Duncan sight unseen. A subsequent meeting between Duncan, Hill and Nancy Dowd convinced the director and the writer that the newcomer was perfect for the job. Like Strother Martin was doing with John Mitchell, Duncan began to study his real-life counterpart, WJAC sportscaster Bill Wilson, and he shopped for a toupee that would fit the bill. He ended up at a Johnstown department store called Glosser Brothers.

"George Roy Hill said, 'I don't care what you get, just get something outrageous,'" Duncan told Mike Mastovich of the *Johnstown Tribune-Democrat* in February 2007. "I went to Glosser's and went to the wig department. The stylist started showing me wigs that made it look like you didn't have a wig. I said no. Then I saw one she pushed aside and I said that's the one. I stuck it on my head and looked in the mirror and started laughing. George looked at me and started laughing. He said, 'If you dare, I dare.'"

Forty years after a young boy was stirred by a hockey broadcast on his radio, that boy, for all intents and purposes, became a hockey broadcaster. Nothing that Duncan ever said as Jim Carr will resonate quite as much as "Henderson has scored for Canada!" or "Do you believe in miracles? Yes!" Not quite. But Duncan's work will live forever just the same; he has cemented a place for himself in hockey broadcasting history.

Chapter 6

The Story on That Dog

——— ● ———

He's known as Morley's Dog. A fixture in Johnstown's downtown for decades, it was appropriate that he was featured in the first scene as principal photography began on *Slap Shot*. It was March 22, 1976.

Morley's Dog was a lawn ornament swept away from its original home in the flood of 1889. Returned after the disaster to its owner, Bethlehem Steel executive James Morley, it was eventually donated to the city. At some point, the dog's story became entwined with those of actual animals that had performed heroic deeds during the flood. One legend even claims the dog came briefly to life in order to rescue citizens. It's not true, although Nancy Dowd apparently thought enough of Morley's Dog to credit him with saving Charlestown in 1938, two years after another real-life killer flood in Johnstown.

But he does deserve credit for ensuring Johnstown became Charlestown in the first place — the 700-pound canine tipped the scale in the decision to film *Slap Shot* there in the spring of 1976.

After realizing that the number of actors who could skate well enough to convincingly play hockey players was woefully low, George Roy Hill agreed with screenwriter Nancy Dowd and her brother, technical advisor Ned Dowd, who suggested real-life players be given chances to work in the film. They also suggested the movie itself be filmed in Johnstown, where, conveniently, lots of hockey players could be found. The director wasn't immediately convinced, though. He asked Henry Bumstead to look into it.

Bummy, as he was popularly known during his 70-year career as one of the film industry's foremost art directors/ production designers, had a keen eye and Hill trusted him implicitly. They first worked together on *Slaughterhouse-Five* in 1972, by which time Bummy, who started at Paramount Pictures in 1937, was already a legend in the business. He won his first Oscar for *To Kill a Mockingbird* in 1962.

The working relationship between Hill and Bummy paid quick dividends as both won Oscars for 1973's *The Sting*. Bummy and Hill worked together for the duration of Hill's career, and Bummy also regularly collaborated with Clint Eastwood; the war movies *Flags of Our Fathers* and *Letters from Iwo Jima* were the final films of Bummy's career, both completed not long before his death at age 91 in 2006.

Bummy scouted a number of American communities — Minneapolis, Duluth, Utica, Syracuse, Binghamton and Johnstown. He told Nancy Coleman of the *Tribune-Democrat* that Morley's Dog had been the key factor in his pick of

Johnstown. "It's amazing, but in these other cities there are no other parks in the center of town. We wanted the park and that dog," he said. "I've fallen in love with the dog. I guess it's because I have a big dog myself, a Labrador, and I'm homesick for him."

His call would not have been questioned by Hill. Universal likely would not have taken issue with Hill's decision, since he had successfully shot several films on location before — *Hawaii* in Hawaii, *Butch Cassidy* at a number of sites in Colorado, Utah, New Mexico and Mexico, *Slaugherhouse-Five* in Czechoslovakia and *Waldo Pepper* in Texas. The only question was: did Johnstown want to be the site of the film?

Ned Dowd and representatives from Universal showed up in February 1976 to find out. They were preceded by a call to the Johnstown Chamber of Commerce from the Pennsylvania Film Commission, which had recently been established to help attract film projects to the state. John Rubal, the chamber's executive director, contacted Denny Grenell, a life-long Johnstown resident and a civic booster with a reputation for making things happen.

"Believe me, we rolled out the red carpet," Grenell says. "We promised them everything and we didn't know if we could deliver one thing. We promised them discount rates at the hotel; you name it, we said we could get it for them."

———— ● ————

Johnstown needed some good news. It had begun to feel the effects of a downturn in the American steel industry. The market for steel was decreasing and the amount of imported steel from other countries was growing. Smaller steel operations, known as mini-mills, were springing up and taking increasingly large bites of the pie.

But the city had bounced back from tough times before. Nestled in a deep valley in the Allegheny Mountains and named after early settler Joseph Johns, it became the home of the Cambria Iron Company in 1852. The company used the region's ample natural resources — timber, huge deposits of coal and iron ore, and the waters of two rivers, the Stonycreek and the Little Conemaugh — and turned Johnstown into the top steel-producing city in the United States. It did not retain this distinction, soon falling behind Pittsburgh and other cities, but it remained a major production center well into the 20th century.

That was despite a horrific disaster that all but destroyed the city on May 31, 1889. About 14 miles outside of town, upstream on the Little Conemaugh, a badly maintained dam gave way and sent millions of tons of water barreling down the river valley and into Johnstown with a force estimated at the time to be the equal of Niagara Falls. The tragedy was compounded by a fire that started in flood debris that pushed up against a bridge in town. More than 2,200 people died in the Johnstown Flood, the largest single-day civilian loss of life in American history until the terrorist attacks of September 11, 2001.

Johnstown rebounded. It was home to about 67,000 people by 1920, and its industrial base got a boost three years later when the Bethlehem Steel Company took over the steel operations and began to reshape them, upgrading old plants and building new ones. The local coal industry was also thriving, as about 150 different companies in Cambria County supplied the factories with their fuel.

Another major flood struck on March 17, 1936, killing about two dozen people and causing an estimated $40 million in damage. With help from the federal government, which pledged to create a channel system in town to prevent its rivers from overflowing in the future, the city again bounced back. It was during this five-year program to make for a "flood-free" city, in 1941, that Johnstown's first pro hockey team was established — the Blue Birds of the Eastern Amateur Hockey League.

The team lasted only one season due to the Second World War, but was replaced in 1950 by the Jets. They quickly established themselves in the community and their players became local celebrities. Most of them were Canadians who came to Johnstown out of junior hockey in the hope of moving up the hockey ladder. One was Dick Roberge, who arrived from Saskatoon in 1954. He was the property of the Toronto Maple Leafs, one of the most prestigious franchises in the best hockey league on the planet. And yet they weren't above skimping on whatever they could, including boots from old skates — Roberge was given a pair of boots that had once belonged to legendary Leafs captain Syl Apps. He didn't literally follow in Apps' shoes, because he never made it to the NHL. But Roberge became a legend in his own right. By the time the right-winger retired in 1972, he had scored 756 goals and 1,740 points and remains the only player in minor league history to ever reach the 700-goal plateau, a mark he hit on February 4, 1970, in Utica, NY.

Roberge spent 17 seasons as a player in Johnstown, leading the Jets in scoring eight times and finishing among the EHL's top 10 scorers on 12 occasions. He scored 38 or more goals and/or 90 or more points 14 times and was the only man in the post-war history of the EHL to win three league scoring championships. He did it all, and he rode far more than his fair share of buses up and down the east coast. It was a grueling life, and he remembers that he was paid $85 a week as a rookie.

"We'd leave Johnstown on Friday morning and go to Clinton, NY to play on Friday night. Then we'd drive all the way back to Johnstown for Saturday night, then play in New Haven or Long Island on Sunday afternoon," says Roberge, now retired from post-hockey life as a golf pro and living in Myrtle Beach, SC.

"It was unbelievable. You just had to love the game."

Roberge and Toronto-born left-winger Don Hall, a Montreal Canadiens prospect, were the cornerstones of a powerful offence that carried the Jets to the top of the EHL heap. They won three straight playoff championships between 1960 and 1962. More importantly, these men were among those who pioneered the concept of settling in Johnstown and making their homes there. Roberge, for example, worked as a golf pro in the summers. Hall studied to be a stockbroker on his way to becoming the first pro hockey player to register 1,000 points in a career. He retired with 414 goals and 1,038 points in 12 seasons, all but the first of them with the Jets.

"It got to the point where I could make more money as a stockbroker than I could playing hockey, which was in 1962. I was 31 years old, and I wasn't an old 31, either," says Hall, who invested in the Jets, becoming a director of the club and eventually its president.

"I was always guaranteed a job in the summertime," adds Roberge, the longtime pro at the Windber Country Club just outside Johnstown. "I was just happy to be there. It was my home."

Practically anyone in Johnstown who wanted to work was guaranteed a job, or so it seemed. More often than not, the jobs were tied to Bethlehem Steel; nearly 12,000 people worked there in early 1973. At the same time, Johnstown learned that the National Civic League had designated it an All-America City for 1972–73, an annual honor given in recognition of overall civic excellence. The designation was marked by a patch on the shoulders of the Jets' jerseys, later replicated on the uniforms of the Charlestown Chiefs.

But it was costing more for Bethlehem Steel to bring raw materials to Johnstown and to ship the finished product where it was needed. The Johnstown facilities were also aging and were coming under greater scrutiny due to higher awareness of the environment and the resulting need to reduce the steel industry's negative impacts on air and water quality. In June 1973, Bethlehem announced that it planned to reduce by more than half the capacity of its Johnstown operations and to slash its workforce there over the next four years. Few people in the city, if any, realized that company chairman Lewis Foy was already being pressured to simply shut down the whole works. It was a move that Foy refused to consider; he was a Johnstown native.

As Bethlehem retrenched and Johnstown fought to diversify, the prospect of a major motion picture pumping hundreds of thousands of dollars into the local economy was impossible to ignore. The city administration, led by Mayor Herb Pfuhl, joined the chamber of commerce in pledging whatever Universal needed to cinch the deal. In the end, Grenell says, every promise that had been made was kept. "We even closed down parking meters for a couple of days without telling the mayor," he laughs.

The Jets also needed to be okay with it. Ned Dowd honestly didn't know who owned the team when queried by his sister, and this became a running joke in *Slap Shot* — "who own da Chiefs?" But it was well known in Johnstown that the

Jets were owned by a group of investors based in the community. Thirty-five people were part of the ownership group, which took over the club in May 1974 from the Johnstown Hockey Company, a smaller group comprised of 19 investors. Don Hall was among them and he became the team president. He remembers the day he was approached about the film, a visit that took him by surprise even though he had been aware that Nancy Dowd was writing a screenplay.

"I was sitting in the office one day and my assistant came back and said, 'There's a couple of guys from Universal Studios here to see you.' I couldn't imagine what they were doing there," Hall says. They explained the purpose of their visit and he wondered, given his job in the investment business, if they were there to borrow money to make this film they were telling him about. As it happened, they were only looking for the hockey team's approval and cooperation. After Hall read the script they gave him, he wasn't necessarily sure the approval and cooperation would be forthcoming.

"It was pretty risqué, for the '70s. I was a little leery about this," he says. But he agreed to talk with his fellow directors, who said they would go along with it if John Mitchell and Dick Roberge thought it was all right. They did. Hall went back to Universal and said the Jets would cooperate as long as the film didn't interfere with the team's schedule.

"I said, okay, I think we can work this thing out. Well, it worked out for about two weeks," he chuckles. "After about two weeks, we were revolving our stuff around the movie. They were paying the players more than we were. It was a tough situation, you know?"

Nobody in minor-pro hockey got paid well in that era, but members of the Jets were hampered by the fact that they played in a comparatively small community and didn't have a great deal of revenue. Not only that, John Mitchell controlled the purse strings.

The Hamilton, Ontario, native had spent most of his life involved in hockey. Mitchell refereed in junior and in the NHL when his playing career ended. He later worked as a scout, coach and manager for Eddie Shore of the Springfield Indians, for Toronto Maple Leafs boss Conn Smythe and for Jack Adams of the Detroit Red Wings.

"If there was ever anybody whose whole life was wrapped up in hockey, it was John," says Glen Sonmor, Mitchell's son-in-law.

But he was "infamously frugal," says Jets netminder Ron Docken. Mitchell was indeed the kind of executive who could turn a nickel into a quarter by squeezing it hard enough and long enough. Extra hockey sticks were difficult to come by. During at least one post-season, Mitchell refused to buy any more hockey tape for the players, who resorted to using electrical tape. They also really were forced to participate in area fashion shows to increase the team's exposure and sources of revenue. That's what they had to do to survive in one of the league's smaller markets, with a locally owned and operated club that did not receive much in the way of support from the powerful teams of the NHL.

His tight-fisted nature notwithstanding, Mitchell was loved by his players, even though he may not always have been able to remember their names — he called everyone "son." The players say he was portrayed to perfection in *Slap Shot* by the veteran character actor Strother Martin, who shadowed Mitchell closely while preparing for the role of Charlestown Chiefs GM Joe McGrath.

"Johnny Mitchell was just like that. He was a fantastic motivator. He was like five-foot-four and he would jump on the medical bench and start hollering and trying to get you going," Roberge says. "He was a character. He was beautiful."

———— ● ————

Paul Newman visited Johnstown for the first time on February 22 and filming started exactly one month later. Many of the actors and crew moved into the downtown Sheraton Inn hotel on Market Street, only a block away from the War Memorial, although Newman and his wife, Joanne Woodward, moved into a home in the nearby town of Ligonier. Calls for extras were answered by scores of community residents looking for a chance to get in front of a camera, maybe rub shoulders with Newman and make some money — $2.30 per hour, the minimum wage in Pennsylvania at the time.

Some extras were given small speaking parts, which paid more but necessitated them to become members of the Screen Actors Guild. One was Gracie Head, wife of Jets captain Galen Head. She was asked by Nancy Dowd to read for a part as a player's wife and was hired to play Pam, who, although it was never explicitly said in the film, was the wife of Jim Ahern, Steve Mendillo's character. Ned Dowd's then-wife, whose name was also Nancy, was cast as another hockey wife, Andrea. She was credited as Nancy N. Dowd to differentiate her from her sister-in-law the writer. Her husband was supposed to have been Jerry Marsh, who didn't make the cut, although his name inexplicably survived — "I thought I'd get Jerry one of those 'Great Ideas of the World' sets."

The shooting process was difficult for people like Head who had other jobs. She worked as a nurse at Lee Hospital in

Johnstown and it was sometimes a challenge to balance her schedules, but she stuck it out and was well-compensated for her efforts.

"The amount of money that you got paid was just unbelievable," she says. "I was getting maybe $900 a week, but then I think it was after you worked 30 hours a week, you got time-and-a-half. And it started from the time you were in makeup, even if they didn't need you for the day.

"I remember my first cheque, it must have been about $1,900. At that time, that was a lot of money. I was walking up the hall and Paul Newman was walking down and I said to him, 'I think I got your cheque by mistake.' He goes, 'Why?' I showed him how much money I'd made and he laughed and said, 'Oh no, I make a lot more than that.'"

Other extras quickly found that it wasn't what they thought it would be. Hall recalls his wife, Jean, telling him she wanted to be in the film. He tried to talk her out of it, but she would not be dissuaded. "So I talked to Henry Bumstead and he said, bring her down early in the morning. We get down there about 6:30 . . . I picked her up at 7 o'clock that night and she said, 'I don't want to be in the movie anymore,'" Hall laughs.

The extras, hockey players, actors and crew all hit it off famously. The key, according to Ron Docken, was that no one in Johnstown was in awe of the film company, not even of Newman.

"We didn't know who they were, and we didn't care. They were coming to our town. We would walk up and down the streets and people would ask for our autographs, not theirs. That kind of leveled the playing field," Docken says. "After a while, Paul Newman found out that we were decent guys, we liked to have a lot of fun. He would say, 'Hey, can we go out and drink some beer and shoot some pool?' And we would. We'd go out and have a good time. He just thought that was fabulous."

Morley's Dog was temporarily moved into Central Park for his big scene, in which he graciously shared screen time with Newman and Lindsay Crouse. Appearing with Newman so early in the process must have been daunting for Crouse, appearing in only her second feature film, but the filming went well. By contrast, Mike Ontkean, the actor playing Crouse's husband, had some early difficulties. The men who would play for the Chiefs were all presented with brand new hockey equipment so they would look like a real team as opposed to a bunch of guys who just happened to be wearing the same jerseys. But Ontkean had his own gear and had been using it for quite a long time; note the numeral 8, from his university days, marked on both sides of his shoulder pads. Some of the equipment had seen better days, but he wanted to keep it anyway.

"The gloves I wore in *Slap Shot* were my own and falling apart," Ontkean says. "I used them in my last year of Junior A, plus four years of college hockey at UNH, plus three years of semi-pro. I had been using them in all the weeks of rehearsals in LA and Johnstown before actual shooting began and just assumed they would be fine for the movie."

George Roy Hill wasn't happy, as Ontkean recalls, but he gave in after realizing the "ancient brown rags" were to the actor what the blanket was to Linus in the *Peanuts* comic strip. "He shot something else for an hour while the prop department painted and dried all the bits and pieces to resemble the rest of the team. First day and already Braden is odd man in the barrel."

That was a trend that carried through the filming. Ontkean often kept to himself, which was noticed not only by his fellow actors but also the residents of Johnstown. Given the friendly nature he consistently displayed while attending school and playing hockey in New Hampshire, it's reasonable to assume he wasn't being standoffish and simply wanted to create for himself an environment that would allow him to better understand and portray the loner that Ned Braden was.

The casting process continued even as filming began. The players who would work in the movie were still playing for their NAHL teams, including the Jets, so the filmmakers had to work around various schedules. They almost got a break when the Minnesota Fighting Saints ran out of money and folded in late February 1976, about three-quarters of the way through the WHA regular season. The hope in Johnstown was that Jack Carlson would return to the Jets, a move that would serve two purposes. First, it would give a huge boost to the team as it battled to retain its championship. Second, it would allow him to slot right back in alongside his brothers when the cameras started to roll. He would be able to play his alter ego, Jack Hanson, in *Slap Shot*.

It had been decided that the Carlsons, after doing a satisfactory reading for Hill, would play the Hansons, three lookalike brothers who wore thick black glasses on the ice and terrorized their opponents and became local folk heroes. And, contrary to popular belief, Reggie Dunlop's reading of that line in the police station was not an inside joke/tribute to Butch Cassidy; it was in the very first draft of the script, before Paul Newman signed on.

The Carlsons' partner in crime, Dave Hanson, would likewise play a character very much like himself, rugged young defenceman Dave "Killer" Carlson. Two other Jets, Guido

Tenesi and Jean Tetreault, were slated for featured roles. Ron Docken would perform double duty — with his goalie mask on, he would do the action sequences as Denis Lemieux, who was portrayed the rest of the time by actor Yvon Barrette. With his mask off, Docken would play backup netminder Yvon Lebrun, a character whose first name was initially Louis. It was changed because of the similarity to Louis Levasseur and the character was renamed for Yvon Barrette. Confused yet? To make matters even stranger, Lebrun's character was never even identified during the film.

Plans had to be changed when Jack Carlson didn't return to the Jets. The Saints players were dispersed throughout the WHA and he was snatched up by the Edmonton Oilers. The Oilers were a sad sack bunch who managed to finish five points behind the Saints in the overall standings even though Edmonton played 22 more games than did Minnesota. But it was still the big league, and Jack was determined to stay. He was out of the movie.

Dave Hanson filled the vacancy, taking on the role of Jack Hanson as if he had been born to play it. He was about three inches shorter than Jack Carlson, but the two men were the same age and both had long blond hair. All that was needed was to put a pair of black horn-rimmed glasses on Hanson's face and a No. 16 sweater on his back — he wore No. 20 with the Jets — and the transformation was complete.

Fitting in as a fictional Hanson and becoming a "brother" to Jeff and Steve was fairly easy, he says, noting their shared Minnesota backgrounds and the fact that they spent so much time together in Johnstown. "You take on complementary personalities to each other. We literally saw each other every day and every night, whether it was on the bus or at the house," he says. "So when Jack got pulled up, it was no big deal for me to just slide right in and be like the guys. The only problem was I'm much better looking than they are. I don't look as horrible as they do."

Getting used to the glasses, well, that wasn't quite as simple. Hanson says even Jeff and Steve had problems with the eyewear. "The glasses were beveled. They were round glasses, and right in the middle of them they had a flat spot. We put those on and wore them for about 45 minutes, and after that we got seasick. My gosh, we can't see with these, we're gonna puke. That's when they came out with the Coke bottle glasses. You could see somewhat better, but it was still tough."

Actor Jerry Houser was then tapped to play "Killer" Carlson. He says the biggest surprise for him was finding out what tremendous athletes the hockey players were, even though they may not quite have been WHA or NHL caliber.

"When you're all going slow, you kind of look like them, but there's this whole other gear they can shift to," he says. "It's amazing. It was such a cool privilege being out there with those professional athletes. They're just a whole breed of their own in what they're able to do, how good they are."

The presence of both Houser and Allan Nicholls on the set led to a problem for Hill, as both men had dark, curly hair and might be mistaken for one another. The director asked Nicholls to wear a helmet. Although he had never worn one before, Nicholls recognized that it made sense as he was older and his character, the team captain, was ostensibly a family man — more careful, more concerned about his post-hockey options at the "fuckin' Chrysler plant." Nicholls added his own touch, a Fu Manchu mustache he says was inspired by Montreal Canadiens defenceman Larry Robinson.

Tenesi and Tetreault were the other Jets who were enlisted to play Chiefs throughout the film, as opposed to the first game, which marked the first and only appearance of several players in Charlestown uniforms.

"They just said, 'You're going to be in a movie.' I said, okay, here we go," Tenesi says. "It was something different to do."

Neither man spoke on camera but both were prominently featured, with Tetreault as the unidentified-on-film Andre Bergeron, who is seen removing his false teeth before one game. He also delivers a believable look of impending doom when told by Blake Ball, as goon Gilmore Tuttle, that he will be "straightened out" in the last playoff game. Tenesi was cast as the narcissistic Billy Charlebois, the handsome blond babe magnet who never met a mirror he didn't like. He says he originally wasn't supposed to have a speaking part, then he was, and then Hill changed his mind again.

"We'll keep you where you are. There's a character within a character that doesn't say anything the whole movie," Tenesi remembers Hill saying to him, adding with a laugh, "That was my chore."

"Guido is a man of little words. He's very, very quiet," says his wife, Leslie Tenesi. "When he speaks, he's always dead on, very to the point and very insightful."

John Gofton was among the Jets who did not join their real-life teammates on the Chiefs. He was given the part of Hyannisport Presidents center Nick Brophy after Jets player-coach Jim Cardiff, who replaced Dick Roberge for the 1975–76 season, turned it down and bowed out of the film altogether.

"When a part came up, whoever was next in line took that part," Gofton says. "I guess Jimmy was a born-again Christian and he took the part of Brophy. The next part that came along was McCracken. That's the part that I read at the reading. After it was all done, Jimmy went to George Roy Hill and said, 'Thank you very much for the offer, but I will not be participating in this movie.' He didn't swear, he didn't drink, he was immaculate. I was right there and Hill said, 'Well, you take his part.'"

That meant having to face off against Paul Newman, in more ways than one. Yes, Brophy took the draw against Reggie Dunlop to start the game, but he was also the first character to have dialogue with Dunlop. This is when Brophy confesses to Reggie that he is drunk and will "piss all over" himself if anybody checks him into the boards — a tidbit Dunlop is quick to share with his teammates.

Seven takes were needed to film the first scene. Thirteen punishing takes were needed for the scene in which Mike Ontkean, as Ned Braden, hammers Brophy into the boards and causes him to lose control of his bladder.

"I said, 'Don't worry about me, just swing in there and hit it.' But one time he hit me pretty good. I hit the boards and my head hit the glass and, geez, I thought I was going to drop. No helmets in those days — you couldn't put a helmet on; nobody would know who you were.

"The part that I play, everybody loves it. I look at it and think, shit, if I had known it was going to turn out like that, I'd have tried to do it a little bit better. But it was fun and it was very enjoyable. We had lots of laughs while we were doing it."

———— ● ————

The most difficult thing about filming the movie was coming up with ways to shoot the hockey action. Much of what Hill had in mind in terms of getting out onto the ice and directing from there had simply never been done before.

The first hockey movies were produced in 1936–37, three cheapie B-films that painted hockey as a violent sport operated and/or infested by crooks. *The Game That Kills* starred Charles Quigley as a man who joins his dead brother's team to investigate the death, which of course turns out to have been a murder; the brother had apparently refused to cooperate with a gambling ring controlled by his team's owner. This film is noteworthy only because the main character's love interest is played by a little-known 18-year-old actress named Rita Hayworth.

Dick Purcell starred in *King of Hockey* about a cocky player who comes under the influence of gangsters and gamblers. A fight with a teammate costs him his sight but it is restored by an operation and the player, redeemed also by the love of a beautiful and devoted girl, returns to lead his team to victory.

The capper, though, was John Wayne in *Idol of the Crowds*. The Duke played Johnny Hanson — things that make you go hmmmmm — a retired star who returns to the sport so he can earn enough money to enlarge his chicken farm. Yes, John Wayne as a chicken farmer. Maybe that's what all hockey-playing Hansons did for fun before the invention of slot cars. Anyway, Hanson is bribed to throw the championship. He refuses and his younger brother, the team's mascot, is injured by crooks. Hanson avenges his brother, wins the championship, gets the girl — you know the drill by now.

For some reason, Wayne kept the gloves he wore in the film. Nearly four decades later, he presented them to Mike Ontkean, who brought them along to Pennsylvania. "He used to watch my show *The Rookies* — don't know why — and gave me the gloves for good luck on my first major movie role," Ontkean says. "Great guy. I kept his gloves set up like a little altar in my hotel room for months in Johnstown."

The early '70s Canadian movies *Face-Off* and *Paperback Hero* didn't do any more than the old B movies had done to advance the idea of actually filming hockey from the best possible vantage point — on the ice. It was left up to Ned Dowd and cinematographer Victor Kemper to figure out how to make *Slap Shot* work, and they came up with some novel ideas.

"It was trial and error," Dowd says, noting an early idea to have a camera operator wear golf shoes on the ice didn't pan out. "The best thing we came up with was to put an operator in a wheelchair. When we got a fresh sheet of ice with a wheelchair and somebody who could skate, like myself, pushing it, they were able to do a lot."

Bobby Rose worked as the key grip, meaning he was the film's chief technician, and both Dowd and Kemper credit him with the design and construction of innovative rigs that allowed cameras and their operators to go places they hadn't previously gone. For instance, he installed a camera on a lawn mower. He also built a sled on which operators like Kemper could lie while holding a camera in their hands. The sled's runners left tracks on the ice, but they were shallow and almost indistinguishable from skate marks.

Kemper, like Paul Newman, hadn't skated since childhood. He says he was nervous at first about skating with a camera in his hands, but the apprehension went away as his skating ability came back to him. Before long, he forgot he was even on skates.

"It's an interesting psychological thing, like when I used to hang out of a helicopter with a camera and people thought

I was nuts — 'How can you hang out like that?' Well, once you're looking through the viewfinder, your vision is limited to that little tiny square. You don't even think about anything else. You're thinking about getting the shot."

The native of Newark, NJ, had been in the entertainment business for nearly 30 years when he was hired for *Slap Shot*. He got his start at a TV station in his hometown after graduating from Seton Hall University and serving in the military during the war, and by the late 1960s he had worked as a sound mixer, sound recorder, floor manager and technical director and assistant cameraman.

Although he had skated as a child, Kemper had never actually watched a hockey game prior to *Slap Shot*. He became a fan from working on and seeing the movie. "I must say I was inspired by the excitement and the roughness of the game," he says, adding his skating became so proficient by the end of the shoot that he was able to skate backwards while holding a camera and remain in front of the action moving forward, towards him. It helped that the hockey players had been asked to perform most of the time at half- to three-quarter-speed, making it easier on the camera operators as well as the actors, all of whom needed to be able to keep up to them.

Kemper cites the inventiveness of the job as particularly exhilarating and enjoyed the freedom bestowed upon him by director Hill, who trusted him not only to get the necessary shots but also to figure out how he would do it.

"George pretty much let me do what I felt was right. He was wonderful," Kemper says. "He would tell me what he wanted out of the shot, what the end result should be, and then he would skate away and leave me standing on the ice with the dilemma in my lap. But it's that kind of challenge that I always enjoyed, and I really appreciated that George worked that way.

"I didn't find it a frightening challenge at all. People will say, 'Were you challenged by the prospect of doing it?' I usually think they mean that I was concerned about how I was going to accomplish it. But rather than being concerned, I'm always excited by the possibilities. And we really came up with some terrific stuff, visually. I had a wonderful time on that movie."

Chapter 7

Believing Your Freaking Eyes

———— ● ————

For all the praise *Slap Shot* has earned over the years for its realism, let's face it — there are some hockey scenes that just can't be taken at face value.

A good example is seen during the Chiefs' first game against Hyannisport. While the play is going on around the Charlestown net, defenceman Billy Charlebois ambles back and forth nonchalantly and doesn't seem to be too interested in preventing goals from being scored. Dave Hanson and the Carlson brothers, in their commentary on the 2002 DVD release of the film, have some laughs at the expense of Guido Tenesi, Charlebois' portrayer.

"Guido's working hard," one of them scoffs, as another suggests he's more interested in staying in the camera frame than in playing defence. Sure enough, Hyannisport scores.

"Another minus for Guido," is the commentary, referring to his plus-minus rating.

Ron Docken, who played goalie Denis Lemieux in all the game scenes, said Tenesi was far from lazy and nonchalant in real life. "Guido was a fabulous defenceman. He was probably the best skater in the league," Docken says. "He's a player that could easily have played in the NHL, given the chance. But that could be said of a lot of players."

Tenesi acknowledges he was directed to do certain things that weren't familiar to him. More realistic, he says, are the scenes where he is making out with a girl or two. "That was natural," he laughs.

"Of course it was," says his wife, laughing too. A Johnstown native then known as Leslie Brotemarkle, she says she wasn't too upset to see her future husband being mauled and the object of other women's desires. "Who cares?" she says, smiling. "He was going home with me."

A more obvious touch of realism could be found in the teams of the fictional Federal Hockey League. They bore more than passing resemblance to actual clubs, particularly those of the NAHL. The Chiefs jerseys were direct copies of the uniforms worn by the Johnstown Jets. The digs of the Syracuse Bulldogs were inspired not by the real-life Syracuse Blazers but by the Beauce Jaros, a Quebec-based team. The actual Long Island Ducks were no more by this time, but they were revived for the Federal League and given the uniforms of the Binghamton Broome Dusters.

Binghamton's team was renamed the Broome County Blades, possibly after the NAHL's Erie Blades, and given the colors of the Philadelphia Firebirds. Hyannisport's team was inspired by the Cape Codders, but an old EHL club, the

Washington Presidents, likely served as the inspiration for the jerseys. Lancaster, like Johnstown, is a small city in Pennsylvania. It has never had a pro hockey team and the origin of the Lancaster Gears uniforms is unknown. The same went for the equally fictional Peterborough Patriots. They were ostensibly from Peterborough, NH, near Nashua.

Ned Dowd and Art Newman wanted to get approximately 60 players, other than the Jets, to be in the film. They approached the other NAHL teams and Dowd specifically tapped some personal connections. He had met Ross Smith of the Mohawk Valley Comets at a St. Louis Blues training camp. Smith was happy to take a film role for substantially more pay than he was drawing as a hockey player.

"We weren't making great money and we were battling the battles that the movie portrays," says the native of Westlock, Alberta, adding he made $200 per week at the time with the Comets.

Smith was a rugged forward with Mohawk Valley and spent some time with the Comets parent club, the Indianapolis Racers of the WHA. He was cast as Broome County Blades center Barclay Donaldson, who engages in a war of words with Reggie Dunlop prior to a face-off. Donaldson ends the argument by telling Dunlop he's "too fucking old to play this game," but more than a few takes were needed because, among other glitches, Smith accidentally put the adjective in the wrong place.

"He was very good. He coached me through it all," Smith says of Newman, adding that director Hill "was very understanding that we were not actors. It was a total thrill." When Smith finally completed his exchange of dialogue with the star, Newman smiled and held up the player's hand as though he had just won a fight. "Next week, kid, Hamlet!" Newman announced, to the appreciative laughter of all present.

But Smith's real fight was yet to begin. After Donaldson insults Reggie, "Killer" Carlson jumps to Reggie's defence and two fights ensue. Before the first bout, Smith and actor Jerry Houser rehearsed and worked to make the fight look realistic. Unfortunately for Houser, Smith forgot to hold back on some of his punches once the cameras were rolling. "He beat the crap out of me," Houser laughs.

The camera was set up in such a way that Donaldson would look like he was punching "Killer" in the face, but in reality Smith would be hitting Houser's right shoulder. As Smith's fist came across Houser's body, Houser's head would snap back as though the punches were really to the head.

"We had it all laid out," Houser says, and then pantomimes what really happened. "Boom! Boom! Boom! I've never been hit in the face that many times, that quick. I'm just bleeding everywhere. George is going, 'Good, keep going, keep going! Looks good!' After, (Smith) said, 'I'm really sorry, I forgot.' I remember that so well."

"Jerry ended up taking a couple of punches," Smith acknowledges, "but Jerry wanted to make it as real as we could and, when you're trying to pull punches, sometimes they don't get pulled.

"Personally, I'm biased, but I thought it was the best fight scene in the whole movie."

———— ● ————

A number of Smith's Comets teammates also wound up with Broome County, and two of them had memorable scenes in the same game. Bob O'Reilly, of Verdun, Quebec, who had played with Ned Dowd at McGill, was a defenceman and a legitimate tough guy. He engaged in a legendary battle with Goldie Goldthorpe of Binghamton in January 1976, bashing his opponent over the head with a chair to keep Goldthorpe from continuing the fight in the penalty box.

O'Reilly remembers it like it was yesterday. He had heard all about the notorious thug and, as had happened when Goldthorpe was playing junior, fact and fiction melded together to present a scary picture of a demented criminal element. He was a martial arts practitioner who supposedly carried nunchuks. He had reportedly been suspended from one team or perhaps an entire league for biting a game official on the leg and drawing blood after the official tried to break up a fight. The way O'Reilly heard it, Goldthorpe ended up in Binghamton after an abortive stay with the Erie Blades, who dumped him after he allegedly beat up the president of the fan club at the team Christmas party.

"You just kept hearing these wild stories about this guy," O'Reilly says. "And you didn't know what he was going to do."

On the night O'Reilly and Goldthorpe fought, Goldie spent the pre-game warm-up standing in a corner of the Binghamton zone, trying to shoot pucks into his own net by banking them in off the goaltender. None of the Dusters appeared to take issue with this. When the teams left the ice at the end of the warm-up, Goldie confronted Mohawk Valley players Bobby Whitlock and Murray Heatley — father of San Jose Sharks star Dany Heatley — and told them he would get them during the game. Neither Whitlock nor Heatley wanted anything to do with that scenario, so, in true Reggie Dunlop fashion, they put a bounty on the goon's head when they got in the locker room. "Whoever takes him out won't have to buy a drink for a month," O'Reilly laughs, remembering the offer from the terrified twosome.

When the game started, Goldthorpe faced off against Bobby Jones, a minor league veteran and scorer who had plenty of savvy about him. The puck dropped and Jones immediately jumped from in front of Goldie, just in time to avoid an attempt to spear him in the groin. Neither player went for the puck right away until Goldthorpe, after a couple of seconds, shot it into the Comets zone.

Defenceman O'Reilly soon found Goldie in his face as the Binghamton player forechecked. Actually, cross-checked is a better description, as that's just what he did to O'Reilly, who responded with a two-handed slash. The gloves came off and they fought, only 42 seconds after the face-off. O'Reilly thought that would be the end of it. That is, until they traded insults and an enraged Goldthorpe tried to get at him in the penalty box. Goldie put his hands on top of the boards to boost himself in, but O'Reilly punched him in the face and knocked him down. Goldie got back up and tried again, but O'Reilly knocked him down a second time. Again, Goldie was right back up. O'Reilly, realizing that he couldn't hurt this man with his fists and that his life would be in peril if Goldie actually got in the box with him, resorted to the chair. That finally ended the battle. A year later, Goldthorpe made a point of shaking O'Reilly's hand and praising him for being even crazier than Goldie himself.

Ironically, O'Reilly would play a victim in his big movie scenes. His character, Heckey, first takes a stick in the gut from Jeff Hanson — falling to the ice with an audible "oof" — and then gets sucker-punched by Steve Hanson after having the temerity to lightly check Steve in front of the Blades net. Steve

Chapter 7

then straddled and throttled the prone Heckey, but you won't see a close-up of Heckey's face during this sequence; O'Reilly was laughing through the whole thing.

"We had no idea what it was going to be about," says O'Reilly, who was paid $700 for seven days of work, "other than the fact that it was Paul Newman, Strother Martin, Jerry Houser and Michael Ontkean. We were too stupid to even ask. Frank Hamill was the only one smart enough to bring a camera."

Hamill, another Comet who made the grade, grew up in Sudbury, Ontario, the son of former NHLer Red Hamill. A Montreal Canadiens prospect who never played in the NHL, he bounced around the minors before signing on with Mohawk Valley in late 1975. Hamill did bring a camera and took a number of pictures which he copied and shared with his teammates, but he was eager to get in front of the bigger cameras as often as he could during his one week of work. He finagled several appearances in the film, including three notable ones during the Hansons' first shift. In the first, his character, No. 12, was slammed into the boards by Steve Hanson and then chopped by Jeff as he lay prone on the ice. Luckily, it was a balsa wood stick so there was no real danger of Hamill getting hurt by the chop. Moments later, he was ganged up on and beaten along the boards by all three Hansons; when they finished and departed, Hamill slumped to the ice.

"We did that scene 10 times," he says. "They're whacking the hell out of me for about 30 seconds each time, then I fall down. I told them, 'Take it easy, it's just a movie!' They said, 'We've got to make it look real.' They beat the hell out of me — it was just like playing hockey against them in the league."

Hamill had an idea, though, that director Hill liked enough to incorporate. He suggested a camera be placed on the inside of the glass, looking out at the rink. Hamill would, after absorbing the beating, let his hand slide down the glass before he toppled over. George Anderson, the entertainment editor of the *Pittsburgh Post-Gazette*, watched the filming of that scene and wrote about it in the April 30, 1976, edition of his newspaper. "That I like," Hill said of Hamill's work.

The player's third and final big moment with the Hansons came as the brawl was erupting. Hamill's character was tangled up with Billy Charlebois of the Chiefs when Jeff Hanson came flying past and walloped him with a right hand. Hamill, his head twitching as it snapped back, filled the screen for an instant after the blow, which might have been an even better movie punch than the one Alex Karras, as Mongo, threw to knock out the horse in *Blazing Saddles*.

"I had a lot of fun," Hamill says, adding that neither he nor any of the other visiting pros understood at the time exactly why a hockey movie was being made in Johnstown. "We didn't really know what was going on as far as any plots or themes or anything like that."

The whole sequence was basically the Hanson Brothers skating around and pulling dirty tricks on their opponents, according to Ned Dowd. It was something the players in question were used to, which made it easy. For all intents and purposes, they wound up playing themselves on film.

"Obviously there was a script to follow. We tried to do it, and obviously it was kind of robotic, especially with Jeff," Hanson says, noting Jeff would write his dialogue on his hands or try to read it from cue cards. After talking amongst

Chapter 7

themselves, they decided to improvise and found that the director was pleased with the result.

"We did it and George Roy Hill would say, 'That's great. Forget the lines. If you guys don't want to say what's on the sheet and you've got something else, go ahead and give it a shot.' Most of the time, that's what we did. There was so much ad-libbing, it got to the point where we weren't acting, we were just being ourselves. That's probably one of the reasons why it worked so well on camera. Everybody else was acting, but we weren't — we were just being ourselves."

"He gave us the free rein of making him laugh," Steve Carlson says of Hill. "The first couple of weeks, we pretty much did what they wanted us to. Then they would see what we would do, joking around, and they thought it was funnier."

It meshed with the freedom Hill had already given to seasoned pro Andrew Duncan, as the team's announcer Jim Carr. "There's more improvisation than I'm used to doing," the director told Nancy Coleman of the *Tribune-Democrat*, "but there are a lot of sequences that just say what the game result is. We have to figure out as we go along how the sequence is going to be staged, what the action is going to be on the ice."

Former Jets coach Dick Roberge, who had stepped down after the 1975 championship, played referee Ecker in three games, including the Broome County contest. His first line of dialogue was "too much, too soon" in reference to Round 1 of the "Killer" Carlson-Barclay Donaldson fight. "What a great line, eh?" he says, laughing.

He then got to eject the Hansons from the game and argue with Reggie Dunlop about it. It's a sight to behold, really — the man and the character he inspired. "I thought I was such a star. I don't know why they didn't take me to Hollywood," Roberge says, laughing again. "It was fun."

Ted McCaskill had retired from playing and was coaching Mohawk Valley but he signed on to appear in the film — he's No. 18 with the Blades and is most notable for getting sandwich-checked between Jeff and Steve Hanson and left face-down on the ice. He's also one of the two players who skate over to gaze at Frank Hamill after he's been left for dead by all three Hansons. In another scene, he can briefly be seen grappling with Dunlop while "Killer" and Barclay are fighting their first round. McCaskill fondly remembers that scene because, as hard as Newman had worked on his skating, he still wasn't very sturdy on his pins. When the gloves dropped, McCaskill grabbed Newman by the shoulder pads and started to shake him around.

"He didn't have any traction at all. It was kind of funny. It was like shaking a rag doll," McCaskill laughs. "And the director says, 'Cut! Cut! Don't hurt him!!' Needless to say, that scene did not get in the movie."

Comets general manager Brian Conacher agreed to two things, neither of which really worked out as he had intended. He signed to appear in the film as a referee but his scenes were cut from the final product. He also rented out the team's bus for use as the Chiefs' "Iron Lung," not realizing the vehicle would have a sledgehammer taken to it — on screen, no less — in order to "make it look mean."

The cross-pollination of hockey figures led to a breaking down of the barriers between people in the NAHL. As in other hockey leagues, opponents were to be barely tolerated at best. When someone became part of your team, they were fine. Team members who were traded often became *persona non grata*.

Chapter 7

"They were your enemies. They were taking money out of your pockets," says Ron Docken. "It's not like it is today where they're laughing and clowning around with each other. We never talked to another player. But when they were filming *Slap Shot*, some others from other teams came in. Well, okay, it's summer, we'll let our guard down a little bit. And we found out they were pretty decent guys too."

The sentiment was the same from the other side. "We were always fighting against them and competition was high," says Rod Bloomfield, captain of the Dusters. "All of a sudden we were put in with them in a social scene, but it was a lot of fun and I really enjoyed it. After that, whenever we played each other, there was still competition but there was no rivalry any more. Everybody got along so well."

You won't find Bloomfield's name in the credits and it's difficult to pick him out on screen, but he had the pivotal job of working as Paul Newman's double. While the superstar was competent enough to do much of his own skating and stick-handling, a fact he was proud of, the script did call for some moments when Reggie Dunlop was called upon to move faster than Newman was capable of going. Or when Dunlop, in the final playoff game, was mashed into the boards by a leaping Oggie Oglethorpe.

Bloomfield and another player were considered for the job of doubling Newman. Bloomfield was more Newman's size and build than was the other player, but that man was chosen instead and Bloomfield returned home, content to wait until he was called back to the set to play an extra like his Dusters teammates. About two weeks later, he received a phone call asking him if he was still interested in being Newman's double. Bloomfield asked what had happened to the other guy.

"They said, 'We made a bit of a mistake. We shot for two weeks and figured out he was shooting right-handed. You and Paul both shoot left. We've had to scrap all the film,'" Bloomfield laughs. "That was a great negotiation — I had the upper hand."

He eventually negotiated for himself a salary that paid him far more than Universal wanted to pay him, but Bloomfield did indeed have the edge; the studio knew it and eventually it gave in. Universal balked at giving Bloomfield an on-screen credit for his work, but he hadn't asked for one and didn't care. He did, of course, accede to the demand that his blond hair be cut short and painted — not dyed — grey every day to match Newman's hair.

"That was one of the best experiences I ever had," he says. "I think that was the greatest thrill. I had a really good time. Paul Newman was just the greatest guy. He'd sit in the bar every night and drink beer with us. He was really down to earth."

Reg Kent, having retired from pro hockey and returned to Johnstown, also worked as an extra. He appears as a Chief in the first Hyannisport game but is more proud of the contribution he made to Newman's development as a believable hockey player. Kent remembers approaching the actor after seeing the way he was holding a stick. "He was holding his arms way out from his body. I skated up to him and I said, 'Just let your arms hang and get them closer to your body. You'll have more control with the puck.' That was all foreign to him."

Newman was grateful for the advice, but there was something else he wanted from Kent. The hockey player wore a Jets team jacket with his first name and his uniform number on one of the sleeves — Reg, 7. Newman wanted it as a lasting memento of his experience as Reg, No. 7. When filming was over, he gave Kent the skates he had worn in exchange for the jacket. Unfortunately, Kent no longer has the skates. "I gave them to my son because he was playing hockey. He went up to Penn State, and who knows where they are now?" he laughs.

The extras included future NHL coaches Bruce Boudreau, Dan Belisle and Steve Stirling. Boudreau was a rookie who split his first season of pro hockey between Johnstown and the Minnesota Fighting Saints. While with the Jets he roomed with Dave Hanson in a small apartment that was turned into Reggie Dunlop's apartment in the film.

Paul Newman and some associates turned up on the door-step one day as Hanson was preparing for a pre-game nap, Newman telling the stunned player he wanted to see what a hockey player's apartment looked like. Hanson told them to make themselves at home and then went to bed. Newman and friends helped themselves to beer from the fridge and watched an auto race on TV as Hanson slept. This may have inspired the scene where Dunlop is trying to sleep before a game but is interrupted by a ringing telephone and Lily Braden pounding on the door. Just like Hanson, Reggie welcomed his visitor inside and promptly fell asleep.

Boudreau apparently wasn't home at the time of Newman's visit, but he made up for it by spending as much time in front of the camera as he could. He wore No. 7 for the Hyannisport Presidents and can clearly be seen several times during the two games between the Chiefs and the Presidents. "I knew I wasn't going to get a chance at too many major motion pictures," he told the *Fort Wayne News-Sentinel* years later, "so I was going to make the best of it."

For the final Syracuse-Charlestown clash, the Bulldogs management brought out of retirement a number of former

Federal League thugs who were portrayed by actual minor-league tough guys. Andre "Poodle" Lussier was played by Mark Bousquet, of the NAHL's Philadelphia Firebirds. Gilmore Tuttle was played by veteran Blake Ball. Connie "Mad Dog" Madigan, the oldest rookie in NHL history when he made the St. Louis Blues in 1973 at age 38, played Ross "Mad Dog" Madison. In a real blast from the past, "Indian" Joe Nolan was asked to play Clarence "Screaming Buffalo" Swamptown.

Nolan, in particular, intrigued the young bucks of the Jets, for whom he had once played back in the late 1950s. "The Carlson kids were kind of looking at him," Don Hall remembers. "They said, 'How tough is Indian Joe?' I said, 'Guys, with one hand behind his back, he could take all three of you.'"

Ned Dowd was chosen to play the most fearsome goon of them all, Oggie Oglethorpe, a decision he says was made the day of the shoot. "When we got to the final game, George had no idea what he was going to do, because it wasn't written, per se. We just went out there on the ice and mucked around until he said, 'That's it, that's it, I've got the ending!'"

Dowd's curly hair was teased out to make it more the style of Goldie Goldthorpe's Afro and he was set to play "the worst goon in hockey today," as the character had been dubbed in the script. Oggie uttered not a word but made his presence known right away, simply glaring at Steve Hanson after Steve's cheerful offer to buy him "a soda after the game." He suckered Steve on the opening face-off and fought with Jeff during the epic game-ending brawl. "It was great fun because I got to actually be something that I wasn't," Dowd says.

Dan Belisle, who spent most of his playing career in the minor leagues, was coaching Syracuse when the call came for extras. He signed up and was also assigned to the Blazers.

Chapter 7

When the players prepared for the final brawl, they were told to skate around until they heard the sound of a horn, at which moment they were to pair off by grabbing the nearest opponent. Belisle's veteran savvy led him to the perfect dance partner.

"I said, I know damned well where the cameras are going. They're going to Paul Newman. So I slithered up to him. As soon as the horn went, I grabbed him," says Belisle, who later coached in the NHL with Washington and won three Stanley Cups as a scout with Detroit.

The old adage soon rang true about being careful what you wish for. Belisle spent much of the next five or so hours flat on his back on the ice, with Paul Newman straddling his chest, punching him in the shoulder — the camera angles made it look like the punches were landing on Belisle's face. Both men were made up to look like they were bleeding profusely. Newman, his hands sore from punching Belisle's shoulder pads over and over, asked his opponent if the pads could be shifted just slightly to spare Newman a bit of pain. Of course, with Newman now punching skin instead of the protective pads, the pain quickly shifted to Belisle.

"It was quite a new experience. I was stiff all over. I was black and blue in the shoulders. I said, this is the movie business, is it?" Belisle says, adding with a laugh, "but there were three thousand women in the stands and they all wanted my job."

His son, Dan Jr., was also cast in the film as a Chiefs stickboy who reassures the team they won't have to face Oggie Oglethorpe in their game against the Lancaster Gears because the goon has been suspended. He was one of two stickboys the team employed — Will "Woody" Espey of Johnstown also appeared in a number of scenes but, unlike the younger Belisle, had no speaking parts.

In another nod to irony, the Chiefs win the final game and the championship not by outscoring the Bulldogs, but by forfeit. The Chiefs prevailed only when it came to outrageousness, Ned Braden tipping the scales by shucking his uniform and most of his equipment. It was a move that so sickened Syracuse captain Tim "Dr. Hook" McCracken that he lost it and eventually punched the referee, portrayed by Myron Odegaard. How Braden got his long underwear off without removing his jock and his skates, though, will forever remain a mystery.

As good a skater as Mike Ontkean was, he needed to be taught how to move on the ice gracefully, like a figure skater, for the scene to come off as desired. Universal hired Eileen "Bibi" Zillmer, a figure skater and coach then living in Johnstown, to coach Ontkean and prepare him for the scene. Zillmer, although born in the United States, was a three-time West German champion who represented that country at the 1968 Winter Olympics, when she was only 15. Two other Johnstown skaters, Barbara Shorts and Renee Roberge, one of Dick's four daughters, were hired to play Bluebirds in the Ice-Stravaganza, a take-off of the Ice Capades.

For winning the Federal League championship, the Chiefs were presented with a trophy that looked very much like the actual Lockhart Cup. As an aside, the Syracuse Blazers won the final Lockhart Cup the following year, 1976–77. When the NAHL folded, Dan Belisle is rumored to have kept the trophy. Supposedly, it remains in his home to this very day. Belisle won't confirm or deny the story.

Chapter 8

Letting 'Em Know You're There

————— ● —————

Filming on *Slap Shot* continued in the spring of 1976 as the NAHL regular season wrapped up and the playoffs began. The expanded league had been divided into two five-team divisions and the Johnstown Jets finished atop the West Division with a 47–25–2 record. They drew the Buffalo Norsemen in the first playoff round, a best-of-five series.

The Norsemen finished 36 points behind Johnstown in the standings but the Jets were already taking some heat for not necessarily putting forth their best efforts on the ice. They were spending their days at the rink, skating with the actors, and some were doing quite a bit of drinking in order to try to keep pace with Paul Newman, a champion beer drinker by anyone's standard. His favorite beer at the time was Coors, which was not then available east of the Mississippi River — a fact which served as the plot point for another movie of the period, *Smokey and the Bandit* — but Newman got around that by having 100 cases of the beer shipped in for his own personal use. He could reportedly put away a case per day and drinking competitions on the set were not uncommon.

"I drank more beer on that shoot that I did in my entire life up until that shoot," says Allan Nicholls. Coming from a Canadian-born and raised hockey player/musician, that's saying something.

"George Roy Hill spent a terrific amount of time with the skaters and with the actors," says cinematographer Vic Kemper. "We'd be all set up to do the shot and it would seem like hours they would stand and talk about the shot. I would skate over sometimes to find out what was going on. And I found out they were talking about how many beers each of them could drink at any given time. It was like a contest between them. That's a fun anecdote."

The bottom line was it didn't bode well for an organization hoping for a long playoff run and a second consecutive championship. The Jets found themselves in a real dogfight with Buffalo in their first series, and it really could have gone either way after the teams split the first four games. But Johnstown prevailed much the same as the Charlestown Chiefs would in their series against the baddies from Syracuse — by forfeit.

The Norsemen had a rookie named Greg Neeld, who had gained some notoriety after a junior game in December 1973, when he was struck in the eye by an opponent's stick. The eye could not be saved and was removed, replaced by a glass eye, although Neeld later returned to junior hockey and continued to dream of playing in the NHL. The Buffalo Sabres drafted him in 1975, but the NHL had a bylaw against one-eyed players and Neeld's subsequent lawsuit against the league was unsuccessful.

The WHA and the NAHL didn't have similar rules, so Neeld signed with the Toronto Toros and played part of the 1975-76 season in the WHA. Most of the campaign was spent with the Toros NAHL affiliate, coincidentally located in Buffalo. It was with the Norsemen that Neeld would generate even more notoriety for himself.

Kicked out of Game 2 of the Johnstown series and suspended for the next two contests, Neeld kept up a running battle with the Jets from the sidelines. A *Slap Shot* cast member who saw Game 4 in Buffalo recalls seeing Neeld, in the stands, holding up a sign that accused the Carlson brothers of being gay. Others remember another sign targeting Jets forward Hank Taylor, a 19-year-old black man who had been named the league's rookie of the year after leading the Jets in scoring with 50 goals and 93 points. The sign allegedly used a vulgar insult to suggest that people of Taylor's race should be playing basketball instead of hockey. The Jets, rattled, lost the game. When they left the ice at the end of the contest, Neeld was waiting for them at the gate. Johnstown forward Vern Campigotto, among others, went after him but nothing of note transpired.

That would not be the case in the fifth and deciding game — once again, the Jets were united and had found a sense of purpose. Word quickly spread through Johnstown that the score would be settled in Game 5. Campigotto, in particular, was determined to not even wait that long. Neeld wore a helmet with a special visor, unique at the time, to protect his one good eye. It also kept people from picking fights with the player, concerned about hurting their hands on the helmet. But he only wore it during games, not in pre-game warm-ups. Campigotto decided he would get Neeld then.

The cast and crew of *Slap Shot* weren't kept out of the loop. M. Emmet Walsh remembers a member of the Jets going from table to table in the hotel dining room, spreading the word. George Roy Hill was inspired to set up a camera when he got to the arena, hoping to catch something that might be of use in the film.

"I would imagine our trainer probably leaked that to the actors — 'If you're going to go to the game tonight against Buffalo, if it's a 7:30 game, make sure you're there by about quarter to seven. Don't miss the warm-up,'" says Ron Docken. "I know I didn't say it that way, but I do know that the vast majority of the crew was there when we came out on the ice for the warm-up."

One account said there were more than 4,800 spectators on hand. As planned, Campigotto went right for Neeld when the teams came onto the ice. To Neeld's credit, he didn't shy away or turtle — he dropped his gloves and fought. But he was no match for the veteran Jet, who pounded him mercilessly. No officials were on the ice to stop the fight, and the Norsemen were unable to come to Neeld's rescue because each of the Jets had grabbed someone and, if they weren't hammering away themselves, they were at least holding their opponents at bay.

"Buffalo had no clue what was coming," says John James of the *Tribune-Democrat*.

When the brawl finally ended, both teams went back to their dressing rooms. The Jets came out a while later for the start of the game, but the Norsemen did not. Despite repeated entreaties and warnings, they refused to emerge for the game.

Chapter 8

The Jets were awarded the game and the series by default. They were off to the semifinals against the Philadelphia Firebirds. Unfortunately, because a hockey game hadn't actually been played against Buffalo, they also had to refund all the admission money they had just taken in — an estimated $20,000.

"That was a lot of money, and we were operating on a shoe-string," says Don Hall, adding the Jets applied to the NAHL for restitution. But the Norsemen folded, so there was no way for the Jets to recover any of the lost money. "We never got a nickel.

"I think they learned a lesson," Hall says of the Jets players, laughing. "If they're going to beat the other team up, they'd better do it in the third period, not before the game."

———— ● ————

The Jets lost the next round 4–2 to Philadelphia, which went on to win the final series against the Beauce Jaros and succeed Johnstown as Lockhart Cup champions. At least the Johnstown players were now free to focus entirely on the film. More players began showing up as their teams were also eliminated from the playoffs.

Among them was a Massachusetts-born college graduate who had begun to make a name for himself in the NAHL, although he had not chosen the pacifist path of Ned Dowd. Paul Stewart liked to drop the gloves and slug it out with the league's established tough guys, whether they were on the other team or not.

A Binghamton rookie in 1975–76, Stewart remembers being sucker-punched by Goldie Goldthorpe at a team party not long after Goldie joined the club. There was only room on the Dusters for one goon, or so Goldie told Stewart. Goldie bit Stewart in the ensuing fight, sending the rookie to hospital for a tetanus shot. The mutual animosity continued to fester, and it culminated in the thrown pop bottle in the dressing room that ensured Goldthorpe would be on the outside looking in once the filming of *Slap Shot* started.

No grudges were held against Stewart, though, and the future NHL referee was assigned to the Long Island Ducks. You can see him in the scenes right before goalie Tommy Hanrahan goes berserk; Stewart, intelligent Ivy Leaguer that he is — he's a graduate of the University of Pennsylvania — donned a yellow helmet to ensure he would be able to pick himself out from the crowd of hockey players.

"It was a fun time. I think we made about $500 each," he says, "but what I got out of it was a *Slap Shot* script, signed by Paul Newman. I still have that, and I have the memories of being in the movie."

Chris Murney, the actor who played Hanrahan, has his own cherished memories. "We shot that fight scene for a long time. I jumped into that damn penalty box more times than I care to count," he says.

Murney is from Narragansett, Rhode Island, and he attended the University of New Hampshire while Mike Ontkean was also a student there. Murney, who owns two degrees from UNH and a master's degree from Penn State University, remembers watching Ontkean play hockey and Ontkean, in turn, watching Murney act in plays.

Filming of the fight scene with Paul Newman began in the morning one day and extended into the afternoon. Lunch included some beers and, after getting back to the rink and into his heavy goaltender's equipment, the 5'3" Murney found he wasn't quite as able to jump into the penalty box as before. Not to be deterred, director Hill ordered the construction of a small ramp which, when placed on the ice against the boards, gave Murney an extra four inches or so.

The repeated takes, combined with the difficulty of pulling punches on skates, unfortunately, took their toll and Newman and Murney both suffered groin pulls. Murney's injury happened the next day. "Something's got to give at some point," he says. "I was playing softball when it happened to me, running down the first-base line. It was like somebody shot me."

Of course, the Murney–Newman scene served as an inspiration to a generation of hockey trash talkers, and Murney is delighted to sign pictures for fans who ask him to personalize the autographs with things Reggie Dunlop told Hanrahan. He also treasures memories of reminiscing with Newman in the years following *Slap Shot*. "I ran into him a couple of times and he still remembered doing that scene. We had some good laughs."

There were other, more serious injuries on the set. Yvon Barrette took a puck off an unprotected part of his leg and wound up hospitalized briefly. Steve Mendillo suffered a serious cut on his cheek, opened up by a deflected puck during a scrimmage. It was later suggested he had been hit in the eye and his vision had been in danger, but he says that's an exaggeration and his eyesight is still perfect today. Still, the cut required 30 stitches to close and Mendillo, accompanied by Nancy Dowd, chose to drive to Pittsburgh to have it sewn up. Part of him was concerned about his acting future, and he wanted a clean stitch job that would not leave him with a visible scar. Another part of him just accepted it for the hockey injury it was; he had gone through many similar hurts in his youth in New Haven.

"I've been cut so many times," he says, recalling how he used to wake up his father to have his skin stitched back together with a needle from his mother's pincushion. Dr. Mendillo would sterilize the needle with a match. "He'd be half asleep. No Novocaine or anything. He sewed me up many times late at night, six stitches here, eight over there."

———— ● ————

Although Morley's Dog was featured in the film, George Roy Hill was concerned about using anything that could possibly identify Johnstown. For that reason, he declined to film anything connected to one of the city's most prominent attractions, the Inclined Plane, a self-contained cable railway built in 1891. With a grade of 70.9 per cent, it is billed as the steepest of its type in the world.

But other elements of the city and the surrounding area were used. Of course, the Cambria County War Memorial was the home rink of the Chiefs, and was referred to several times in the film as the War Memorial. The Bethlehem Steel operations, unidentified as such, served as a backdrop for the whole thing.

A vacant downtown building was transformed — at a cost of $30,000 — under the direction of production designer Henry Bumstead into "Big King Drugs," where the Chiefs sometimes hung out. It was there that an uncredited pharmacist gave goalie Denis Lemieux "a double dose" of some kind of painkiller. When Reggie Dunlop gave the pharmacist a ticket to the Chiefs' next game — "Thanks, Reggie!" she replied brightly — it marked the first and only time Paul

Newman ever shared screen time on a feature film with any of his six children. The pharmacist was played by the eldest of his five daughters, Susan.

Susan had launched a fledgling acting career when she reached adulthood, initially billing herself as Susan Kendall in an unsuccessful attempt to keep people from connecting her with her famous dad. After a number of stage roles, including a very short stint in a Broadway bomb called "We Interrupt This Program," Paul asked her to work with him on *Slap Shot*.

Susan was in two scenes as the pharmacist and later referred to the job as a "mannequin part." She was on the shoot mainly as an assistant but fell in with Swoosie Kurtz and Nancy Dowd and basically just soaked up the atmosphere in Johnstown, which was markedly different from anything she had ever experienced before. One gets the impression she felt much like Dowd probably felt a year earlier when she had stumbled into the foreign environment of minor-pro hockey.

"Coming from a world where — how can I put this? — my daintier male friends were ballet dancers and writers, it was suddenly very caveman. Ugh-want-water-sex-sleep-play-money. I fell in love with several of those guys," Susan told Martha Smilgis in a July 1978 issue of *People* magazine.

Susan collaborated with the Hanson Brothers, along with Allan Nicholls and Jerry Houser, in an impromptu musical group called The Loogans. Nicholls was a musician, of course, and Houser also liked to play the guitar and sing. The sextet created several little songs and went to the local radio station to record one of them, called "It Had to Be Johnstown."

It's been said that Susan dated Jeff Carlson, but Gracie Head isn't sure that's exactly true. "She had a crush on Jeff Carlson, but I don't think Jeff would even talk to her. I think Jeff stood her up, and nobody stood up Paul Newman's daughter."

———— ● ————

While set builders back at Universal City in California were constructing a replica of Bruce Boudreau and Dave Hanson's apartment, Hill decided the McQuillan home in Johnstown would be realistic enough to serve as home base for newspaper reporter Dickie Dunn.

It was the home of Dr. Bernard McQuillan, a Jets director, and his family, and it's where Ned Dowd had lived while he played in Johnstown. Nancy also stayed there when she came to visit Ned and his team. Young Mickey McQuillan was chosen to play Dickie Dunn's son, who argues with his pretend sister over what to watch on TV as Dickie does his best to ignore the squabbling children and focus on a conversation with Reggie Dunlop.

M. Emmet Walsh remembers the scene best for a bit that did not make it into the finished product. Newman was notorious for pulling pranks on film sets, and he and Hill had come up with a doozy that, if it had come off as planned, likely would have sent jaws dropping all over Hollywood.

Dailies, also known as rushes, are unedited footage that is developed after each day of filming. The footage is screened the next day for the director and key members of his crew so they can see what they have captured. In the case of *Slap Shot*, the dailies were viewed at the end of the following day of work in a room at the War Memorial.

The dailies were likewise being seen by Universal executives back in California, and possibly also by producers Bob Wunsch and Stephen Friedman. Universal's parent company,

Chapter 8

MCA, was headed by two men named Lew Wasserman and Sid Sheinberg. If you can find the common religious denominator in those four surnames, you're on to something.

"The whole business is Jewish back here in LA," says Walsh, who was to be the set-up man for the prank. It would revolve around Dickie asking Reggie who would want to buy the Chiefs. With a straight face, Dunlop was to reply, "kikes."

"That's one you can't get away with (in a theatrical release), but it would be on the reel and they would fucking go crazy . . . they'd have been screaming back at Universal," Walsh says. "All hell would have broken loose. But we could not pull it off. I fed it to Paul 20 times, very serious, and Paul couldn't say it. He'd crack. George wanted it and Paul wanted it, but Paul could not keep from cracking."

It's unknown whether Newman, the son of a Jewish father, the actor who portrayed Israeli freedom fighter Ari Ben Canaan in the landmark film *Exodus*, simply found the irony of the situation too funny to keep from laughing. At any rate, the prank was dropped.

———— ● ————

Reggie did manage to relate to Dickie that the prospective buyers of the Chiefs, whatever their religion might have been, had "already built the rink!" Although it might have seemed strange for most hockey fans in the 1970s to think of Florida as a place where their sport might realistically be played, hockey had already established some footholds in the Sunshine State, starting with the Miami-based Tropical Hockey League in 1938–39.

The NAHL's forerunner, the EHL, spearheaded hockey's first real push south in 1956, when the Baltimore Clippers were forced out of their home arena by a fire. They set up shop in Charlotte, NC, a move that was intended to be temporary, but the team caught on there and stayed for the next 21 years. Charlotte, which eventually renamed its team the Checkers, remains a hockey hotbed today; its current ECHL franchise, also called the Checkers, is consistently among the league leaders in attendance.

The unexpected success of hockey in Charlotte led to the quick establishment of more EHL teams in the southern US — Greensboro, Knoxville, Nashville and, in 1964, the Jacksonville Rockets, Florida's first truly professional hockey team. They were joined in 1971 by the St. Petersburg-based Suncoast Suns. In fact, the Suns roster in 1972–73 included the real-life Denis Lemieux, in his first season of pro hockey — "we go to Florida and I *get* da money."

Alas, hockey in Florida eventually petered out again. The Rockets folded in 1972. They were followed by the Jacksonville Barons of the AHL but that team failed within a year. Also in 1972, the Miami Screaming Eagles were to be an original franchise in the WHA but never got off the ground. The Suns folded in 1973. When the WHA's Cleveland Crusaders were looking for a new home in 1976, a prospective move to Florida fell through and the Crusaders ended up in Minnesota as a new version of the Fighting Saints.

Of course, the Charlestown Chiefs never made it to Florida either. That doesn't mean hockey fans in St. Petersburg didn't appreciate the thought. When Paul Newman visited the city in 2003 for a Grand Prix auto race, he welcomed *St. Petersburg Times* sports columnist Gary Shelton to his trailer for an interview, and Shelton reminded him of Reggie Dunlop's machinations. "I had forgotten that," Newman told Shelton, laughing.

Chapter 8

"He was laughing so hard the trailer shook," Shelton says, recalling the moment. "It really was one of the cooler afternoons I have spent as a journalist."

The point where Reggie learns that Florida will never be more than a figment of his imagination is easily the most notorious scene of the entire film. It involved Newman and an actress who was in town only long enough to shoot the scene in question. Her name was Kathryn Walker and she was hired to play Anita McCambridge, the owner of the Chiefs.

Landing Walker was a real coup, as she was at the height of her profession at that very moment. It was May 1976, the same month she won an Emmy Award for her portrayal of Abigail Adams in the PBS miniseries *The Adams Chronicles*. The Harvard-educated Philadelphia native had been working steadily on and off the Broadway stage and had appeared on three different TV soap operas between 1972 and 1976. Walker was working for Joe Papp in "Rebel Women" at the Public Theater in New York when she was invited to fly to Johnstown and play Anita.

"I flew in the day before the shoot, had dinner with Paul, did the shoot the next day and flew out," she says.

"I guess the scene is controversial. I never gave it much thought since it didn't amount to much of a scene for me except as a sort of set-up. Not a particularly enhancing role. I've never actually seen the film and was surprised years later to hear how popular it was from an ice-hockey enthusiast I met."

Newman, as Dunlop, pushed all kinds of boundaries in his confrontation with Anita, the attractive young widow who seems to flirt with him while telling him, yes, she most likely could find someone to buy the Chiefs. The lie he had created could very well come true, and Reggie is overjoyed. But the joy is short-lived. Anita informs him that, based on her accountant's advice, she has decided to fold the team instead and take a tax loss. His initial response is shock, which gives way to escalating anger, which leads to Reggie storming out — but not before the macho hockey player, his pride wounded, knowing he has nothing left to lose, unleashes the crudest insult he can think of at that moment:

"You know, your son looks like a fag to me. You'd better get married again, 'cause he's gonna wind up with somebody's cock in his mouth before you can say Jack Robinson."

Jack Kroll, the longtime drama critic at *Newsweek* magazine, wrote that it was "the single most profane sentence ever uttered by a major American actor."

Universal Pictures president Ned Tanen called it "one of the best lines in the history of movies." As foul as the insult was, Tanen said, it worked because it elicited laughter at Anita's comeuppance as well as a sympathetic reaction for Reggie.

"He gets clearly what this is all about, and nothing in our society has changed, it's only gotten worse. It's nothing more than a tax write-off to her and it doesn't work for her any more. She doesn't care a fuck about the community."

Reggie appears to find no peace in his parting shot. His frustration is exacerbated by listening to a radio interview in which Dave "Killer" Carlson pays a heartfelt tribute to his coach. Reggie pulls his car off the road and sighs. What follows is a line that Paul Newman said years later was his favorite of all he had ever delivered in front of a camera:

"What a fuckin' nightmare."

———— ● ————

George Roy Hill endured a short-lived nightmare during the filming. The prank that he and Newman had attempted to perpetrate on the Hollywood bigwigs had fallen through, but Newman was determined to put one over on Hill.

The actor was known for his on-set pranks, although they were hit and miss. Sometimes they paid off beautifully, like when he filled Robert Altman's trailer with baby chicks on the set of *Buffalo Bill and the Indians*. He and Robert Redford had a running gag involving a demolished Porsche that they kept passing back and forth to each other. Newman also once sawed Hill's desk in half with a chainsaw. Hill, after getting over the surprise, nailed the desk back together and refused to admit there was anything wrong with it. Universal later sent Newman the bill for a new desk, whereupon Newman responded by telling Universal that while he would pay for the desk to be replaced, this meant he now owned the old desk and was renting it to Hill, with the result that Newman was now owed several hundred dollars.

Sometimes the jokes were not well received. During the shooting of *The Mackintosh Man*, Newman constructed a dummy of himself and had it placed at the top of a tower. The dummy was then thrown off the tower, convincing director John Huston that the star of the movie had just plummeted to his death.

Hill had the same reaction after Newman staged a fake car crash and made it look as if he'd been, at the least, seriously injured. It was while Reggie was driving out to the cabin where Ned Braden was staying after being benched and leaving the Chiefs. Newman, after arranging for the Carlson brothers and Dave Hanson to assist in the prank, told Hill before shooting the scene that there appeared to be something wrong with the car but he would try to get through the scene anyway. He drove out of the camera's range, whereupon Hanson and the Carlsons began smashing trash cans and creating as much noise as possible to make it seem like Newman had collided with something.

"It was a scary moment," recalls John Hill. "It really sounded like he had killed himself, or someone else."

John's father rushed to the scene, as did everyone else. They found a laughing Newman, who thought the prank was the height of hilarity. The senior Hill didn't feel that way. He immediately announced that the film was over and everyone was fired. Newman hurriedly tried to calm Hill down, and succeeded, but a chill existed between the two men for a few days. Newman remembered the prank during an April 2004 interview with Heather Mills McCartney on CNN's *Larry King Live*.

"It scared him and scared a lot of people, actually," Newman said, "and there were a couple of days when he wasn't speaking." The director finally confronted the actor and made him understand that the pranks carried with them "an element of maliciousness" and were more often hurtful than they were funny. "So I've cut down on my practical jokes to people who I really don't like."

There were other pranks on the set. Hockey players would set fire to the shoelaces of assistant directors, to the delight of lowly crew members who would never have gotten away with such behavior. The Carlsons and Hanson hazed Jerry Houser repeatedly and capped their treatment of him with a fabled rookie initiation known as "the shave," an old hockey tradition in which the victim is pinned down while his pubic hair is roughly shorn away. Allan Nicholls says Houser once came into the dressing room to find his street clothes nailed to the wall, but Hanson says Nicholls was actually the victim of that prank. Newman himself was victimized when his portable sauna was filled with popcorn.

"There was no common theme to anything, it was just disruption," Nicholls says. "Well, I guess disruption *was* the common theme."

Hill quickly got over his anger at the fake car crash and more or less encouraged the carefree atmosphere. Houser says the director was captivated by the Carlsons and Hanson and their natural exuberance. "George loved that about the guys. In Hollywood, on a movie set, there's kind of a hierarchy — who's the director, you go through the proper channels, you don't bother this person or that person. These guys, we'd shoot all day and go out at night and get hammered, and they'd call George at 1 in the morning: 'Hey, George, what time you want us there tomorrow?' But George appreciated that too. They didn't care; they weren't looking to have acting careers. They were hockey players that happened to be in this movie. He enjoyed the fact that nobody was kissing anybody's butt. They were just being real."

Of course, the kidding stopped when the three hockey players, bored from the seemingly endless waiting around, bailed out on the project and went their separate ways. Steve Carlson alone remained in Johnstown, and it was up to him to track down Jeff and Dave and get them back to the set amid threats of lawsuits. All was forgiven when, suitably chastened, all three returned to the film.

Joking aside, everyone on the shoot knew Hill was in charge. He didn't necessarily need to make a big show of the fact that he was the boss. That attitude didn't apply, though, to people who didn't belong on the set, and as far as he was concerned there were two prominent names at the top of that list — Bob Wunsch and Stephen Friedman. The producers were told in no uncertain terms to stay away from Johnstown while filming was underway.

Hill had coped with a number of instances earlier in his career where his creative control was either limited or even usurped. He clashed with producers Walter Mirisch and Ross Hunter on the respective sets of *Hawaii* and *Thoroughly Modern Millie* and was removed from the latter project during post-production. The only way he could guarantee the artistic freedom he wanted was to serve as his own producer, and he finally accomplished this with *The Great Waldo Pepper*. It was something he intended to do again with *Slap Shot*. He figured Wunsch and Friedman would be content with "executive producer" credits. He was wrong.

"George wanted to have a producer credit desperately," Wunsch says. "George said, 'I always have a producer credit on my movies.' I said, 'When you develop them, yes, but I developed this . . . it's my project.' He said, 'Well, maybe I won't do it.' He threatened us, indirectly, through lawyers. And Stephen and I conferred and we said, basically, fuck him, we'll go somewhere else. It's a great project for him and he's an idiot if he doesn't do it. If he doesn't do it, we'll go somewhere else with it."

Hill did back down and leave Wunsch and Friedman with the producer credits, but the ban was his retaliation. Bob Crawford was the line producer, responsible for the day-to-day activity on the set, and he remembers that Hill had been more wary of Friedman than of Wunsch, concerned about the power he might wield if given the chance.

"It was unfortunate, because Bob Wunsch is a pretty decent guy. Steve Friedman was a much more hard-driven entrepreneurial son of a gun, a sharper personality," Crawford says.

Chapter 8

"But George felt that he couldn't play favorites . . . and he was just a tough enough nut to say, it's my baby, I'm going to create it, I don't want anybody to mess with it more than necessary. In his opinion, he didn't think they were going to bring enough creative value to be worth the hassle. He was clearing the deck. If they were going to bitch about it, he felt that was the cost of doing business.

"It's a harsh thing to do to a producer. I've been in the inner circle with George where he was counting on me to fill all the needs of a working producer . . . somebody that I could be candid with him but I wasn't going to be in competition with him for power and control . . . but I've been shunted aside myself for the same reasons."

Ned Tanen sympathized with the producers. He knew they were in a difficult situation but was unable to be of any assistance because the studio wanted the movie finished with the least possible amount of difficulty. Any attempt by Universal to try to force Hill to accept the producers on the set would certainly have jeopardized that.

"I will tell you Bob Wunsch did a terrific job in impossible circumstances, because Hill was not one to take advice," Tanen said. "That's the way he was, that's who he was. But he didn't need the advice. He just went his way and knew what he was going to do. He just pointed the line and he went to it. Not always with a lot of grace, with which Wunsch would be the first one to agree.

"Poor Wunsch. I had some tough times with him which were totally my fault, they weren't his. I was just trying to get the movie made and stay out alive."

Wunsch and Friedman knew what was at stake, so they didn't push the matter. They stayed away from Johnstown.

Although it hurt them to not be part of the project they had discovered, nurtured and helped bring to life, they ended up with absolutely no complaints about the job Hill did.

"I think he did a great movie, of which I'm very proud, and I'm thrilled that he did the movie," Wunsch says.

"George was not an easy person at all. He was a very difficult person. He was a wonderful director, enormously talented, and his whole body of work contains some of my favorite pictures. But he was a very, very prickly, tough, difficult human being."

Whatever Hill's attitude may have been toward the producers, apparently it was kept from the actors and the hockey players. He may not always have known in advance exactly what he wanted to capture, but he was very much a hands-on director who was constantly looking for ways to improve the production.

When he did know what he wanted, he meticulously planned it and got exactly what he had in mind. The scene where Reggie takes Francine back to her apartment is a perfect example of this. It begins with a shot of a wedding picture on a table — Reggie and Francine's wedding picture. But it is not a retouched photo, with the heads of Warren and Newman placed on the bodies of an anonymous bride and groom. Rather, Hill arranged for an actual wedding picture of the actors to be taken at a photography studio in Johnstown. Newman donned a tux and had his greying hair darkened so he would look younger and the black-and-white picture would look as if it had been taken years earlier.

"He had that in his head right from the beginning," Jennifer Warren, Francine's portrayer, says of Hill. "We just thought it was perfect."

Chapter 8

Ongoing improvements included script changes. Nancy Dowd was kept busy by Hill's requests for rewrites while the filming was going on. Her original screenplay had Reggie ending up with Lily Braden *and* with a catatonic Ned Braden, who went off the deep end as a prelude to his striptease. The part was rewritten so that the stripping was a calculated move on the part of Ned, maintaining his sanity.

Despite the extra work, Dowd said she was happy with how the movie was progressing, but Newman's portrayal of her primary character was somewhat bittersweet. "I'm pretty pleased with what Newman is doing with the film," she told Nancy Coleman of the *Johnstown Tribune-Democrat*. "It's strange to have a character in mind. You've lived with him, and now to see it happen and see Newman sort of become Reggie is at once pleasing and very dismaying."

One line in the script that has frequently been criticized is Reggie's reference to "the big apple" when he announces at the end of the film that he will be coaching the Minnesota Nighthawks of the Iron League. The Big Apple, of course, is a well-known nickname for New York City, which is nowhere near Minnesota. But Dowd was clearly using "the big apple," not capitalized, as a synonym for the big time, or the big leagues. If the Minnesota Nighthawks and the Iron League are to Charlestown and the Federal League what the Fighting Saints and the WHA were to Johnstown and the NAHL, then "the big apple" in that context would be appropriate.

In the original script, after Reggie is fired from the Chiefs, it is Joe McGrath who brings word of the job in Minnesota. Reggie tells McGrath to stuff it. The ending was rewritten to bring a semblance of a happy ending to a story in which the dying town and the dying hockey franchise are not saved at the last minute. The Bradens are reconciled, but the Dunlops are not; Francine does not run back to Reggie. Rather, she is allowed to say a final goodbye to him and to Charlestown on her own terms.

"I don't think it was ever in anybody's mind that Francine would ever go back to him," Warren says. "It was pretty clear. I mean, you know, you can love Reggie only so much. He's just such a boy. You can't get angry at him. He's just a boy who'll never grow up. My approach was that I understood him so totally and knew he wouldn't change. Because I'm out now, I could be patient with him like you would a child.

"But talk about a hard job — I had the hardest job there! I got cast in a part where I had to leave Paul Newman!"

She has fond memories of that final scene together because of the look Francine gives Reggie when he tells her she doesn't have his number. The knowing smile tells all of us — with the exception of the oblivious Reggie — that that isn't at all true.

"It's one of my favorite moments of my career," she says. "What worked for me was the thought that went through my head at that moment: 'Honey, do I have your number. I've got your number.'"

The outcome of the Tim "Dr. Hook" McCracken-Dave "Killer" Carlson stick fight was also changed. When Carlson was knocked down, that was originally the end of the battle. McCracken was hauled away by the officials before he could inflict more damage on the Chiefs defenceman, who went down fearing his eye had been carved out of its socket by a flick of the wrist. A few days later, the actors filmed a new ending which saw Carlson, down but not out, emerge victorious. Jerry Houser laments today with a laugh that Carlson never collected on the $100 bounty Reggie had placed on McCracken's head.

Paul D'Amato relished the opportunity to play the villain, regardless of whether or not he won the stick fight. Today, he is still recognized by fans who love to parrot Dr. Hook's better-known lines back to him, primarily the first words he speaks to Reggie Dunlop in the hallway outside the locker rooms.

"The line started out as, 'Dunlop, you suck cock in your spare time,'" D'Amato says. "When we got to the looping process, the ADR (additional dialogue recording) where you add your voice to the final print, they cut the 'in your spare time.' It was redundant."

While he brought a certain look to the character that was invaluable — "the maddest looking face you have ever seen!" marveled Ned Tanen — D'Amato needed assistance in the ways of hockey violence. A genuinely warm and friendly man, he prides himself on his general lack of malevolence on the ice. "I'm a Lady Bynger," he says, referring to the NHL's annual award for sportsmanship and gentlemanly play.

Dr. Hook was originally a more "showy" character who, in the final game, was to wear a cape onto the ice. While skating past the Chiefs bench, he was to jump into the air and click his heels. As good a skater as D'Amato was, that was beyond his capability. He convinced the director to lose that feature and found that Hill was quite willing to allow the actor to explore the character.

"He said, 'You can do anything you want.' I realized I had an opportunity. He was saying, 'I have confidence in you. Whatever you do is going to be right.'"

He took some inspiration from a clash he witnessed between Dave Schultz of the Philadelphia Flyers and Bobby Schmautz of the Boston Bruins. "I saw Dave Schultz drop his gloves. Dave

Schultz was the toughest guy in the league at that point. But Schmautz didn't drop his gloves. Schmautz had his stick in his hands. He turned it around and he just sorted of taunted Schultz with the stick. And I realized a guy with a stick in his hands was worth a hell of a lot more than a guy with his gloves off."

———— ● ————

There was a hint of the controversy to come when the film company journeyed to nearby Ligonier for some shooting. This is where the infamous "mooning" scene was filmed, as well as the impromptu bus exchange party that was marked by a streaking episode. Residents who had come to watch the filming were unprepared for what they saw, and municipal officials dashed off an angry letter to Hill.

Two members of the cast said later they had serious concerns about the content of the film. Brad Sullivan was in the process of becoming a Christian, a decision that astonished other cast members who were enthralled at how he transformed himself into the lecherous character of Mo Wanchuk. Jennifer Warren, in particular, recalls how he took it upon himself to add the wagging tongue to the scene in the bar where the Chiefs learn they might be going to Florida. "He was just outrageous. He was great," she laughs. "He threw himself into being the scummiest of scumbags."

"I just went and did it," Sullivan said in rationalizing his work. "If you're going to play a character, you've got to play it fully honestly or not do it at all. Besides, I think (Mo) was in a dream world. He was in a fantasy world."

Jerry Houser had recently made the same commitment to Christ that Sullivan was making. "My situation was slightly different than Brad's because my character wasn't as directly lascivious as his," Houser says. "Nevertheless, I was involved in the movie. I was a fairly new Christian at the time and I did give it a lot of thought and prayer before taking the role. I recall my feeling being that taking the role didn't make me that person. I was who I was and if I was going to be shining any light as a Christian I needed to be out in the world where it could shine.

"As I recall there were a number of wonderful things that happened during the filming of that movie that confirmed to me that I was right where I should be. I remember the paper doing an article about my faith and many people meeting me and asking about it."

Features reporter Nancy Coleman wrote many articles for the *Tribune-Democrat* prior to and during the filming, interviewing actors and crew members for stories that were eventually compiled into a commemorative *Slap Shot* tabloid section published by the newspaper in May 1976. She has very fond memories of the experiences, especially having the opportunities to speak with people such as Paul Newman and Hill, neither of whom really cared to give interviews, and with Nancy Dowd, who would become increasingly reclusive over the years.

"The proudest thing that I did was get an interview with George Roy Hill. The publicist on the film said, 'He won't give you an interview, he hasn't given an interview for 20 years,'" Coleman says. She used her imagination to make an end run of sorts around the publicist, penning a personal letter to the director in which she mentioned that, like him, she was a licensed pilot. She professed her love for his most recent film, *The Great Waldo Pepper*. "I laid it on so thick," she laughs, "and I got an interview with him."

The extensive article that followed was well received by the filmmaker, as Coleman found out just before she left for vacation. "We got word that he liked the story so much, he had ordered 40 copies of the edition that it was in. I went to Mexico and I was really flying on Cloud 9."

So was Art Newman after one particular episode on the ice. A superb skater, he was gliding around the rink during a lull, with extras populating the stands, when he realized Mike Ontkean and two other actors had joined him. Curious to see what would happen, he picked up the pace. "I knew they were right behind me and so I started to jack it up a little bit. They were hanging right on me," Newman laughs. "All of these (spectators) started to get excited because what they had was a race. That last loop down the length of the rink and around the back of the goal, I won and there was a lot of screaming."

Ned Dowd, noticing how well Art skated, asked if he wanted to play a referee or a linesman in the film. "Paul was agreeable to that," Art says, "but I couldn't do it. I had to be a member of the Directors Guild and there's a rule . . . that if you're on a picture as a member of the Directors Guild, you can't fill another slot. Mainly it was so some actor couldn't complain and get a director replaced or something like that. So I couldn't do it, with my DGA card.

"But I had had one other time in a film — been there, done that. I didn't need to do that any more. My brother had already established the fact that at least one person in the family had some talent. There was no reason to prove the fact that I didn't get any of it," he says, laughing again.

Chapter 9

Right Back Where We Started From

———— ● ————

The filming of *Slap Shot* took 68 working days to complete. Sundays were the only days off. The cast and crew had various ways to unwind on their off days, and Paul Newman was not the type of person to unwind on his own, without the company of his new friends.

There was a dirt race track not far away from Johnstown and Newman, an avid auto racer, visited a few times. He took Jennifer Warren there once and the estranged Dunlops spent an afternoon zipping around the track in borrowed race cars. On another occasion, Newman, Dave Hanson and Jeff and Steve Carlson rented cars, bought insurance with $100 deductibles, and proceeded to have a demolition derby.

On still another occasion, a contingent of actors and hockey players piled into a limousine to make the jaunt. It was pouring rain that day, which put the kibosh on any thought of racing, but didn't prevent an epic beer-drinking session. Ron Docken remembers that when the car pulled up to the gate, which had to be opened and closed by hand, it was Newman who jumped out to do the honors so no one else would get wet.

But it was that type of attitude that endeared Newman to everyone on the *Slap Shot* set, and they showed their appreciation by treating him as just another guy. This often had unexpectedly hilarious results. Don Hall remembers one night in a Johnstown bar where everyone had to buy a round when their turn came, and Newman was no exception. He went up to the barmaid to place the order and found that she was very excited about being in the presence of a star.

"She didn't know who he was," Hall says, "but she said, 'Do you know who those guys are you're sitting with? That's Ron Docken and the Johnstown Jets!' Newman laughed like hell. He thought that was the funniest thing that happened the whole time he was here. He told that story on himself all the time.

"It was a fun time. I used to skate in the afternoons with Newman. He called me Corporation, because that's what it was in the script — you know, the corporation owned the team. He'd say, 'All right, Corporation, let's go skate for a while.' He was a pretty good skater, and he could handle the puck okay. I was surprised."

Docken says the environment was such in Johnstown that the hockey players were the stars and their fans came from every sector of society. It was common for the players to hang out at local bars with garbage collectors and bank presidents, with everyone getting along famously. "Nobody cared what you did. Everybody was in it together."

Chapter 9

The party atmosphere permeated all aspects of the production. Actors such as Warren regularly showed up to watch scenes and even rehearsals in which they weren't involved. And one night, the collective naivete of Allan Nicholls, Dave Hanson and the Carlsons took them up to a room in the War Memorial where Newman, George Roy Hill, line producer Bob Crawford and editor Dede Allen were watching the dailies. Their appearance was unexpected, because viewing the dailies was supposed to be real work, removed from whatever fun might have been taking place during the actual filming.

"That's something that I must take full credit for," Nicholls says, "because I learned it from Robert Altman, whose dailies were always the reward at the end of the day for the crew and the cast and everybody.

"I got the Hansons and Ned Dowd and a couple of others — Guido Tenesi, I think. We all went and bought six packs. We went into this room and there were the four of them, and they looked at us like, what are you guys doing here? I said, 'We came to watch the dailies.' Bobby Crawford said, 'That's not how we do it.' I said, 'Really? I thought that's how everybody did it. That's how Bob (Altman) does it — we sit around and drink beer and watch the dailies. It's funny, you get to laugh and see what you did.' George Roy Hill piped up and said, 'Okay, let them stay.' So we stayed, and it became a regular thing.

"Hill was a genuinely nice person, and he was really having fun on the shoot. It was different than what he had done before. It had a certain looseness and a certain kind of disturbing reality that not many of his films up to that point had."

Watching the dailies became a nightly extension of the fun and in turn sparked more fun in front of the cameras.

Unintentional mistakes revealed on celluloid brought peals of laughter from the beer- and popcorn-consuming crowd, so the cast then began to screw up on purpose in the hope of making everyone laugh the next evening. The dailies had, in effect, become blooper reels.

"We would walk in front of the scene bare-ass naked, wiggling our dicks or something," Dave Hanson says. "It's a shame they didn't keep that kind of stuff. That stuff would be priceless."

Naturally, the dailies were also being seen at Universal, which sent a watchdog of sorts to Johnstown to try to get things back under control. Things did settle down somewhat but not completely — the camaraderie that had been established between all concerned would simply not allow for things to become too serious.

"We really did become close," says Steve Mendillo. "We all lived together in the same hotel. We'd go out afterwards and hang out. We enjoyed each other."

Mendillo could be forgiven for acting as if it were a family affair, because he had three members of his own family along for the ride. Mendillo, a single father at the time, had brought his son Tag and his daughter Kirsten with him to Johnstown. His brother John came along and was hired to play the ambulance driver who appears in two scenes prior to the Syracuse playoff games. Mendillo also began dating Nancy Dowd.

Many other members of the film company didn't have their families with them on location, though, which helped draw them together into a little community of their own. That community, in turn, found kindred spirits in the egalitarian environment of Johnstown, creating a very rare atmosphere that is fondly remembered today by all who were part of it.

Chapter 9

"There was the feeling we were doing something good," Dowd told Philadelphia morning radio host Michael Smerconish of WPHT 1210 AM in a July 2007 interview, crediting George Roy Hill and Strother Martin with facilitating that kind of feeling. "We all kind of hung out and got along, and that isn't always the case."

"You gravitate toward each other in order to not feel lonely, to feel part of something, and we all just bonded," adds Swoosie Kurtz. "It was a really good feeling, very warm."

She says that helped a little in terms of keeping from "freezing our asses off" inside the War Memorial, where Kurtz, Gracie Head and the other Nancy Dowd — Ned's then-wife, not his sister — spent many hours watching their "husbands" play hockey. While the men on the ice could at least play shinny to help alleviate the boredom while waiting to film a scene, the women in the stands had no comparable relief. Head passed the time by knitting, an avocation that she continued to do with Hill's approval while the cameras rolled. Kurtz's time was also well spent, as her role grew throughout the shoot. Initially she had very few lines, not many more than her companions, who were after all only local extras. But Newman took notice of her delivery of her scripted one-liners — "Good crowd!" — and he urged Hill to pay more attention to her.

"Newman goes, 'She's got the best goddamned line in the whole goddamned movie!' Those were his exact words!" she laughs, referring to the above line. "He said, 'We've got to put her in more of the movie. We've got to give her more to do.'"

She still marvels at the unselfish behavior he demonstrated that day. Some stars might have felt threatened by an unknown actor displaying Kurtz's kind of talent and timing.

And yet here was Newman telling the director that she didn't have enough to do. Kurtz's resulting performance, of course, helped to launch her career into the stratosphere.

"I worked with him a couple of times after that, and what a decent guy, just a great human being," she says. "He always saw the big picture. It was never about him or what's in it for him — ever."

———— ● ————

At some point, word began to slip out that the film being created was going to be controversial. Newman did some interviews during the production and tried to set people's minds at ease, explaining that the violence in *Slap Shot* would be cartoonish, in the vein of *Tom and Jerry*. He stressed that he wanted nothing to do with other films that depicted violence in much more graphic ways.

"Look at *Apocalypse Now*," he told Clarke Taylor of the *Los Angeles Times*. "It's a marvelous script but I wouldn't do a film like it. That kind of violence is terminal . . . *Slap Shot* is realistic. It shows that the wrestling aspect of a sport — the show-biz aspect — pays off in greater proportion than does style or competence. Even the vulgarity in this film is merely indigenous to this subculture."

"I suppose some people will be a little taken aback by the language. It's got that kind of bathroom humor I enjoy," he said to Margaret Daly of the *Toronto Star*. "But it's not just simple vulgarity; if it were, I wouldn't do it, any more than I would if it were just a dark downer about hockey and violence. It's the wildly imaginative, inventive quality of it all that makes it funny." He also told Daly he loved his character, calling Reggie "a Machiavellian primitive, and his dialogue is not George

Bernard Shaw. But there's something lovable about him. He's full of contradictions."

In a talk with Nancy Coleman of the local *Tribune-Democrat*, Newman said he was comfortable with the movie's "hockey violence . . . a lot of blood drawn and a lot of teeth knocked out" and discussed the Hanrahan scene and its relation to the film as a whole. "I think the picture is profane, but it is funny — genuinely funny.

"This scene is hysterical. I don't want to give it away, but when the people know what I'm doing in the scene, and then they see the garbage goal afterward . . . I think it's hysterical."

Hill told Coleman in a separate interview that preparing for and making this particular film was very different from any other picture on which he had worked. Shooting had started when it did to catch the tail end of the 1975–76 hockey season, the amount of improvisation from the performers was far more than what Hill had previously allowed and the location setting could have been problematic. But it was coming together nicely and he was very happy with the process.

"It's a very exciting town to shoot in," he said of Johnstown. "For our purposes, we couldn't have found a better town in the United States. Cinematically, it's just marvelous."

By the end of May, though, the film company's time there had come to an end. There was still filming to be done at rinks in upstate New York and back home in California, but it was time to say goodbye to the place that had been home for the past two months.

One of the last major scenes to be shot there was the championship parade which would conclude the film. As it turned out, there really was a parade going on in Johnstown to celebrate Armed Forces Day, and the film company simply joined in. And yes, there really was a porno double feature — *Deep Throat* and *Meatball* — playing at the time at the Embassy Theatre on Main Street.

The parade was the cap of a surprisingly upbeat ending that did not mesh with Nancy Dowd's original vision, in which Reggie, disgusted by the violence and by his role in it, turned his back on the "big apple" job offer. In the finished product, Reggie looked forward with great anticipation to the move to Minnesota, even though Francine was headed in the other direction, to Long Island.

But Universal president Ned Tanen felt the ending was not upbeat enough, calling the Chiefs' title run "a pyrrhic victory." The team was folding anyway despite its championship, the town was still sinking into economic despair and the hero had not won back his wife after all. Nothing would change. In other words, it wasn't a typical Hollywood wrap-up in which all the good guys got what they wanted. But that wouldn't have been an accurate portrayal, and it wasn't until later that Tanen realized the brilliance in the ending as Hill saw it.

"Here's this parade at the end of the movie which, frankly, is about nothing," he said. "They're leaving, breaking up, (the team) has not been sold to anybody in Florida . . . and that's the end of the movie. I disagreed with George Roy Hill because that was my problem. In fact, he was totally right and I was totally wrong.

"That is the movie that Hill wanted to make. We had some disagreements about that, but in fact, he was right and I was wrong. That was what the movie was."

Johnstown said goodbye in a couple of different ways. The Greater Johnstown Chamber of Commerce staged a dinner on

Chapter 9

May 19. Jennifer Warren, Art Newman, Henry Bumstead and Strother Martin all spoke at the event.

Martin had felt at home in Johnstown. He told Nancy Coleman that his family had also been affected by a devastating killer flood, a 1937 disaster that engulfed a number of communities along the Ohio River. "They lived in Jeffersonville, Indiana, and for a week or 10 days I didn't know where they were," he said.

He was interested in poetry and a music lover who told Coleman he hoped to take in the symphony orchestra in Johnstown and do some antiquing. Paying a visit to the nearby town of Indiana, the hometown of friend James Stewart, was also on his to-do list. "He was so sweet," Coleman says.

"I want to thank everyone for being so hospitable," Martin said at the chamber of commerce dinner. "I've been asked 10,000 times, 'How do you like Johnstown?' And when people ask me that, they study me carefully as they wait for my answer. I like how the people of Johnstown ask me that question. I can tell from the way they ask that they love their city very much. And I like the smiles on their faces when I say I like it too."

Art Newman received a key to the city on behalf of his brother, who was busy filming. He remembered the two of them walking and talking inside the War Memorial after a hockey game there. "Paul turned to me and said, 'Arthur, we couldn't have been in any other city and found the people so polite and thoughtful.'"

Warren said the film they were completing was unique and one of a kind, just like Johnstown itself, calling the city "one of the few places left in the nation that is individual. There's no other place like it.

"It's been exciting to be part of a film of this quality. It's an unusual and original film. It may shock some of you when you see it, but it is an exceptional film."

A May 26 article written by Bill Jones of the *Tribune-Democrat* quoted production manager Wally Worsley as saying Universal had spent $1.3 million in Johnstown during the filming. Approximately 5,100 people had been hired to work as extras, he added. Combined with the personal funds spent by the film company, involving about 150 people, Worsley estimated $1.5 million had been injected into the local economy.

"There's no question it gave an economic boost to the community," John Rubal, the chamber of commerce's executive secretary, told Jones. "The chamber has been most pleased with their entire stay in Johnstown. It has been a real pleasure working with them."

Two letters to the editor were printed in the May 28 edition of the newspaper. One was by George Roy Hill. "When I first arrived in Johnstown," he wrote, "it was not with the intention of actually filming here. It was only as a result of meeting with John Mitchell and out of his spirit of cooperation and helpfulness, that I reached the decision to bring the company here."

The other letter was by Nancy Dowd. "Even as a writer, I am at a great loss today to be able to adequately express my thanks to the people of Johnstown for their kind support during these past two months. *Slap Shot* is my first script to be produced and I will long remember the generosity and patience of this community with affection. I wrote *Slap Shot* as a tribute to the exuberance of American cities like Johnstown and, of course, to the great vitality of minor pro hockey."

Chapter 9

The last day in Johnstown was Saturday, May 29. The final scene filmed there was an early-morning shot of the Chiefs bus pulling away in the darkness. Hill, according to the notes of script supervisor Marvin Weldon, was overcome by emotion and excused himself before the end of the shot. Neither John Hill, the director's son, nor longtime collaborator Bob Crawford witnessed this. But both say that even though it would not have been a typical reaction by the director, they don't doubt that it happened.

"Directing movies meant everything to my father," John says. "And he loved camaraderie, especially male. And I think what happened on a movie set to him was as intimate as what happened away from a movie set, if not more so.

"He was not someone who revealed his feelings often. But he valued feelings. And he showed his feelings more on a movie set than anywhere else. I could see him change as he worked with actors, put his guard down. He would become much more expressive and accessible as he would read a line for an actor or show him the timing of a reaction. In those instances, even surrounded by a whole crew, directing became a very intimate activity."

When the buses and trucks did pull away from Johnstown for real, townspeople lined the route to see them off, waving as the caravan passed and holding up signs that read things like, 'Goodbye, Slap Shot' and other heartfelt messages of farewell.

———— ● ————

Filming continued after the Memorial Day long weekend in Syracuse, where the Charlestown Chiefs once again met the Hyannisport Presidents. This was the game in which the Hanson Brothers led their teammates into the stands, a re-enactment of the infamous January 1975 game between the Jets and the Mohawk Valley Comets. Dave Hanson remembers that the fans in Syracuse, who weren't inclined to be kind toward Johnstown hockey players, took it a bit too seriously when the Chiefs invaded the stands, and they actually tried to take him and the Carlson brothers out. When you see Hanson, in particular, flailing around with people on his back, it's for real.

A couple of Syracuse residents had prominent parts here. Matthew Weinberg, a graduate of Syracuse University, was cast as the fan who hits Jeff Hanson with the keys and is then beaten up. Local actress Ruth Fenster portrayed another fan who smashes Denis Lemieux over the head with a bottle and tells him to "go fuck a moose, froggy." That scene required a number of takes because actor Yvon Barrette, knowing what was coming, invariably closed his eyes each time before Fenster clobbered him.

An announcer was needed to call the carnage for the benefit of radio listeners unable to be at the game. Unfortunately, as someone from the film company belatedly realized, no one had been hired to portray the announcer. Director Hill asked Andrew Duncan if he knew anyone who could fill the role on short notice and Duncan recommended his longtime friend Paul Dooley, another Second City alumnus. They had worked together throughout the 1960s and '70s, creating and recording thousands of commercials for radio and TV.

The West Virginia native had been in the business since the 1950s, working on the New York stage, on TV and in movies. He also worked as the head writer for the first season of the children's educational TV series *The Electric Company* in 1971. As luck would have it, Dooley was available when Duncan told

Chapter 9

Hill about his friend who could play the unnamed but agitated Hyannisport announcer. "I took a train up there (to Syracuse) at night and worked the next day," he says of his *Slap Shot* experience.

Like Kathryn Walker, Dooley worked on the film for only the one day after arriving on the set. Unlike Walker, he did his work alone. He also did not have the benefit of seeing what his play-by-play was describing, because it was shot entirely separate from the hockey game he was supposedly watching.

"George Roy Hill had been allowing Andrew to do a great deal of improvisation, because Andrew is one of the kings of it, and I largely improvised it too," he says of his work. "George said, 'Imagine what's going on down there on the ice and report on it excitedly.' I think he maybe said something like, 'They're having a fight.' But what's unusual about that?"

What did prove unusual was Dooley's frenzied commentary, far different from the staccato delivery of a legend like Foster Hewitt yet equally as homerish. He also managed to throw in a Ralph Kiner moment; Kiner, one of the most renowned sluggers baseball has ever seen, became as famous for his malapropisms in his second career as a New York Mets announcer.

"Ladies and gentlemen, look at that!" Dooley commanded his listeners, instantly realizing his mistake and continuing without missing a beat. "You can't see that — I'm on radio."

"I had no idea I was going to say that. It just came out," he says now, chuckling. "I just tried to bring some excitement to it."

The next stop was Utica, where the Chiefs brawled with the Peterborough Patriots, keyed by a spectacular pre-game clothesline of Bobby Labrecque, another former McGill teammate of Ned Dowd. Labrecque later wrote to Hill and thanked him for the opportunity to be in the film; Hill replied to his letter and told Labrecque his fall was the best he had ever witnessed in all of his years of filmmaking.

Hamilton, NY, was the last stop before California. A smaller community located about midway between Syracuse and Utica and a bit to the south of both, its attraction to the film company was that it was home to Colgate University, and thus also to Starr Rink. It was the site of Charlestown's game against the Lancaster Gears, a contest shown early in the film. A photograph of the entire film company was taken on the ice after the shoot, the scoreboard still displaying a score of 3-0 for the home team over the visiting Chiefs.

The filming in California included Reggie's encounter with Suzanne Hanrahan, played by yet another Second City alumnus named Melinda Dillon, and the scenes in Reggie's apartment, modeled after the Johnstown apartment of Dave Hanson and Bruce Boudreau. As principal photography had begun with Reggie and Lily Braden, it was appropriate that scenes with those same characters ended the shoot. Actually, the final scene featured only Lindsay Crouse, as Lily, putting groceries away in Reggie's kitchen and asking if he wanted any spaghetti. Reggie had fallen asleep next to Ruby, the Bradens' dog, but Paul Newman filmed that shot first.

With that, *Slap Shot* was a wrap. Budgeted by Universal at $6 million to make, it came in slightly above that number — $6,324,918.

———— ● ————

George Roy Hill and editor Dede Allen worked through the rest of 1976 on the footage. Allen had been on the shoot from the very beginning and no one had any doubt that she would be able to help Hill make the necessary cuts and pull the film together.

"She's a marvelous woman, very elegant, very smart. She was George's favorite editor, and she was a legend by that time," says producer Bob Wunsch, noting Allen's credit on the theatrical posters may have marked the first time any film editor ever received such distinctions. "She deserved the credit, because she was a brilliant editor. Whether she negotiated it or George negotiated it for her, I don't know, but I think you'll find it's the first time that (editing) was a front credit. It was never on a poster before."

Allen started in the business in the 1940s and worked with Hill for the first time on *Slaughterhouse-Five* in 1972. She said in an April 2007 interview that she was attracted to the *Slap Shot* script and to the characters, which she felt had been so clearly delineated by Nancy Dowd. "She's a wonderful woman. She's very funny," Allen said. "The story was fun. The characters were great. It helps if you get to know the characters. I'm not just talking about the actors, but the characters."

The movie made such an impression on her that, after filming wrapped in Pennsylvania, she bought a new Jeep and excitedly asked the director and his son to come and see it. She proudly showed them how she had stenciled "Slap Shot" on the rear window of the vehicle. "It was evident that she was just as excited by that as by the prospect of owning a new Jeep," recalls John Hill.

Elegant as Allen, the foul language in the script did not shock, offend or upset her. She was also not hindered by her lack of hockey knowledge, which consisted of a couple of NHL games in the company of Jerry Houser. She pointed out that she knew nothing about billiards before tackling *The Hustler*, a job that was more difficult than you might think because it was made in black and white, not color. "A prop man had somebody shoot Polaroids of all of the different balls in black and white so I could tell one from the other. I had them slapped up where I worked so I could always pick which ball was which," Allen said.

She worked closely with Hill throughout the filming of *Slap Shot*, traveling with the troupe and soaking up the atmosphere. "I went on all the tours. It was a ball!" she laughed. Traveling with the company helped Allen to get to know the various actors and their characters, and that helped her to maintain her focus on the ensemble cast. While Newman was unquestionably the star of the film and the glue that held everything together, appearing in almost every scene, he was most generous in his willingness to work with his castmates, standing back when necessary and sharing the spotlight with them. Allen said this is typical of many great actors because they know this will only improve the movie. "Others sometimes leave and just go sit in their trailers while the other parts are being done. That doesn't make for the best movie because they don't have that electricity between them."

But Newman was no mere straight man, content to let everyone else steal the laughs. Having overcome any question in his own mind as to whether he could be funny, Newman had some comedic turns of his own and he played them wonderfully. "He went a little over the top at times but he was funny as hell," Allen said, laughing again.

John Hill got a great education working with and for Allen on *Slap Shot,* and delights in telling about the unique way in which she worked, in the days before editing was done on computers.

"She would use a grease pencil and slash at the film, cut it and whip the trim behind her back," he says. "At that point I, being the apprentice, would grab the trim as fast as I could without goosing her and hang the trim under the appropriate cinetab in the film bin. I swear the process happened as fast as it does now electronically except possibly for my slowness.

"As I was looking at the cinetabs, I would hear the whipping sound again and turn to see another trim waiting for me, impatiently shaking. I soon realized how important my job was. If I didn't hang the trim quickly, Dede would not have use of both of her hands. And Dede couldn't make a cut without both her hands. And Dede wanted to cut."

Sometimes, depending on John's slowness or on her desire to rearrange certain shots in a particular manner right then and there, Allen would hang trims of film around her neck or even hold them in her mouth while she determined what would go where. This turned out to be a common practice and it gave her a certain look. Barry Sonnenfeld, who worked with Allen on *The Addams Family*, told Hill she looked like Medusa at times.

All the editing work for *Slap Shot* was done in a room next to the senior Hill's office at Universal. Numerous rules were broken in order for this to happen, John remembers. "Editing rooms were not allowed there, but we got away with it. In fact, we even had a projector in the editing room, which was definitely not allowed. We called the projector 'Oggie' after Oggie Oglethorpe and Dede made sure I always tucked 'Oggie' in with a sheet in case a suit came by and noticed 'him.'"

As capable as Allen's work was on *Slap Shot*, some "oops" moments did make it into the finished product. Most occurred early on in the film. Ned Braden is shown wearing two different sets of gloves — brown, and blue and white — during the intro-ductions before the first Hyannisport game. Or it may have been the same old pair, shown once before the paint job and once afterward.

When Hyannisport scores its first goal, the players on the ice skate to their respective benches and are replaced, but some of the same Presidents who were just on the ice are now seen coming off the bench. Bruce Boudreau, No. 7, is one of them. And when the Chiefs score their only goal of the game, Reggie starts the play by taking the puck behind the net and back-handing a pass to Jean-Guy Drouin on his left side. But if you look closely, just as Reggie prepares to make the pass, the puck actually slides harmlessly off his stick to his right. Oops.

—— ● ——

While Allen and the younger Hill worked on the film, his father spent much of his time playing the piano in his next-door office. He had maintained his love for and interest in music and was always very hands-on when it came to includ-ing music in his movies, working closely with talented music supervisors like Elmer Bernstein. Hill's instincts were gener-ally good too, at least from a commercial standpoint — he included a Burt Bacharach-Hal David song called "Raindrops Keep Fallin' on My Head" in *Butch Cassidy and the Sundance Kid*, and it won an Oscar (as did the film's score) and became one of the biggest hits of 1970. When Hill made *The Sting*, he insisted the score incorporate the ragtime music of Scott Joplin even though ragtime had long been passé by the 1930s, the era in which the movie was set. Marvin Hamlisch's score won an Oscar and his recording of the song "The Entertainer" went to No. 3 on the pop chart and won a Grammy.

Chapter 9

As *Slap Shot* was a rare contemporary film for Hill, he needed contemporary music. Nancy Dowd and, fittingly, musician-actor Allan Nicholls helped show the way, giving Hill a mix tape that included several current or recent hit songs. They included Fleetwood Mac's "Rhiannon" and "Say You Love Me," Elton John's "Sorry Seems to Be the Hardest Word," "You Make Me Feel Like Dancing," by Leo Sayer and "A Little Bit South of Saskatoon" by Sonny James.

The centerpiece of the soundtrack would be a song called "Right Back Where We Started From," which had peaked at No. 2 on the pop chart in May 1976. Maxine Nightingale was a singer-actor from London who had made a name in her homeland by appearing in the rock musicals *Hair, Jesus Christ Superstar* and *Godspell*. It was in *Hair* that she met a fellow performer named Vincent Edwards.

In 1975, Edwards established a partnership with Pierre Tubbs, a writer and producer with United Artists Records. They had first met in the late '60s when Tubbs worked on Edwards' UA single release of "Aquarius," from *Hair*. Several years later, they met up at a show in London and decided to work together again.

"He gave me the title and I started the lyrics. I already had a tune and feel written down from a couple of years before," Edwards says. Tubbs already had a singer in mind to record their song, when it was finished. He mentioned Nightingale's name to Edwards, who was delighted with the choice. "I knew Maxine from *Hair* so there was no problem — I knew she was good."

The two men finished writing the song in Tubbs' car while they were driving to Hammersmith Hospital, where Tubbs' wife was about to give birth. They recorded a demo the following day and Tubbs gave the demo to Nightingale so she could learn the song. "We recorded it within a week," Edwards says. "I did back-up vocals and Pierre got it released on UA Records."

The driving disco song went to No. 8 on the British chart before crossing the Atlantic and nearly topping the US list. Once Hill decided he had to have the song in *Slap Shot*, a deal was made with ATV Music, the song's publisher in the US.

"The Stripper," made famous in a 1961 hit recording by its composer, David Rose, was an obvious choice for the scene where Ned Braden peels off his uniform piece by piece. The pop standard "Lady of Spain" was played at least twice by the Chiefs' organist, most infamously when an exasperated Reggie tears up the man's sheet music and yells at him to never play the song again.

"The Star Spangled Banner," or an abbreviated version of it, was picked for what appeared to be a throwaway scene, the opening credits. The playing of the national anthem has long been a tradition at hockey games. But the American flag was used as the scene's backdrop, indicating that the anthem's use served another purpose here. Dowd and Hill were saying, "This, what you are about to see, is America right now." Given that the fans are depicted as more interested in brawling than in hockey and in substance more than style — "They don't want you to score goals, they want blood! They're booing you!" Reggie Dunlop tells Ned Braden — it's clear the writer and the director wanted to drill this home from the very beginning.

Chapter 10

Violent, Bloody and Thoroughly Revolting

———— 🏒 ————

Slap Shot was scheduled to be released in February and March 1977, right when the hockey season was heating up.

There were staggered release dates because movies back then opened gradually and built their audiences over time, unlike today, when most big-budget films open across the United States and Canada on the same release date and hope for huge box-office success right out of the gate. February 25 was the date chosen for *Slap Shot*'s dual premieres in New York and Los Angeles.

Hill decided, though, to launch the film eight days early at a special benefit screening at Yale, his alma mater. It was something he had done to great success with *Butch Cassidy and the Sundance Kid*, and it made sense since Paul Newman had also attended Yale. The proceeds would go to film studies at the university. Also in attendance were Mike Ontkean, Strother

Martin, Jennifer Warren, Lindsay Crouse, Steve Mendillo, Nancy Dowd and Dede Allen, among others.

Jeff Carlson was playing in the NAHL with the Mohawk Valley Comets. When he joined the Comets, he informed them of the upcoming benefit screening and insisted on permission to go as a condition of his signing a contract. They agreed. But when he attended as planned, the club suspended him. He eventually returned and finished the season with Mohawk Valley, but there were undoubtedly some hurt feelings.

There was also plenty of animosity left over from the filming as far as Hill was concerned. He made it clear that he did not want producers Bob Wunsch and Stephen Friedman to attend the Yale screening. Since Wunsch is also a Yale graduate, Hill couldn't have simply expected to be able to prevent Wunsch and Friedman from coming. So he pulled a different kind of power play — even though he had organized the benefit, he announced he would leave if the producers showed up. As they had done during the shooting, Wunsch and Friedman stayed away. They staged their own screening five days later, on February 22, at the Writers Guild Theater in West Hollywood.

Both men loved *Slap Shot* and, despite Hill's feelings toward them, were immensely proud both of the film and of the director's work.

"His choice of music was superb. His choice of Dede Allen was superb. His choice of the supporting actors was superb. His choice of location — everything that a director does, he did wonderfully. Everything having to do with the physical making of the movie, all the choices were his and they were great choices," Wunsch says. "He deserves an enormous amount of credit for his eye, his taste, his balls, his gut instincts, and I don't have a single negative thing to say, only highly positive things to say, about how wonderfully he made this movie."

Wunsch admits to having been somewhat torn over the controversy generated by some of the more colorful dialogue. It hurt the movie's box office showing, although that initially didn't seem apparent to the producer. He remembers seeing a very long line outside Grauman's Chinese Theatre and figured it was great news, but the theater's manager pointed out to him that the customers were almost exclusively young males, who would not see the movie more than that one time because repeat audiences were unheard of then. Ominously, there were very few women in line, and women were seen then as the customer base that would drive a movie to success.

"It was quite clear that this movie did not appeal to women," Wunsch says. "The psychological profile that the distributors sort of chatted about was that women simply were offended that Paul Newman, who had been in so many movies with such charm, was all of a sudden so vulgar and crude and rude and low-class, and they didn't like it. I don't know if it's true, but it was a speculation at the time as to why the movie, which was brilliantly made and starred Paul Newman and was so original, didn't really succeed, did not make a lot of money."

Like anyone involved in the film industry, Wunsch was certainly interested in the product making as much money as possible. But he also realized that to have toned down the foul language would have meant a compromise that would have made for a far less accurate portrayal — and that was against everything Hill stood for.

"The studio asked George to remove some of the worst lines, like when he screams, 'Suzanne sucks pussy,' like when he says, 'Your son's gonna have somebody's dick in his mouth before he knows it.' They felt that was going to hurt them at the box office. George, to his credit, said 'Absolutely not. This is the movie and I think it requires that level of vulgarity. That's what makes the movie sing, that's what makes it great. I won't do it.' It was a very big battle . . . ultimately, I think, it was part of the reason that the movie was not a runaway success. It was a better movie, but less successful. The studio, correctly, prefers a more successful movie. Even I would have preferred a more successful movie. But it wouldn't have been as *good* a movie."

Studio president Ned Tanen acknowledged that he had to fight off those at Universal who were adamantly opposed to the level of vulgarity, particularly the infamous line spoken by Reggie to team owner Anita McCambridge. "I remember going to the first preview," he said. "My associates were screaming at me, 'You can't do this!' And when that line came out, the audience, there was this hesitation and then the theater just erupted. It was like a whole volcano erupted in the movie business."

The positive response from the preview audience convinced the executive to go with his gut and okay the release as is, with all the dirty words intact. But he expected even more opposition to come from the Motion Picture Association of America, the board charged with the responsibility of assigning one of four possible ratings to the film: G, recommended for general audiences; PG, parental guidance suggested; R, restricted, viewers under age 17 required accompaniment by an adult; or X, no one under 17 admitted. In those days, a rating meant everything to the potential box office, and companies would often appeal what it felt was an unduly harsh judgment by the board. M. Emmet Walsh remembers such an episode involving *All the President's Men.*

"The review board gave it an X rating because they had the vernacular for copulation in it twice. There were two 'fucks' in it. Any time 'fuck' was used in a movie, it was an automatic X rating. *All the President's Men* appealed and got it reduced from an X to an R, and it was the first time the code had been busted a little bit."

Which was a good thing in the case of *Slap Shot*, because Walsh also remembers a fellow actor counting 168 instances of swearing, mostly "fucks," in the script. "We weren't even playing with R," he laughs. "We were playing with X from the get-go."

But the ratings board passed *Slap Shot* with an R rating, much to the everlasting amazement of Tanen. "The fact that I ran it for the board in New York and they didn't toss it still astonishes me," he said, adding he thought it went right over the heads of the board members.

He remembered waiting for that particular line and wondering how harsh the reaction would be when it was uttered. "I sat there with the board, which by the way was located in between two porno theaters in New York, in Manhattan, and I said, oh, shit, here it comes. And they didn't even get it."

Audiences did. Line producer Bob Crawford says it had the impact of "a sledgehammer to the forehead."

"It hit you — wham! — between the eyes. It was pointed and it was telling for all viewers who came to our movie: we were profane, and shocking, and effective, and violent, and funny, and entertaining, and seductive, and bewildering.

When you came away from it, you thought, 'What happened to me? I loved that movie, but I was shocked and embarrassed and mortified, and I like violence much too much, and I would go see it again. I've been seduced here and I don't know, psychologically, if this is good or bad for me, but I sure enjoyed it.'"

Many people, however, did not enjoy it. The infamous line and others like it did not pass unnoticed by those critics who were soon foaming at the mouth over *Slap Shot*. Some, like Rex Reed, came across as almost hysterical in their reviews — his words are the title of this chapter. Regis Philbin, on KABC-TV's morning show *AM Los Angeles*, said that if this was what pro hockey had come to, Idi Amin should be its commissioner and Adolf Hitler and Joseph Stalin should be resurrected in order to settle World War III on the ice.

A number of reviews made fun of the film's title, suggesting it should have been called *Slap Dash* or *Slap Stick* or some variation. One such review was written by Richard Cuskelly of the *Los Angeles Herald-Examiner*, who went on to say that, "*Slap Shot* comes on like a nervous comedian at a topless bar anxious to keep the customers satisfied with bawdy one-liners while the girls change from nothing to nothing."

Reed made a more reasoned argument in his claim that Universal had refused to make private screenings available for reviewers. Instead, critics were invited to attend preview showings for the public. He charged this was a deliberate attempt by the studio to influence the reviewers, believing the writers "too dense to understand a noisy movie about violence without the ambiance of an audience of civilians screaming their heads off to remind us which scenes are 'working.'" Stephen Friedman responded in *Variety* by pointing out

Chapter 10

the final mixing of *Slap Shot* was completed only two weeks before the opening and it had been thought the February 25 release date would have to be pushed back because of the tenuous timeline.

Some film distributors also felt the movie was entirely inappropriate and questioned its R rating. Edward S. Shaw, writing to the *Los Angeles Times*, said he was happy to have been able to preview the film so that he wouldn't waste $3.50 on a ticket to see Paul Newman, "the man who *was* my favorite star." Shaw claimed the film's advertisements noted that certain language may have been too strong for children. "I think it should have read, 'Certain language may be too strong for children and adults who haven't done time in the slammer or worked in a whorehouse.'"

———— ● ————

Criticism was not limited to those whose job it was to be critical. While researching his book *War As They Knew It: Woody Hayes, Bo Schembechler and America in a Time of Unrest*, author Michael Rosenberg uncovered a gem of a story about Hayes, the autocratic longtime football coach at Ohio State University. The Buckeyes would gather to watch a movie on the night before a game, a bonding exercise. One night, in Champaign, Illinois, assistant coach Mickey Jackson and trainer Billy Hill decided the team would watch *Slap Shot* at a local theater. They were unaware of its content, knowing only it was a sports movie and Paul Newman was its star. It wasn't long before they realized they had screwed up.

Hayes stewed as the profane language and sexual comments came rapid-fire. The bedroom scene between Reggie Dunlop and Suzanne Hanrahan was the last straw, a topless

Suzanne confessing her lesbian interludes to Reggie and asking him if he was shocked.

"Woody Hayes was sure as hell shocked," Rosenberg wrote. "He stood up in the middle of the theater and shouted, 'This is TRASH! This is TRASH!' Mickey Jackson slunk as low into his seat as he could so Hayes would not see him. The Buckeyes did not have the theater to themselves — there were other paying customers there — but the Old Man was too pissed off to care. He walked out to the candy counter and asked for the manager, and when the manager came out, Hayes barked, 'You're fired!' Hayes then went outside and left a note on the team bus to let everybody know he was walking back to the team hotel, the Lincoln Lodge. And he did."

Steve Mendillo took a bit of heat for his character's complaint of looking "like some cock-sucking faggot" in the fashion show scene. "I don't think my old man appreciated it much," he says. "He took some of his friends in Fort Lauderdale to see it and I think the color of the whole movie put him off a little.

"But he didn't care for the arts, anyway. He was a very literate guy, very well read, but he just wasn't interested in the arts."

Some writers saw the movie as the satire it was intended to be.

Vincent Canby, *New York Times*, February 26, 1977: "People as thick-headed and slow-witted as are most of these characters aren't very interesting when seen in close-up for very long. Seen as a collective spectacle in a long-shot, though, they make a sometimes bitterly comic comment on one aspect of the industry that is professional American sports."

Chapter 10

Bill Foley, *Oswego (NY) Palladium-Times*, June 10, 1977: "*Slap Shot* may be the best thing to come along since the hockey helmet. The movie is making people see how ridiculous the sport has become. More importantly letting some people see themselves as they really are."

Other critics were generous with limited praise, if that's possible.

John Simon, *New York*, March 7, 1977: "*Slap Shot* is an amusing movie as long as you don't look at it very closely, and forget it as fast as you can."

Part of Simon's problem with the film stemmed from what he saw as Hill's and Newman's unwillingness to clearly state a point of view — is hockey violence good or bad? He wasn't alone in this belief. Newman responded by telling an interviewer that the lack of overt comment was itself a statement. "I think that short of lecturing it demonstrates very, very effectively what the American mentality is. I see *Slap Shot* as a very dark picture, actually," he said.

Newman said he had seen the film with an audience and wasn't at all surprised or even dismayed that the crowd cheered the violence. "What you saw, then, was an American audience at work. We're not manipulating *them*."

Many reviewers found the movie salty but entertaining.

Bob Thomas, *Associated Press*, March 1977: "George Roy Hill's direction and Nancy Dowd's script provide lusty entertainment, combining human touches with ample mayhem on the ice . . . See it now, because its bleeping language will not allow TV exposure, except as a silent. Rated R, as in raunchy."

Ruth Batchelor, *Los Angeles Free Press*, February 25, 1977: "*Slap Shot* is the most exciting, enlightening, perceptive picture I've seen this year."

William Wolf, *Cue*, March 5, 1977: "This comedy about grubby, lower-echelon hockey teams should easily be among the most enjoyable pictures of 1977. Sitting at the typewriter, I find myself laughing again at the thoroughly outrageous scenes."

Janet Maslin, *Newsweek*, March 7, 1977: "(Newman's) obviously well-pondered decision to come out of the four-letter closet is going to blow a million minds. Actually, you've never heard dirty words uttered with such endearing cleanliness, such innocent sweetness, as Newman utters them."

George Anthony, *Toronto Sun*, February 27, 1977: "It's a terrific movie, brimming with life and gutsy humour and stunning action sequences and rich performances . . . *Slap Shot* is scripted in locker room vernacular, and brilliantly so, giving the movie a cinema-verite thrust that makes it utterly hypnotic. What makes crude epithets so acceptable — and to my knowledge never have so many been strung together before at one time — is the fact they are delivered with that sweet naivety and innocence that is the exclusive property of every red-blooded American jock. These guys aren't cursing each other; they are merely communicating."

That was something many jocks didn't even consciously recognize until they were presented with the evidence.

"The first time I saw the movie, I was a little taken aback by the language," says Paul Stewart. "It was even a little bit more than we would do, or maybe I was just oblivious to how much players do swear.

"Even now, sometimes I forget myself with my kids and blow a couple of F-bombs out. But going to the theater with my wife and a bunch of the neighbors and seeing this film, they didn't know that side of me, the drinking and the smoking and the women and the f-ing this and the f-ing that and the life on the bus. But it was all true."

"The hockey community didn't want people thinking that's what professional hockey was all about," says Ric Seiling, who began his 10-season NHL career in 1977 with the Buffalo Sabres. "But there was a lot of truth behind it. Believe me, I know of places where buses needed escorts out of town, not just in (the minors) but even in Junior B hockey in Canada."

Many pro hockey players disavowed the film. Ron Docken recalls listening to Pittsburgh radio station KDKA after the movie was released. "Some of the Pittsburgh Penguins would get on the radio and say, 'That was totally false, none of that happens,'" he says. In fairness, it's safe to say that a lot of those in hockey who were critical of the film had never spent any time at the NAHL level.

Even in Canada, hockey's birthplace, *Slap Shot* was not immune from criticism. "I remember when I was out promoting it," says Allan Nicholls. "There were a few hockey purists who really didn't want to know anything about that film, (broadcaster) Dick Irvin Jr. being one of them. He didn't want to see a film that made fun of hockey. They forgot it was just a celebration of all that was hockey, a celebration of the minor leagues and all that you could and would go through in that system."

Nicholls attended the premiere in Montreal with Nancy Dowd and Yvon Barrette. "A guy came out from the movie. He was an Irishman, something like 70 years old, and he came straight to me, saying, 'You're a disgrace to hockey,'" Barrette says, laughing. "I was really surprised by the reaction of the spectators."

Those who "got" the film did so on merit, according to Jennifer Warren, because she believes *Slap Shot* got lost in the shuffle between critics who didn't understand it and a studio that didn't really know how to promote it to those critics or to audiences. There were too many facets for it to be easily given a label.

"It was not one thing, it was several. It wasn't just a sports film, it wasn't just a silly comedy . . . They didn't know how to sell it," she says, adding the realism depicted in the script and in the performances, and Hill's direction, kept the movie from crossing the line into farce and also prevented the studio and critics from pigeon-holing it.

"I think he knew so clearly what that line was, and I don't think it ever goes over into where they're commenting on their characters. They're outrageous people, but you don't believe that they're commenting on, 'Aren't I outrageous?' That's just the way they were, and that's why it works . . . that's why it's so successful."

———— ● ————

Pauline Kael wrote perhaps the most thorough and detailed review of the movie. It first appeared in the March 7, 1977, edition of *The New Yorker* and was later reproduced in *When the Lights Go Down*, one of many published collections of her works. She devoted a big chunk of the review to fulsome praise for Newman's work, writing that the film was held together by "the warmth" he supplied in delivering "the performance of his life — to date." Kael goes on to compare Newman to Humphrey Bogart, describing him first as "an actor-star" who is "peerless" in the right role. "What Newman does here is casual American star-acting at its peak; he's as perfectly assured a comedian as Bogart in *The African Queen* . . . What he does as Reggie isn't very different from what he's done before: it's that the control, the awareness, the power all seem to have become clarified. He has the confidence now to value his own gifts as an entertainer."

He was also confident in his appearance, Kael argued, noting he had retained his youthful look even though Reggie, while childlike, "is scarred and bruised, and there are gold rims on his chipped teeth . . . the childlike quality is inner, and the warmth comes from deeper down. He makes boyishness seem magically attractive." But there was more to the character than that. Kael noted Reggie's "desperate, forlorn quality" and his vulnerability, fed by physical pain from various injuries and by despair which stems from the seeming hopelessness of his situation.

"How and why Newman broke through in *this* picture, I don't know," the critic wrote. "But this is the kind of breakthrough that doesn't often happen with movie stars. And when a star grows as an actor, there's an extra pleasure in it for us. We know Newman so well in his star roles — he is so much a part of us — that we experience his development as if it were our triumph. Newman proves that stardom isn't necessarily corrupting, and we need that proof as often as possible."

Naturally, many reviewers expressed surprise that *Slap Shot* had been written by a woman. Batchelor wasn't as much surprised as she was delighted, writing that she wanted to cheer the fact. Kael also wasn't surprised. "Nancy Dowd has proved that a woman can write a script as profane and manipulative as a man's — but did anybody doubt it?" she asked. Dowd's father was apparently surprised. In a July 2007 interview with Philadelphia morning radio host Michael Smerconish of WPHT 1210 AM, she said her father actually thought she had written the swear words phonetically. "I don't think he thought I had any understanding," she laughed.

Some took a patronizing view of Dowd and her writing. Stephen Farber, writing in *New West*, thought it "perverse that at a time when there are so few good women's roles in movies, even the rare women writers center their scripts on men . . . Once women agree to play by the industry's rules, they can only perpetuate the sexual prejudices that Hollywood approves." Dowd responded by telling freelance writer Carol Mithers that if Farber "had any genuine concern about my rights as a woman artist, he would never say what I *should* write about. I can write about whatever I feel like."

The *Los Angeles Times* took a particular interest in *Slap Shot*. Very little of this interest was positive. Kevin Thomas fired the first salvos in his February 25 review, calling the movie a "cynical little piece . . . shabby and calculating."

"*Slap Shot* has the ingredients of a movie that could be both a lively entertainment and a comment upon the public's blood lust for violence in sports. Instead, *Slap Shot* uses its mill-town milieu and its third-rate athletics to justify the foulest dialogue yet heard in a mainstream commercial movie, a nude sequence that if not unwarranted plays exploitatively, and dosages of violence (mixed with mealy-mouthed protestations that violence is awful) that make the movie into the objects of its own hypocritical scorns . . . Newman's gutter talk hits some kind of pinnacle in a scene with frosty Kathryn Walker as the team's secret owner. Few scenes have ever been at one swoop as unconvincing and as offensive."

Charles Champlin followed up on March 10 with his own review, although he couldn't help but open with a shout-out to his colleague, noting that *Slap Shot* had already been "checked

Chapter 10

into the boards fairly resoundingly" by Thomas. Champlin then focused on the seeming lack of a viewpoint, on the inability to believe in the character of Reggie as portrayed by Newman and, of course, on the "locker-room vile" language.

"The defense of Newman's exit speech to the woman who owns the hockey club, like the defense of much else in the film, is that, well, that's the way those jokers are. They talk crudely about women and nastily about homosexuals of either sex because of deep fears about their own masculinity . . . You don't have to be gay to be sad at the gratuitously offensive and reactionary ideas Newman has let himself say . . . The language alone has outraged viewers who are neither prudish nor easily shocked. It is impossible to believe that *Slap Shot* would not have been better served at the box office by a less raunchy handling of its basic contents."

Well, sure it would have. But, as Bob Wunsch says, a better box-office tally doesn't necessarily make for a better movie.

The *Los Angeles Times* did allow for both sides of the story to be told. Mithers wrote a major feature about Nancy Dowd in which she eagerly defended the film. While she said the film's objective was to mock violence in hockey, her intention "was not to condemn hockey players for being violent; that's like condemning truck drivers for polluting the air. I'm more interested in who owns violence, who profits from it; like the woman who owns the team congratulating Reggie for helping her profits and at the same time making the statement that she would never let her children watch hockey because it's too violent."

She also discussed her decision to make the owner of the team a woman, saying the fact that she had doubts only convinced her to do it. "I believe that if women are to have any sort of equality in terms of portrayal, then we should be able to be portrayed not just as heroines or victims, but also as bitches, the terrible people we sometimes are; we can be rich, we can be poor. It's just inverse sexism to say otherwise."

Dowd scoffed at charges the film was "calculated," pointing out that each move that was made along the way would seem to have been the antithesis of calculation. "How you can take a 52-year-old star playing a hockey player, a studio opposing a picture, a first-time screenwriter with a screenplay full of obscenities writing about a minor league sport, a cast of unknowns and non-actors, shot on location, on ice, and call that a sure-fire exploitation picture, I don't know."

That 52-year-old star spoke his piece too, in an interview with Lee Grant of the *Times*. He reiterated and expanded upon his earlier thoughts about the cartoonish violence. "I have a theory that if something is truly funny, it isn't vulgar," he said. "In *Slap Shot*, there is cartoon violence like a *Tom and Jerry* cartoon or *Alley Oop* or *Popeye*, like when a guy goes out for a long pass and crashes into a tree. It's not real and lingering. It's all funny, all so damn funny. But then again, my humor comes straight out of the toilet.

"In the final analysis, we tried to make a funny picture. One critic said, 'The lady next to me fell out of her seat laughing.' That's what it's all about. I've never done a violent picture in my life. I've turned down all the famous violent pictures made in Hollywood. I'm certainly going to differentiate between our film and *The Enforcer* or *Dirty Harry*."

Hill was also given an opportunity to comment, in a bylined column written for the *Times*. He took Thomas and Champlin to task for what he considered their hypocrisy, noting they were "offended" by the "ultraviolent" nature of *Slap Shot*. "A film that has no guns, no knives, no weapons of death or torture, no rapes, no killings, no broken bones and in which no one expires even in bed — is ultraviolent? And this from two critics who have admired recent releases that have featured amputations, guts spilling out, stranglings, kids burned to death, mad women impaled by flying knives and so on?"

The director argued that what really bothered the critics is that the supposed violence and the dirty language was being shown and heard out of its accepted realm, in much the same way that Tim "Dr. Hook" McCracken was upset by Ned Braden's striptease. "It is their sense of place that is offended; a convention has been flouted," Hill wrote. "To McCracken a hockey rink is a place for brawling and a little hockey playing, not for skating about in one's underwear, just as to our critics language acceptable in a locker room is simply not acceptable on the screen. In *Slap Shot* all we did was decide . . . that if we were satirizing a particular subculture in our society, we should use the language of that subculture. Simple as that."

His film's violence, he insisted, was depicted as "outright farce" and suggested this may have been why the critics were offended. "They like their violence slow and serious, not fast and hilarious; laughter is the one thing violence and super-macho cultists cannot withstand. And laughter is what *Slap Shot* is getting, lots of it. There is no question that our two critics' moral outrage, like McCracken's, is perfectly genuine, but, alas, like McCracken, if they haven't gotten the joke by this time they probably never will."

McCracken's portrayer, by contrast, loved the film. So did Paul D'Amato's friends, although they were taken by surprise.

They had seen him act and they had seen him play hockey, but nobody expected what they saw on screen. "It wasn't like they didn't know Chekhov. They knew Sam Shepard as well as they knew Harry Sinden," he says.

"A bunch of us got together after the film came out. They all said, 'Paul was the nicest guy. We had him around because he was fun. And he turns out to be the goon — he's nastier than Wayne Cashman!' he laughs. "But they were all extremely proud."

Strangely, with all the criticism directed at the film, Newman's wardrobe apparently escaped unscathed even though it's not certain the fur-collared coat and the brown leather suit were even in style at the time. Ironically, as the reputation of *Slap Shot* grew over the years, Reggie Dunlop's choice of clothing has become more and more a point of ridicule. It's generally accepted now that the way he dressed was far more offensive than anything that came out of his mouth.

"Don't you love his clothes?" Jennifer Warren asks, laughing. "He loved (the wardrobe) because it was such great character stuff. He was willing to have no vanity. He was the one that suggested all these things. He loved his costume."

"All I can think about is Newman in that House of Suede suit," Ned Tanen said, laughing hard. "Oh, Christ, the guts!"

If Hill and Universal had thought the critical reception for *Slap Shot* might be more favorable overseas, they certainly must have been disappointed by their experience at the Cannes Film Festival in France.

Cannes, even then, was the world's pre-eminent festival and Hill had actually enjoyed good experiences there. He entered a film in the competition for the first time in 1972 and that entry, *Slaughterhouse-Five*, won the Jury Prize, the third most prestigious award after the Golden Palm and the Grand Prize. Hill was invited to be part of the jury in 1975.

Slap Shot was an out-of-competition film at Cannes but it received a significant honor when it was chosen to close the festival on its final night, May 27, 1977. The stage was set for it to make a huge splash — French actors had dubbed the dialogue in their own language and the movie was retitled *La Castagne*, which loosely translates to *The Punch*. It received ample press coverage in the newspapers leading up to its presentation. It debuted in a Paris theater prior to the Cannes showing and was warmly received there; Bob Crawford was among the spectators.

"I was thrilled. We had a great crowd in the theater. They laughed at every moment from the beginning to the end of the movie, on cue, as I had heard them do in the United States," he says.

The response at Cannes was far different, Crawford recalls, laughing. "It was a stony silence that greeted the film. At the end of the film there was just polite applause, after a pause. That's when George said, 'Maybe this isn't a society picture.' We didn't do a lot of business in Paris after that."

The box office business in Canada, however, was very brisk. Strangely, it was also huge in Japan. But it wasn't as big in the United States as had been hoped. Although critic Pauline Kael had fully expected *Slap Shot* to join *Butch Cassidy* and *The Sting* on the list of all-time moneymakers, it topped out in North America with a take of $28 million. That was still a respectable showing, especially in relation to its $6.3 million production cost, but it was also the same amount earned by *Herbie Goes to*

Monte Carlo. Both paled in contrast to the heavy hitters of the class of 1977 — *The Goodbye Girl, Close Encounters of the Third Kind, Saturday Night Fever, Smokey and the Bandit* and *Star Wars.* Even *Semi-Tough* outperformed *Slap Shot* at the box office, bringing in more than $37 million.

When the year's films were honored by the various awards programs, *Slap Shot* was overlooked in almost every instance. Most egregiously, Paul Newman did not earn an Oscar or Golden Globe nomination for his portrayal of Reggie Dunlop. The Writers Guild of America nominated Nancy Dowd's script for the best comedy screenplay written directly for the screen, but it lost to *Annie Hall.* In Japan, *Slap Shot* was nominated by the Japanese Academy and by the Hochi Film Awards for best foreign film of 1977. It prevailed in the latter category, the only film industry award it would ever win.

Chapter 11

We All Saw it With Our Own Eyes

———— ● ————

Slap Shot didn't receive an overwhelming welcome in its hometown. It opened on March 25, 1977, at the Westwood Plaza Theater in Johnstown. A full house was expected. It didn't materialize.

Gracie Head looks back fondly now on the film, but at the time she was among more than a few Johnstown residents who thought it simply hit too close to home in its portrayal of a dreary, declining community. "I remember when I saw it for the first time and people thought it was very funny. I didn't think it was funny, I thought it was sad. This was a true story."

"They filmed every bad section of the city," says Leslie Tenesi, who didn't appreciate the negative depiction of her hometown. "It's not dreary and depressing. It's really green, really lush and it's a nice small town."

Johnstown doesn't have a bigger booster than Denny Grenell, but even he couldn't find fault with the portrayal. "It was accurate. The mill was dying, and that was a very valid point," he says, adding the number of people turned off by the film was "a small percentage" of local residents.

"I went to the premiere of it and I thought it'd be standing room only. The theater was only about half full. People had heard about all the bad language in it, and I think they boycotted it for a while. But that didn't last. In fact, I've often wondered how many DVDs and video tapes of it have been sold."

Slap Shot shook off the inauspicious beginning and settled in for a long stay at theaters in Johnstown, which was feeling pretty good about itself as spring became summer in 1977. A brutal winter with heavy snow loads had people worried about the possibility of floods, but the spring melt came and went with no problems.

Despite its 1973 announcement that it would begin scaling down its operations in Johnstown, Bethlehem Steel was still going strong. It continued to employ in the neighbourhood of 12,000 people and company chairman Lewis Foy, a city native, was doing all he could to keep his hometown from suffering through the decline of the domestic steel industry. Bethlehem even announced in 1976 a future investment of almost $100 million worth of environmental upgrades to its Johnstown works. Unemployment in the Johnstown metropolitan area had dropped to 5.3 per cent by May 1977.

Things weren't terrific on the local hockey front, though. The Jets were only one year removed from one of the best regular-season finishes in their history. But a new ownership group blundered when it abruptly dismissed John Mitchell at the end of the 1975–76 season. The campaign that followed was simply awful as Johnstown plummeted from first place in its division to seventh overall in the eight-team NAHL with a 22–49–2 record. A quick playoff exit followed.

That was just a blip, people figured.

But things were about to get much worse. Disaster was right around the corner for Johnstown's hockey team and for the city itself. No one saw it coming. No one could have seen it coming.

Millions of dollars had been spent after the 1936 flood to ensure such a tragedy was never repeated, and for years the work had been good enough. But the money spent and the preparations made had not taken into effect the possible impact of the type of storm that comes along not once in a millennium — more like once every 5,000 to 10,000 years. The storm of July 19–20, 1977, dumped nearly 12 inches of rain in only 10 hours. It was too much for six dams around Johnstown, which failed and sent 128 million gallons of water pouring into the river valley. It was more than six times the amount of water that had all but destroyed the city in 1889. The newest disaster caused more than $200 million worth of damage, killing 85 people and leaving 50,000 homeless.

Damage to the ice-making plant at the Cambria County War Memorial forced the Jets out of business, a decision that became moot when the entire North American Hockey League folded prior to the start of the 1977–78 season. Suffering even more calamity than the War Memorial in Johnstown were the Bethlehem Steel works — more than $50 million worth of damage. It spelled the real beginning of the end of the local steel industry, as the company abandoned its earlier invest- ment plans and began to immediately slash jobs, cutting almost 4,000 workers loose within a month of the flood.

More than a few residents wondered if the film still playing in town wasn't the cause of all the misery. "Some of the churches were very unhappy when *Slap Shot* came out," says Don Hall. "A lot of people blamed the flood on the fact that God was getting back at us for making that movie. There was a lot of talk about that."

The city rallied again. Hockey returned in the fall of 1978 with a new team, the Wings, and a new setting, the North Eastern Hockey League. John Mitchell was back in charge and Dick Roberge was coaching once again. But they couldn't recapture the old magic, and the Wings finished last in the five-team league. The loop renamed itself the Eastern Hockey League the following season and the Wings became the Red Wings, but they could finish no better than fifth in a six-team grouping. The team folded and the EHL followed suit a year later.

More bad times were in store. The recession of the early 1980s hit Johnstown hard. Bethlehem Steel was winding down and unemployment shot up to more than 25 per cent, the highest rate in the United States. Filmmakers came back to Johnstown to put another steel mill town-gone-bad story on the big screen, a high school football movie called *All the Right Moves*. The film starred Tom Cruise, Craig T. Nelson and Lea Thompson and, while it was a welcome boost to the local economy, did nothing to shake the image that Johnstown — renamed Ampipe for the movie — was a dying city.

While thousands of residents again took jobs as extras, Gracie Head wasn't one of them. Nancy Dowd helped with the casting process and urged her to do it, but Head refused. "I didn't even go and apply," she says, "Nancy said, 'You still have your SAG credentials. They would have to give you a job before they give it to somebody else.' But I wasn't interested."

———— ● ————

Ironically, it was around this time that Johnstown's first movie began to come back to life.

Everyone connected with *Slap Shot* had gone on with their lives. Dave Hanson and Jeff and Steve Carlson had been offered movie contracts by Universal, which was convinced it had found a modern Three Stooges act. The three were interested — their next film would have been a roller derby picture — but they were more interested in continuing with their hockey careers. When Universal could not guarantee that the filming of future movies would not conflict with hockey, the trio said thanks but no thanks.

"They wanted to have the ability to do it whenever they wanted to do it instead of doing it in the off-season," Hanson says. "We said, we love playing hockey and we want to be hockey players. Movie acting is not something we have a desire to do as a profession. We just shot it down. We said no."

All three made it to the WHA with the Minnesota Fighting Saints, and Hanson and Steve Carlson also had brief stays in the NHL, as did Jack Carlson. Jeff never made it to the NHL but he did play in the minor leagues until the 1982–83 season. Dave, who also played with the New England Whalers and the Birmingham Bulls in the WHA and with the Detroit Red Wings and the Minnesota North Stars in the NHL, retired in 1984. Steve also played with New England and Edmonton in the WHA and with the Los Angeles Kings in the NHL before calling it quits in 1987. He has the unique distinction of having suited up with

Gordie Howe in New England and with Wayne Gretzky on the Oilers in addition to Paul Newman in Johnstown, but says his biggest thrill was playing with childhood idol Dave Keon on the Whalers.

Despite predictions that *Slap Shot* would never be shown on network television because of the substantial amount of editing that would be required, the broadcast rights were sold to ABC. It readied the film for broadcast as the *ABC Sunday Night Movie* on January 31, 1982, replacing the adjective "fucking" with "freaking," among other creative changes.

In an interview with Aaron Latham of *Rolling Stone* that was published in January 1983, Newman remembered the day he was contacted by an ABC representative. The representative told Newman he had counted 176 uses of the word "fuck" and the network did not know how it would proceed. Newman then apologized to Latham for his foul mouth and urged the writer to excise the dirty words from his article. "Ever since *Slap Shot*, I've been swearing more. You get a hangover from a character like that, and you simply don't get rid of it. I knew I had a problem when I turned to my daughter one day and said, 'Please pass the fuckin' salt.'"

He touched on the same thing in speaking with Fred A. Bernstein for a March 1984 article in *People*. "There's a hangover from characters sometimes. There are things that stick," he said. "Since *Slap Shot*, my language is right out of the locker room."

Although he looked upon this as a negative trait, Newman never forgot the film or the fun he had while making it. He spoke of this often, both privately and publicly. Sometimes he expressed less-than-positive feelings toward some of his roles and movies but his enthusiasm for *Slap Shot* never waned.

Chapter 11

From the *New York Daily News*, January 21, 1981: "It may not have been the best movie I ever made, but it was the most original role I'd played in years."

From the *Christian Science Monitor*, December 3, 1981: "In all, he seems pleased with his various accomplishments and delighted that he found a few real gems — in his opinion, at least — along the way. *Slap Shot*, for example. 'What a deeply original film that was,' says Newman enthusiastically."

In some of the many interviews Newman gave about *Slap Shot*, he referred to a fondness for toilet humor and commented that nothing is out of line if it's truly funny. It gave an insight into the type of man he was. It should not have been a surprise to people who knew him when he told reporter Denise Worrell of his fondness not only for *Slap Shot* but for Reggie Dunlop.

"One of my favorite movies. Pretty funny," he said in an interview which formed the basis for a major *Time* magazine feature in December 1982 and was later reproduced in Worrell's 1989 book *Icons — Intimate Portraits*. "Unfortunately that character is a lot closer to me than I would care to admit — vulgar, on the skids." He also told Worrell separately that the film was "hilarious" and that his favorite line, of any he had ever spoken in front of a camera to that point in time, was: "what a fuckin' nightmare."

He also told Andrew Horton for his George Roy Hill biography how fond he was of the role. "I like Reggie more than any character I have played in 10 years," he said, laughing. "I look back on him with such incredible affection . . . Reggie is at the end of his strap; he's the eternal optimist, a born desperate loser who will scrap for the last piece of hamburger on the plate."

In an interview with Peter S. Greenberg for *Playboy* in April 1983, Newman said more than once that *Slap Shot* was the most satisfying film he had ever made.

"I loved that movie," he said, again referring to it as a "deeply original" project. "It rates very high as something in which I took great personal satisfaction. It may be about the only one I rate that high."

And the audience response was becoming ever more effusive. These interviews all coincided with circumstances that were now giving *Slap Shot* new life. Around the time of its network television debut, it was also released on home video. Now people who had liked it in theaters could see it again and share it with others who had missed out, people who could now see what all the fuss was about. It didn't take long before *Slap Shot* developed a cachet.

The bright idea to install TVs and video players on coach buses took that cachet to the next level as hockey teams, looking for ways to break the monotony of long road trips, discovered the film and recognized its brilliance. The film did not last long as merely one entertainment option on the team bus — it became *the* option, must-see TV on the way to a game, on the way home, or even both.

Over time, the appeal of *Slap Shot* grew further by comparison to newer sports films that just weren't very good. Critics recognized this as well as did viewers. Gene Siskel was one high-profile reviewer who was happy to admit he had been wrong about it, despite liking it in the first place. In addition to his 1993 Letterman appearance, he talked about it during a 1983 visit he and longtime partner Roger Ebert made to Governors State University in University Park, Illinois.

Chapter 11

John Larrabee, then a student at the university, remembers the two Chicago-based critics discussing Alfred Hitchcock, noting his films were often not well received when they were released, but the same critics would invariably laud them years later. When Siskel and Ebert began to take questions from the audience, Larrabee asked if either of them had ever wished they could have a do-over for a certain film. "Siskel said he would have given *Slap Shot* a better review. 'I thought it was above average at the time, but I've since come to appreciate it as one of the best comedies of the '70s,' he said."

Every once in a while, as other hockey movies were made, they were assessed not only by their entertainment value but also by their resemblance to real hockey life. *Youngblood*, released in 1986, might have been interesting for its casting of Patrick Swayze, then in his early 30s, as an 18-year-old junior hockey sensation, or for Keanu Reeves' film debut as a goalie with a laughably bad French accent. But it failed as a realistic portrayal of hockey — junior hockey teams do not have now and never had open tryouts prior to the start of their playoff schedule. It's also hard to fathom Rob Lowe, playing a kid with no hockey fighting experience, almost overnight becoming a punch-up king who brutally avenges himself and his best friend after capping a magical hat trick, all three of his team's goals, with a championship-winning tally on a last-second penalty shot. It's a miracle on ice far beyond anything Herb Brooks ever envisioned. Compared to that and other far-fetched sports schlock from the era like *The Natural*, *Days of Thunder*, the self-parodying *Rocky* franchise and *Over the Top*, another Sylvester Stallone retch-fest, *Slap Shot* suddenly seemed awfully realistic. Pretty poignant, too, not to mention pretty funny — *Raging Bull* meets *Caddyshack*, if you will.

"It came to be the one film you could show on the team bus that had any relevance. That, in and of itself, is something," says Allan Nicholls.

The relevance stemmed not just from the humor but from the social commentary which became more obvious due to the recession of the early 1980s and one of its lasting effects, a generally more cynical view of life. The honest depiction of a dying steel town and the desperation of one of its inhabitants were seen now not as cruel or harsh but as history that demanded an audience. There was a wider realization that athletes were sometimes caught up between what their public wants — violence, blood, victory at any cost — and what is morally and/or legally right. The public that had long lionized their favorite teams and their sporting heroes was learning to face the reality that, often, these teams and athletes were nothing more than commodities as far as franchise owners were concerned — properties to be bought, sold or disposed of as the owner saw fit. Finally, belatedly, *Slap Shot* and those who had participated in its creation were being recognized for all that they had accomplished in bringing it to life.

"Hill and Newman thumbing their noses at the movie business and embracing their inner punks was a powerful engine," says Mike Ontkean. "The absolute respect they accorded Nancy's investigative daring and personal perspective was a joy to behold."

———— ● ————

As it has done so many times in history, Johnstown has fought back after years of struggle. It will never regain the prominence it had when steel was king, but it has diversified its economic base and continues to move forward.

Nancy Coleman recalls graffiti that was painted on a wall at the time of the 1977 flood that vowed Johnstown would not die — and it hasn't. "There's a spirit here that, nothing's going to get us," she says. "We'll bounce back."

There is no more steel industry there, Bethlehem Steel having closed down its last operations in 1992. The corporation itself no longer exists; it filed for bankruptcy in 2001 and was folded into a new Cleveland-based conglomerate, International Steel Group, two years later. ISG was in turn acquired in 2005 by Mittal Steel, which merged in 2006 with another behemoth called Arcelor. The entity is known now as ArcelorMittal and is based in Luxembourg.

Johnstown has been listed by Pennsylvania as a financially distressed community since Bethlehem Steel pulled out, but things aren't as bad as they once were. "It's really recovered. It's true the steel industry is gone but the coal industry is still booming around here," says Don Hall. "A lot of defence stuff has come in. John Murtha, our congressman, brought a lot of stuff to the community."

Murtha was a controversial figure in Washington. The Democrat represented Pennsylvania's 12th congressional district from 1974 until his sudden death in February 2010 and has been credited with bringing billions of dollars worth of federal funding — earmarks, they're called — to his district. Defence contracts comprised a large portion of that funding. But much of it is seen as wasteful and frivolous by those who accused Murtha of being a pork-barrel politician, the type that funnels government money to his area whether it is needed there or not. The national watchdog group Citizens for Responsibility and Ethics in Washington cited Murtha, before his death, as one of the 20 most corrupt members of Congress.

His name seems to be everywhere in his hometown — the John Murtha Johnstown-Cambria County Airport, the John P. Murtha Technology Center, the John P. Murtha Regional Cancer Center. His supporters, who cross party lines, praise him for having brought money to the district which has built roads and water projects, health care facilities and other public projects.

Hall laughs when he recalls how, in 1974, he considered running against Murtha for the congressional seat vacated by the death of Rep. John Saylor. At the time, Murtha was a state representative and a local businessman who owned a car wash. Jean Hall put a stop to her husband's political dreams. "She said, 'You're not running. You have a job. John Murtha doesn't have a job. You let him take that job,'" Hall says, noting that Murtha became "one of the most powerful guys in America, and a good guy, a really good guy."

The jobs provided by the various projects spearheaded by Murtha have again made Johnstown a promising place to raise a family, along with the variety of post-secondary educational institutions in the area. Tourism is a big industry and sports draw many visitors to the community. The Seven Springs ski resort is about 30 miles southwest of town.

The All American Amateur Baseball Association stages its annual tournament each August at Point Stadium in Johnstown. More than 600 athletes have gone through Johnstown on their way to the major leagues, says Denny Grenell, citing Reggie Jackson, Ken Griffey Jr., Al Kaline, Rod Carew and Joe and Frank Torre as just some of the names.

Chapter 11

The Sunnehanna Amateur Golf Tournament for Champions takes place every June at the Sunnehanna Country Club. The best amateur golfers in the world — Arnold Palmer, Jack Nicklaus and Tiger Woods, among others — have taken part in this tournament, which is still a must-stop for anyone looking to land a spot on the US Walker Cup team for international competition. A win in this tournament earns the champion 75 points toward making the team. "Next to the US Amateur, that's the most points you can earn (in one event)," Grenell says.

Another June event is Thunder in the Valley, a hugely popular annual motorcycle rally. "I think last year we had 50,000 bikers here. When they come into town, you know where they want to go? To the arena — they want to see where *Slap Shot* was filmed."

——— ● ———

Visitors invariably want to see the War Memorial. Although it was upgraded in 2002–03 at a cost of approximately $8 million, it still looks very similar to how it appeared in 1976. As such, it is as much an attraction as anything else in town.

It is the home of various minor, girls and high school hockey teams and, for 23 seasons, was the home of the Johnstown Chiefs. The city had been without pro hockey for almost eight years when the team was founded and put on the ice within a matter of days in the middle of the 1987-88 season.

It was December 23, 1987, when Henry Brabham paid a visit to Grenell. He told Grenell that he wanted to put a pro hockey team in Johnstown and had been told Grenell was the man who could help him do it. Grenell thought Brabham meant he wanted the team ready to begin play the following autumn; Brabham said no, he wanted the team on the ice in two weeks.

Brabham owned three of the other four teams in what was called the All-American Hockey League, so he obviously had the pull to engineer a mid-season entry by a new franchise. Grenell was at that time a member of the War Memorial's board of directors, and in that capacity he was able to quickly arrange a lease agreement for the team. He also connected Brabham with John Daley, a former Jets general manager who agreed to come on board with the new enterprise.

Speaking of the Jets, that name was unavailable to the new club. It's owned by a local businessman and Grenell says he knew the asking price for its rights would be too steep for Brabham to consider. "I said to Henry, 'What do you want to call this team?' He said, 'I don't know, what do you want to call it?' The only thing that came to my mind was *Slap Shot*. I said, 'How about the Chiefs, the Johnstown Chiefs?' That's how they became the Chiefs. And I'll be damned if, two weeks later, we weren't playing hockey."

The Chiefs played 26 games that first season, finishing with a 13–13 record. In the fall of 1988, they, the Carolina Thunderbirds and the Virginia Lancers bolted the AAHL for a new arrangement. They were joined in this venture by two new teams, the Erie Panthers and the Knoxville Cherokees. These were the founding five franchises of the East Coast Hockey League, now known today simply as the ECHL. Twenty-two years later, the Johnstown Chiefs were the only original team still in its original location.

The Chiefs made a more direct connection with their past right off the top in 1988–89, hiring Steve Carlson to coach the team. He had immediate success with the Chiefs, leading them to a second-place finish behind Erie. Johnstown swept Knoxville in the semifinal playoff round while fourth-place Carolina did the same to Erie. Things looked good for the Chiefs when they won the first two games of the best-of-seven final by lopsided scores, but the Thunderbirds fought back and eventually prevailed in the seventh and deciding game at the War Memorial. Still, although they had lost the battle, the Chiefs had won the war; pro hockey had been re-established in Johnstown.

Carlson coached the Chiefs for four seasons before being let go. The team and even the ECHL tried to distance themselves from the movie Chiefs, concerned that NHL clubs would not want to send prospects to play in what may have been perceived as a goon circuit. This was particularly true when Nick Fotiu took the reins in the mid 1990s. The veteran pro had begun his long career in the North American Hockey League and his name almost wound up in *Slap Shot*, but he was not keen on the association. "He said he thought the movie discredited the league," says Don Hall. "He used to talk to me about that."

Mike Mastovich, a city native who covered the Chiefs for the *Tribune-Democrat* for 19 seasons, said popular demand from outside Johnstown eventually necessitated a new embrace of *Slap Shot*. People would come into the War Memorial looking for evidence of the film. He remembers overhearing a coach on a pay phone inside the arena one day, bragging to someone on the other end of the line about where he was. It was Peter Laviolette, later the coach of the New York Islanders and the Carolina Hurricanes and the 2006 US men's Olympic hockey team. It struck Mastovich that out-of-towners like Laviolette were genuinely excited to be there for the very reason that the Chiefs had been trying to ignore. It didn't make sense.

"We take this for granted," Mastovich says, recalling the day he skipped school to watch the filming of the speeding van scene in Franklin Borough, where he grew up. "You'll see players come in, looking around for different landmarks, and they just love it."

The film and Johnstown's hockey past became equally celebrated. In recent years, the Chiefs retired the uniform numbers of four former Jets — Hall (9), Dick Roberge (11), Galen Head (8) and Reg Kent (7). Head served as an assistant coach with the club for a few years and Kent laced up the blades and scrimmaged with the team from time to time. The Chiefs also wore mid'70s-era Jets jerseys during special "retro" occasions.

Johnstown never recaptured the same kind of on-ice success it enjoyed in the past, and the Chiefs never returned to the ECHL playoff final. It can be difficult for teams at this level to put together championship clubs since better players are often scooped up by higher affiliate teams in the AHL or even by the NHL parent. As well, the frequent changing of affiliations — the Chiefs were tied to the Calgary Flames, San Jose Sharks, Tampa Bay Lightning, Boston Bruins, Colorado Avalanche, Columbus Blue Jackets and Minnesota Wild in the 2000s alone, not to mention their various AHL ties — often prevented players from lasting very long in a Johnstown uniform. This kept local fans from building the same kind of identification with those players that they had with their Jets.

The Chiefs continually ranked near or at the bottom of the ECHL attendance lists. It was to be expected considering the city's size compared to that of its rivals, not to mention the smaller capacity of the War Memorial. "We have dedicated hockey fans here, no matter if the team is good, bad or indifferent," Grenell says. "They're just very, very, very loyal."

"Die-hard fans, after a Chiefs game, would complain for 45 minutes about how bad everything was, but they loved this team," Mastovich adds.

Figures compiled by the Chiefs several years ago state the team brought an estimated 100,000 visitors to downtown Johnstown each season and generated more than $6 million in annual revenue. "You need to realize what a valuable commodity asset the Chiefs are," John McGrath, a hockey fan and a marketing professor at the University of Pittsburgh at Johnstown — and, obviously, no relation to the fictional Joe McGrath — told *Philadelphia Inquirer* reporter Frank Fitzpatrick in January 2003. "Emotionally and economically, they would be sorely missed, even by those people who hate hockey."

Declining attendance figures eventually doomed the Chiefs in Johnstown. In February 2010, with the Chiefs drawing an average of fewer than 2,000 fans per home game, the team's owners announced that the team would move to Greenville, SC at the end of the 2009–10 season.

Chapter 12

Still Putting on the Foil

———— ● ————

No one has been more surprised by the Hanson Brothers — their longevity and their continued success — as the Hanson Brothers themselves.

Jeff Carlson, Steve Carlson and Dave Hanson are all now well into their 50s and have established careers away from pro hockey, and yet they are unable to extricate themselves from the sport and the personas that made them famous. Not that they're at all unhappy to still be appearing today as their alter egos, three thuggish brothers in horn-rimmed glasses who espouse a violent style of play disguised as "old time hockey."

"When you've got three great-looking guys with all the talent in the world, I don't think it's going to end," Steve says, deadpan.

It's part of the shtick, as is the claim that the Hansons made the career of Paul Newman — he never won an Oscar until after they taught him how to act, they point out — and it never fails to go over with their audiences. And the act plays not just to older crowds, who have known the Hansons and *Slap Shot* for years, but to children as well.

"If there's anything that really amazes us, it's that we pretty much are spanning three and four generations," Dave says. "You have the little ankle-biters — and fortunately, most of them have not seen the movie yet — their parents and their grandparents. We're great with kids, we just love kids, and we have a blast with them. The kids don't really necessarily know at that time why they're meeting us, but they know they're having a great time while the parents and the grandparents are saying the lines from the movie."

Steve says many kids *have* seen the movie. It's not something they promote to children, given its R rating, but that they have watched it is simply a fact of life. Besides, he says, it's not necessarily as bad as the slasher films and violent video games that are pushed on kids all the time these days.

When the Hansons appear at hockey games, it's funny but clean. They're conscious of their audiences and they promote themselves accordingly, their "violence" obviously comedic with no malice intended. They wear the familiar black horn-rims but, because Jeff and Steve now wear contact lenses, the glass inside the frames is clear and does nothing for their vision. Unless they're looking down, that is. They can't wear these specs on the ice because the glass is just too thick and it's next to impossible to find the puck.

Chapter 12

"What we usually do when we play a game, we'll wear our glasses the first shift or two, then we'll just put black frames on so we can actually see and play," Steve says.

It's a terrific irony, when you think about it — the stars of one of the most controversial films ever released, without having changed a great deal about themselves, have become the epitome of family-friendly entertainment.

So, how did the Hansons find their way back to the spotlight?

It started in 1993. Steve Carlson had left the Johnstown Chiefs and was coaching the Memphis RiverKings of the minor-pro Central Hockey League. Dave was in Troy, NY, managing the AHL's Capital District Islanders. Jeff had established himself as an electrician in Muskegon, Michigan, his final minor league stop. They had fond memories of *Slap Shot* but had all put it behind them, as they had intended to do when they turned down movie contracts in order to resume their hockey careers.

Dave was asked if the three had ever been unhappy with the film's characterization of them as "retards" or "fuckin' horrible looking" or "a fuckin' disgrace" or, as film critic Richard Roeper once described them, "three psychopathic simpletons who could probably send Jason Voorhees heading for the woods in fear." Dave says the only thing that ever bothered them was the claim by Reggie Dunlop that they were "too dumb to play with themselves."

"We got a little offended by that, because we're not. We're not too stupid to play with ourselves. Out of all of them, that was probably the most offensive line," he says, in character. Then the façade cracks. "No, not at all," he laughs. "It was just a blast. When we finally saw it on film, it was even funnier. Nobody took anything personally. It was just a fun time to goof around."

The RiverKings were an expansion franchise in 1992–93 and Steve was trying to get them established in Memphis. Things didn't look promising one night when a college basketball playoff game was scheduled to take place in Memphis on the same night as a regular season home game for the RiverKings. There was a good possibility that the hockey crowd would be all but non-existent. A member of the hockey team's PR staff came up with an idea — bring Dave and Jeff in to visit with Steve and have the three of them drop the puck for a ceremonial face-off. As it turned out, Dave and Jeff were both free on the weekend in question, and the thought of getting together seemed like a great idea. They showed up, dressed casually, the two out-of-towners both sporting mustaches along with short hair. It didn't matter — word had spread like wildfire that the Hanson Brothers would be at the hockey game, and the building sold out. "We sat and signed autographs for four-and-a-half hours," Dave says, still in awe today when he recalls that game.

It inspired him to try the same thing at his own arena, where the minor-league Islanders were drawing flies. This time, though, they would wear Chiefs jerseys and black glasses and skate in the warm-up with the Islanders. Gordie Howe was in the area on a book tour and he happily agreed to show up too. "And I sold my place out," Dave says.

———— ● ————

When news of the Hanson reunions hit the wire service, calls from radio stations and other news outlets began pouring in.

Chapter 12

So did requests for personal appearances. Entirely by accident, the three men had created a market for themselves. Smart enough to realize what they had, they hit the road.

The Hansons donned wigs at first before they decided to grow their hair long again. Jeff and Dave still had mustaches. Fans didn't care, mobbing them everywhere they went. One of those places was a sports bar in Detroit, where a puzzled advertising man named Michael LaBroad had come to see what the fuss was all about. He was working for Anheuser-Busch at the time as the senior brand manager for Bud Ice, a struggling brand, and was investigating ways to promote the beer through sponsorships with the NHL, the AHL and the now-defunct International Hockey League. He wasn't familiar with *Slap Shot* but a brewery field representative suggested he check out the Hansons. Detroit was the first opportunity for him to do that, and he was stunned by what he saw — not only was the place packed, the crowd was made up of people of all ages and both genders.

"I just knew," LaBroad says now. "I always look for what I call relevancy. There's lots of things that you and I may buy as a product, or we remember as a kid, that our kids won't embrace. But the Hanson Brothers have been able to transcend generations . . . and they don't have to go around explaining who they are — people know them instantly.

"It was time to bring them back."

And Anheuser-Busch was prepared to go to great lengths to do just that, in a big way. First up was a celebrity event in Las Vegas, where the Hansons were mobbed while football legend Dan Marino and a bevy of swimsuit models were all but ignored. That was followed by a 100-city world tour which took the Hansons overseas for the first time.

They met a lot of interesting people and were shocked at how much fans knew about the movie. Nothing has escaped the die-hards when it comes to truly obscure details. "Some people come up to us and give us trivia questions that we have no idea — 'What time was on the score clock when Steve hit the organist in the head with the puck?' It's those kinds of things that just blow you away," Dave says.

"Everybody calls it a cult movie, but we literally have been around the world. It's just mobs and mobs of people that have seen the movie. I don't know what defines cult status, but I don't see that there's anything more popular than *Slap Shot* has grown to be."

Going across the Atlantic made perfect sense, as the film and its protagonists already had plenty of fans in the United Kingdom and in Europe. When the Hansons met the British under-16 boys hockey team at a tournament in Windsor, Ontario, in December 1994, British coach Allan Anderson and other parents were just as excited as were the kids. He told Bob Duff of the *Windsor Star* that, in the U.K., *Slap Shot* was "as popular as any World Cup video" and that meeting the Hansons was a bigger thrill than encountering then–Toronto Maple Leafs captain Wendel Clark two years earlier. He said he was glad to have taken pictures of the encounter, otherwise no one back home was likely to believe it.

Another parent, Brian Smith, who at the time was coaching a team in the British Pro League, said *Slap Shot* was always the first movie on the video player when the team took road trips. He was on his third copy of the film, having worn out two previous ones.

The world tour was a huge money-maker for everyone. Bud Ice sales soared and the brand rocketed to No. 1 in the ice beer marketplace. The marketing, which included a TV commercial, earned awards for its creativity and LaBroad was promoted to the Budweiser brand. Bud Ice, meanwhile, is still the official beer of the NHL and still has sponsorship deals with 21 of the 24 American-based NHL teams.

"They were terrific to work with and work for. They did just a phenomenal job for us," LaBroad says. "You couldn't find three more decent, more charitable-minded guys."

Unfortunately, not everyone thought so. The 1996 NHL all-star game took place in Boston and Anheuser-Busch had every intention of taking the Hansons to the game. The NHL put the kibosh on that plan, saying the Hansons did not suit the league's image. A spokesperson said they were "part of a retro, old-time image of the game . . . better suited to the minor leagues than the NHL."

"They wouldn't let us in the building. We were 'a distraction,'" Steve says, adding their appearances in Boston were limited to sports bars.

"They said the Hanson Brothers don't represent the kind of hockey that the National Hockey League wants to promote," Dave says. "But there's not three guys that are more colorful, more fan-friendly, are better ambassadors of the game and make people feel good than the Hanson Brothers. Even though the movie is adult and risqué, that is not what people look at the Hanson Brothers and see. They just see fun-loving guys that bring them back to their youth and have a good time with the game."

LaBroad, who eventually went to work for the NHL, is diplomatic about the Boston incident, saying the league was trying to distance itself from a fighting and "goonism" element. It sounds very similar to what the ECHL and the Johnstown

Chiefs were going through at around the same time. But it's still a sore point with the Hansons, especially since the NHL directive to keep them away from the all-star game was reissued the next year in San Jose; Steve says the league went so far as to tell Anheuser-Busch not to even bring the Hansons to the city. Steve went to the game anyway as a fan, taking his son along, and was appalled by what they saw during a pre-game appearance by various team mascots.

"They started fighting. All the mascots dropped their gloves and had a fake brawl," he says, still incredulous. "They're not going to bring us in because we promote the game in the 'wrong' manner, but they have all these mascots fighting on the ice."

———— ● ————

All the time on the road helped them hone an act with which they were already intimately familiar. Although Jeff and Steve have a real brotherly connection that they can play off, Dave is so accustomed to them after all these years that switching from real to fictional Hanson is no problem for him. And when one Hanson isn't necessarily on, the other two have no trouble picking up the slack.

Steve remembers an appearance they did in Redvers, Saskatchewan, which is in the southeastern part of the province, near the Manitoba and North Dakota borders. The three were all supposed to meet in Minneapolis and travel together, but Dave had flight problems and was delayed. He ended up flying from Pittsburgh to Regina via Detroit and Winnipeg, then riding from there to Redvers, a two-and-a-half-hour drive. It was straight to the event once he hit town. Needless to say, he found it hard to be on as soon as he got there. Yet the event was still a huge success.

Chapter 12

"I just said to Jeff, 'All right, it's you and I, let's make it work,'" Steve says. "But Dave got in, we did the auction, we did our question-and-answers, and it was fine. It was great. Redvers brings in people every year. They've had Walter Gretzky, they've had Tiger Williams, and the guy said to us, 'I don't think we can top you guys. We can't bring anyone in who can do better.' We helped raise $9,000 for that town of 1,000 people, for their youth hockey program."

They also fondly recall a sports trivia contest in St. Louis, billed as the world's largest of its kind. An organizer tried to direct them and asked them to do a scripted bit; they obliged, but they felt it hadn't worked. The Hansons asked for the freedom to entertain the crowd in their own way.

"We said, okay, we've done this before," Steve says. "We know what to do. We don't know how we're going to do it, but we know what we're going to do. Just let us go, have the camera follow us. Let us get into the crowd, get us where we're around people and we can have fun. For six hours, we did this, and they said it was the best thing. It was televised by Fox Sportsnet locally and they said it was unbelievable.

"They say to us, what are you guys going to do? I say, I don't know. Let's just wait until we get there, and we'll figure something out. And we figure it out. It comes to us very naturally. When we play charity hockey games, we have a few skits that we do, but every game is different, and we come up with something funnier every game. We'll do something. We'll go into the crowd and eat popcorn . . . we've done many things like that."

Sticking to the tried and true is what makes the Hansons great, LaBroad says. "Artistry is such that people think they need to change their shtick, they've got to grow, they've got to make it different. What will kill the Hanson Brothers is if they change. They still need to be the foil-wearing thick-glasses guys, water skiing behind the Zamboni, running into officials in the corners, knocking down local players. You and I want to see them in the style which made them famous. And I don't think it's going to be an issue."

After a couple of years of working full-time with Anheuser-Busch, the Hansons decided to scale back their schedule. They wanted to spend more time with their families and resume more reasonable working hours. But they're not ready to give up a sideline that allows them to travel around the United States and Canada to selected appearances, bringing them to thousands of fans each year. They have been able to raise countless sums of money for charitable causes, something that has become very important to them.

While they're pleased to devote their time and efforts to raise money, they're not happy at the thought of someone else making money off their images. There have been a plethora of websites and online stores claiming to sell Hanson items like pictures or autographs. They say that unless you actually see them signing an autograph at a personal appearance, don't believe these sites are legitimate. There are Hanson Brothers action figures out there, created and sold by comic book tycoon Todd McFarlane; he received a licence to do so from Universal Pictures, which technically owns the characters. The Hansons are resentful of McFarlane, saying he did not consult them before launching his toys. In protest, they have refused — politely — to sign or pose with them when asked by fans.

No matter, though, because now the Hansons have their own bobblehead dolls. And now that they have control over their own action figures, they think it's cool to be like cartoons. "It's kind of like Hulk Hogan," Dave says.

Steve, through his company Steve Carlson Hockey, runs the Hanson Brothers business from his home in Islip, NY. The brothers' official home on the internet is www.hansonbrothers.net, which retails pictures, posters, jerseys, caps, T-shirts, sweats, DVDs and bobbleheads and keeps fans up to date with what the three are and have been up to.

One of their appearances was at the Austin Film Festival in October 2000. They reunited there with Ned Dowd for what may have been the first screening of *Slap Shot* at such a festival. It was billed as "George Roy Hill's 1977 tour de farce . . . the capstone to his awesome body of work with Paul Newman . . . Sublime in its use of profanity and sternum-rattling body checks, it's a comic masterpiece that holds up more than two decades later." It was now being seen in a new, positive critical light, spearheaded by Barbara Morgan, the Austin festival's executive director and co-founder.

The Philadelphia native has long considered *Slap Shot* her favorite sports film. In 1999, she happened to be chatting with screenwriter Anne Rapp, an Austin resident taking part in that year's festival. The conversation turned to sports films and Morgan mentioned her love for *Slap Shot*. That's when Rapp floored her by telling Morgan she had been married to Ned Dowd.

"I've always wanted to do a retrospective of that film. I figured it would go over really well here because it's just such a really big sports town," Morgan says. "We also at the time had just gotten a minor league hockey team here, the Ice Bats. I knew people who were working for the Ice Bats and I thought if we did this, we could partner with the Ice Bats to get the word out. We literally finished the conversation and Anne went right into my office and called Ned."

Dowd and the Hanson Brothers conducted a question-and-answer session during the screening of *Slap Shot* at the Paramount Theatre, an Austin landmark and a national historic site. "We just had so much fun," Morgan says. "I wasn't sure how many people would show up, just because it's an old movie, it was on TV a lot and it's not usual film festival fare. But Ned had that great story about how it got written, and we're a writers' festival. The whole thing was awesome; there were probably about 600 people there.

"It was the most alcohol they had ever sold at that theater for a film screening," she adds, laughing. "That should tell you something about the crowd. It was like going to a *Rocky Horror Picture Show* screening. Everybody that came knew all the lines, and they were quoting the lines before stuff happened. They loved it. They were so excited that the Hansons were there. They went and did a show with the Ice Bats the next night."

Dowd had already reconnected with his old friends and teammates earlier in 2000, while he was working in Pittsburgh on the Michael Douglas film *Wonder Boys*. That's where Dave Hanson lives and, as luck would have it, the trio was booked to appear at a Pittsburgh Penguins game. Even if the NHL itself doesn't get it, its individual teams do, and it's very common for those teams to play clips from *Slap Shot* on their video screens.

"You go to any major arena to watch a game and between periods or between whistles they'll throw up a shot of *Slap Shot* or a little segment of the Hanson Brothers and people go nuts," Dowd says, adding he was delighted to see that his friends can still draw a crowd and make some money in the process. "I caught them at one of the Penguins games, doing their thing, and it was amazing, beyond belief. Art copies life copies art. They're good guys. Nobody made any money in those (NAHL) games. You made 500 bucks a week if you were lucky; this was before hockey players made any money at all."

If the Hansons have their way, the money will keep coming in. Steve in particular is brimming over with new movie ideas, saying the Hansons would be perfect hockey team owners and general managers. He points out both he and Dave have been hockey GMs in real life, and the storyline created by two *Slap Shot* sequels has established the Hansons as multimillionaires. As Steve sees it, the Hansons own an NHL team and show up at the entry draft, encountering rival executives like Glen Sather.

"'Hey, Glen, how you doing? You gonna draft this guy? Yeah? No, you're not!' BAM — hit his head against a table," Steve laughs. "Or it could be the Hansons in Malibu at the league meetings, trying to get the rules straightened out, or negotiating with an agent for some Russian that wants millions."

Anything is possible. Then again, considering the incredible history of *Slap Shot* and its equally incredible longevity, maybe it's better and more accurate to say anything is probable.

———— ● ————

While the Hansons were appearing on ice rinks around the world, the popularity of the movie continued to grow. A Hanson visit to a Detroit Red Wings practice in March 1994, around the time Michael LaBroad first laid eyes on them, inspired a slew of NHLers to pay homage to the Hansons and to the film.

"The greatest movie I've ever seen," Sheldon Kennedy told Bob Duff of the *Windsor Star*. "We'd watch it two or three times a night."

The Hansons, meanwhile, formed a mutual admiration society with Wings tough guy Bob Probert. They did the "we're not worthy" shtick from *Wayne's World* when confronted by Probert, who responded by telling the Hansons they were his idols.

A young Russian-born Red Wing in his fourth NHL campaign did not know at the time who the Hansons were but, taken aback by the reactions of his more learned teammates, pledged to find out. "*Slap Shot*, I do not know this movie," said Sergei Fedorov, who at the time was capping a Hart Trophy-winning season as the NHL's most valuable player. "I must see this. I will stop on the way home. Blockbuster Video, eh?"

That's a sentiment Aaron Downey would appreciate. In December 2007, the Red Wings right-winger told Scott Cruickshank of the *Calgary Herald* that any hockey player who hadn't seen *Slap Shot* should "make it a Blockbuster night." He said he had watched the movie at least 50 times and it got better with each viewing. "An Academy Award winner, it should be. It's pretty much part of my life. It's been ingrained in my head."

These days, it's much more common for European players to come to North America with extensive first-hand knowledge of *Slap Shot*. Phoenix Coyotes forward Robert Lang, from the Czech Republic, told the *San Jose Mercury News* in January 2008 that he had seen the movie repeatedly before he left his homeland in 1991. Finland-born Tuomo Ruutu, of the Carolina Hurricanes, said much the same thing to Cruickshank.

Downey told Cruickshank it was his belief that everyone in the NHL had seen the film, an opinion with which Mark Smith, then of the Calgary Flames, fully agreed. "It's a prerequisite, isn't it?" he asked. "If you play in this league, you've got to see it at least three or four times."

In November 2007, San Jose Sharks defenceman Craig Rivet was out of the lineup due to an injury. Eager to remain as involved with the team as possible, he stepped behind the bench to help with the coaching duties. Immediately, his teammates began referring to him as "Reggie Dunlop," the club's new player-coach. Rivet loved it, telling the *San Jose Mercury News* that Dunlop was the pinnacle for a player-coach. "I don't think there's any hockey player on the planet who isn't a fan of *Slap Shot*. That always will be the greatest hockey movie ever made."

The love for the film has moved off NHL ice and behind the benches, not to mention to the executive suites. Philadelphia Flyers general manager Paul Holmgren, who played briefly with the Johnstown Jets during the 1975–76 NAHL season, is a fan. So is Toronto Maple Leafs GM Brian Burke. In fact, Burke had cause to think about *Slap Shot* on the greatest day of his hockey career. On June 6, 2007, the Anaheim Ducks were seconds away from clinching the first Stanley Cup in franchise history. Burke was waiting for the final buzzer. Standing behind him was Joe Trotta, the club's video coordinator. Trotta couldn't resist — "The Chiefs have won the championship of the Federal League," he shouted, in much the same way Jim Carr had done. Burke doubled over in laughter.

Five years earlier, during the 2002 Stanley Cup final between his Hurricanes and the Red Wings, Carolina coach Paul Maurice was asked at a news conference about his club's power play. "Yeah, yeah, we're working on it," he told the assembled journalists, the same line Reggie Dunlop gave an inebriated fan who had confronted him in a Charlestown bar. For the benefit of the uninitiated, Maurice immediately followed up by gleefully noting that he had just quoted from *Slap Shot*. "That's a great line," he said.

It may be an exaggeration that everyone in the NHL has seen the movie, and it certainly is an exaggeration that everyone involved in hockey loves it. Ron Wilson, coach of the Toronto Maple Leafs, has said he is not a fan and has "no idea" why it's so popular. Robbie Ftorek, who has coached the Los Angeles Kings, the New Jersey Devils and the Boston Bruins, says he has never even seen the movie and has no desire to.

But the film's cultural impact has long since transcended hockey. There are at least two punk rock bands named in homage to the the movie — Slapshot, formed in 1985 in Boston; and The Hanson Brothers, formed a year earlier as an offshoot of British Columbia punkers NoMeansNo. The Hansons were formed to play Ramones covers and other original songs that were simpler than the more serious material NoMeansNo were doing. Their recorded product as The Hanson Brothers, which includes the albums *Gross Misconduct* and *Sudden Death* and the songs "Rookie of the Year" and "He Looked a Lot Like Tiger Williams," has been credited with creating and helping to popularize a new musical sub-genre known as "puck rock."

Chapter 13

A Life of Its Own

———— ● ————

Ken Blake lives in Orange County, California, but he grew up in New England and remembers the first time he saw *Slap Shot*.

It was at a theater where his then-girlfriend had dragged him to see the Barbra Streisand film *A Star is Born*. But it was a double feature and Blake, having patiently sat through the first movie, insisted they stay for the second. All he knew was that it was a hockey film starring Paul Newman.

"The opening scene with Denis Lemieux just hooked me on the movie," he says, "but everybody played such an integral part and such a funny part. It made them all memorable."

The years passed and Blake was a fan like any other, swapping one-liners with his buddies. That began to change one night at a Los Angeles Kings hockey game. He was sitting in a luxury box when he noticed Jerry Houser, aka Dave "Killer"

Carlson, in another suite. Blake, who had worn a Charlestown Chiefs jersey to the game, thought it was serendipitous. During a lull in the action, he leaned out of the box he was in and yelled "Killer!" at the top of his lungs. Houser heard him and looked. But so did hundreds of others, startled at Blake's outburst. Blake hadn't considered "that you shouldn't scream "Killer" or "Fire" in a crowded building. All of a sudden security is at the door asking, what the hell is going on here? And Jerry is two boxes down laughing like crazy and pointing at this crazy guy in the Chiefs jersey."

Houser soon came down to say hello and they established a friendship that continues today. That inspired Blake to try to track down some of the other cast members and get their autographs. He found a website that had a picture of someone named Yvon Barrette, and this person sort of looked like he could have played Denis Lemieux, but Blake wasn't sure. The website, built for a movie called *15 fevrier 1839*, was in French.

"I wrote to him and I said, I don't speak French, I don't understand French, and if you reply in French I won't be able to read it. But I'm looking for the guy in the picture — can you tell me if that's Yvon Barrette who was in *Slap Shot*? And he wrote back and said, yeah, it's me."

Barrette laughs when he recalls that first contact from Blake. He didn't know why anyone would be asking him about *Slap Shot*, and he asked Blake that very question. But he agreed to sign some pucks that Blake had sent him, and enclosed an extra treat when he sent them back — some call sheets from the filming. Blake next tracked down Paul D'Amato, who noted that he often saw Chris Murney and Brad Sullivan. After locating Allan Nicholls, Blake found another website that led him to the Sparkle Twins, the cute young blonde women who were Billy Charlebois' biggest fans.

Upon learning that Louise Arters suffers from multiple sclerosis — her twin is Janet — Blake thought about a cast reunion to help raise money in support of Louise. In 2003, the sisters, D'Amato and Mark Bousquet, who had played Syracuse thug Andre "Poodle" Lussier, dropped the puck at a Philadelphia Phantoms AHL game. The following year, the Sparkle Twins, plus Barrette, Murney, Jean Tetreault, Guido Tenesi and Bill Goldthorpe got together in Philadelphia for a golf tournament and another Phantoms game. The troupe was met in Johnstown by Gracie Head and the now grown-up Mickey McQuillan and Woody Espey.

"We signed pucks and jerseys for one hour before the game and all through the game. It was non-stop," Murney says of the 2004 Phantoms game. "It was then we went, holy, we can do something with this. This is a force for good!"

Two golf tournaments at the Angus Glen club in Markham, north of Toronto, followed in 2005 and 2006. On these occasions, funds were raised for the Association of Hole in the Wall Camps, a creation of Paul Newman, who wanted to create a camp for children with cancer and other serious medical conditions. There is now a network of camps in the United States, Europe, Israel and Africa, and more than 100,000 children have been able to participate over the years.

"This is absolutely outstanding," Hege Lauvik, senior development officer with the Hole in the Wall Foundation, said after the 2006 event. "We're just absolutely amazed with what this group has pulled together."

Guido Tenesi helped to organize the event and acknowledges it can be comparatively simple to obtain sponsor support for something like a *Slap Shot* reunion. "If you're talking
to somebody that has a little bit of a hockey background, they
know the movie. It's a little bit easier to get stuff and they'll
help you out as much as they can."

Paul Newman signed some items for a silent auction at
both Markham golf tournaments but was unable to attend
either time. He recorded a video thank you which was played
at both events. "I'm very touched that so many of the cast
from *Slap Shot* worked so hard to organize this impressive
event," he said, also giving thanks to the golf club and others
involved with the tournament, like Blake. "I take my hat off
to you."

Blake operates a *Slap Shot* fan website (www.slapshotfan.
com) and auctions autographed merchandise on eBay, donat-
ing the proceeds to charity. One such item was Brad Sullivan's
Chiefs jersey, which the actor had kept for years following
the film. "They all love doing this," Blake says of the cast
members-turned-friends. "They like being remembered for
Slap Shot. They love interacting with the fans and they're all
just great guys."

"We've had fun," Tetreault says. "That's a special movie.
I'm really proud of it."

"I am amazed, and I truly enjoy doing it," Murney says of
meeting fans. "Who knew that 30 years later, that you could
still exert an influence on people?"

D'Amato feels the same way and is delighted to accommo-
date fans, many of whom ask him to inscribe his famous greeting
to Reggie Dunlop. "Whatever we need to do to help a child, I'll
write it. I'll be happy to do that. I love to help people," he says.

Chapter 13

"It takes a lot more to extend your hand to help somebody than it does to hit that person."

———— ● ————

Extending a hand has gone a long way toward redeeming the image of Bill Goldthorpe, who has been more or less adopted by the *Slap Shot* fraternity. In October 2005, at the first Markham golf tournament in Toronto, Nancy Dowd attended and paid him a heartfelt tribute, acknowledging that she had indeed created the character of Oggie Oglethorpe based on stories she had heard about Goldthorpe.

Goldie could play hockey and was an especially capable defensive forward when he was given the chance to play that role. But more often his job was to fight and cause havoc, and he did that exceedingly well too. In 208 career pro hockey regular season and playoff games, he was assessed an astounding 1,138 penalty minutes. He also accounted for 54 goals and 124 points.

The closest he got to the NHL was some exhibition games with Toronto and Pittsburgh. Unfortunately, his on-ice behavior too often spilled off the ice and got him into problems that couldn't be solved by sitting in the penalty box. Well, not a hockey penalty box, anyway. On 18 different occasions Goldthorpe wound up in a different kind of sin bin — the one with iron bars and a huge lock on the door.

He has freely admitted to copping a confrontational stance when someone would approach, whether maliciously or not, and wonder aloud if this really was Oggie Oglethorpe. Drinking didn't help his attitude. Neither did a knack for finding himself in the midst of bad crowds and worse situations, like the time he got shot in the stomach and almost killed by an ex-girlfriend's drug dealer. Or the time he stepped in to help a woman who was being beaten, only to get slashed and stabbed in the left arm and hand by the abuser. He reportedly needed 300 stitches to repair the damage from that incident.

Part of what hurt the most, though, was the knowledge that *Slap Shot* had made stars out of Dave Hanson and two of the Carlson brothers, while Goldthorpe had been left on the outside looking in. He refused to watch the film for a number of years and has acknowledged some bitterness over the Hanson Brothers' continued relevance and success.

"But when I meet guys who played the game," he told Allan Maki of the *Globe and Mail* in 2002, "they all call me Ogie [sic] Oglethorpe. They all say that. They know."

"I've read some stuff where some people think, oh, you didn't want him because he was going to be trouble," says Ned Dowd. "I don't know, because I wasn't part of that decision, you know what I mean?"

Goldthorpe has thrived in recent years, working steadily in construction and basking in his own belated celebrity. He has his own website now, www.goldiegoldthorpe.com, where fans can buy Goldie pictures, toques and, yes, bobblehead dolls complete with the unique Goldie blond Afro.

But even his inclusion in the *Slap Shot* fraternity hasn't erased all the bad feelings. He took issue with the decision of *Sports Illustrated* in 2007 to feature the Hansons on the cover of its summer double issue and inside the magazine, with a lengthy feature article written by Austin Murphy. "It's a horseshit article," he told Emmanuel Moutsatsos of the *Thunder Bay Chronicle Journal*, calling the magazine cover "kind of like a slap in the face. Not just to me, but to everyone that was in that movie."

He apparently didn't realize that the Hansons don't seriously believe they turned Paul Newman into a movie star as they jokingly claim. "They think that they made Paul Newman, but Paul Newman made them," he scoffed.

Goldthorpe isn't the only person rankled at the Hanson Brothers and the idea of who "made" them.

Dave Hanson published his autobiography in the fall of 2008. It's called *Slap Shot Original: The Man, The Foil, The Legend* and features introductions by Jeff and Steve Carlson, forewords by Bob Costas and Gordie Howe and a promotional blurb by Newman. He went on tour to promote the book and gave numerous interviews and, while he has done nothing but praise Nancy Dowd for her work, she has not taken kindly to the Hanson Brothers' collective contention, reinforced in Dave's book and in his interviews, that the three hockey players more or less improvised their film roles.

In a scathing contribution to the *New York Times* hockey blog, "Slap Shot," which had reviewed Hanson's biography in December 2008 as one of the season's new hockey books, Dowd adamantly claimed, among other things, that no one in *Slap Shot* had ad-libbed their work. "It is flattering for a screenwriter when people consider her lines immortal. However, it's considerably less than flattering and perhaps worse when those who have the good luck to be hired to speak her lines convince themselves and others that they wrote them in the first place, as your book review would have us believe," she wrote, adding that the on-set pranks detailed in Hanson's book had also "never happened."

Dowd went on by, among other things, disputing the right of Dave Hanson and the Carlsons to perform in their "dog and pony show," as she referred to their frequent public appearances, claiming their act is "in clear, prolonged and persistent violation of my author's rights to all live performances made by my characters." In April 2010, she announced she was taking legal action to put a stop to their public performances.

Her contentions raise some interesting questions. If the dialogue scripted by Dowd in fact came from tape recordings of actual conversations — and no one has ever disputed that the tape recorder carried around by Ned Dowd was essential in helping his sister to capture the atmosphere surrounding the Johnstown Jets — who is really responsible for that dialogue? And if a film character or three are speaking dialogue and doing things as directed by a screenplay that was inspired by their own words and actions in the first place, who is really responsible for the creation of those characters?

According to Dowd, she is. The Hansons of the original *Slap Shot* "are my creation," she wrote. "They remain eternally young, amusing, violent, psycho, offensive, offending and, truly, original. In the eternity of genuine creation, they will never be old, bewigged, bloated, straight to DVD, embarrassing, unfunny, cringe-making flops . . . The actors who had the great good fortune to be cast as the Hanson Brothers, as they have proved twice since, created absolutely nothing."

Dave Hanson declined to answer questions regarding Dowd's contentions. But let's face it — if there had not been the Carlson brothers, there would be no Hanson Brothers, no matter how fertile Dowd's imagination. Just like, if not for Dowd, few people today would recall the Carlsons or Dave Hanson other than as minor-pro veterans who played briefly in the WHA and NHL. The bottom line is they all needed each other to attain what they all deserved — hockey and film immortality.

Dowd apparently doesn't see it that way. She continued her tirade after another blog poster chimed in with support for her. "I have been silent about the cheap exploitation of *Slap Shot* for a long time," she wrote, calling Hanson's book "a blatant fraud" that compelled her to throw "down the velvet gloves. It is fans like you that made *Slap Shot* a classic, despite the fake moral outrage that greeted its release and now despite a trio of shamelessly self-promoting poseurs and their bush league self-importance. I hope the fans know that I had absolutely nothing to do with it, Your Honor. *Slap Shot* was good to those of us who made it, and it sickens me to see it trashed. Thank you for ignoring (the sequels). And if there is, God forbid, a *Slap Shot 4: Assisted Living*, please turn away."

———— ● ————

It's unlikely that Dowd's feelings will stop the *Slap Shot* juggernaut. As time passes, its fan base grows exponentially and it gains more and more critical acclaim.

William Goldman is a two-time-winning Academy Award screenwriter who won his Oscars for *Butch Cassidy and the Sundance Kid* and *All the President's Men*. He is also responsible for, among other classic works, the creations of the novels and screenplays for *Marathon Man* and *The Princess Bride* and the screenplays for *Harper*, *The Stepford Wives* and *Misery*. He also co-wrote *The Great Waldo Pepper* with George Roy Hill. Needless to say, his credentials are impeccable. And he said in a March 2000 interview with Drew "Moriarty" McWeeny of the website Ain't It Cool News that he recognized the brilliance of *Slap Shot* the first time he saw it.

"I still remember screaming in the theater, laughing so hard," Goldman said. "Paul Newman's on the phone with someone at one point and the Hansons come up, and he just looks at them and says, 'They brought their fucking toys.' I remember shrieking. Marvelous picture."

In 2005, comedy writer-director duo Peter and Bobby Farrelly (*Dumb & Dumber, There's Something About Mary*) were asked by *Stuff* magazine to come up with a list of what they considered to be the greatest slapstick movies of all time. Their list of 20 films appeared in the October 31 issue that year and they slotted *Slap Shot* in at No. 5. "*Slap Shot* was a fucking classic," they wrote. "It's pretty amazing. You can watch it right now. It's still hysterical."

This accolade followed a trifecta of No. 5 placings assessed by three noted sports authorities in, fittingly, a span of five years. *The Sporting News* was first, choosing *Slap Shot* as its No. 5 best sports movie in its August 24, 1998, edition.

Almost four years to the day later, on August 25, 2002, ESPN.com announced that the writers and editors of its popular Page 2 feature had also placed *Slap Shot* at No. 5 on its list of the Top 20 Sports Movies of All Time. "Paul Newman demonstrates how goofball sports movies ought to be done (this should be required viewing for Adam Sandler)," read the accompanying editorial comment. Each of the 15 voters had listed his or her top 20 selections and ranked them on a sliding scale, with the top selection receiving 20 points and the bottom pick getting one point. *Slap Shot* received 166 of a possible 400 points and, along with second-place *Rocky*, was the only film cited by as many as 14 voters. No one film was chosen by all 15 panelists.

Another year passed, and another No. 5 selection was bestowed upon *Slap Shot*, this time on August 4, 2003, by *Sports Illustrated* in its Greatest Sports Movies list: "Newman's hockey coach, Reggie Dunlop, revives a deadbeat minor league team by recruiting the hard-checking, high-sticking Hanson brothers. Eyes obscured by taped-up glasses, fists swathed in tinfoil, these geeky goons revel in dirty play. So does the audience."

The love for the film has, like the Hansons themselves, crossed oceans. In December 2005, Calvin Shulman and Patrick Kidd of *The Times*, a national newspaper in the United Kingdom, compiled a list of the 50 Greatest Sports Movies and placed *Slap Shot* at No. 12: "Yet another excellent Newman sports movie (the highest of his three appearances in our top 50)," wrote Shulman and Kidd, who picked *The Color of Money* at 47 and *The Hustler* at 16.

Legendary sportswriter and novelist Dan Jenkins wrote in the November 2007 issue of *GQ* that *Slap Shot* was the best sports film of the past 50 years. "I always go back to Mark Twain or whoever said it first: The best humour is grounded in truth," Jenkins wrote. "When sports movies leave out the cussing, they come across as phoney. *Slap Shot* is as casually profane as sports truly are."

In that same month, Terry Frei wrote in his ESPN.com column that, as *Rocky* had inspired many writers to pen a screenplay — "thinking if Sylvester Stallone could do it, so could they" — *Slap Shot* had done that for him the first time he ever watched it. Frei's script remains unfilmed, he said, but his favorite film's greatness also remains.

"Seriously, it's a great movie, great on several levels, great as a comedy and a satire, both laugh-out-loud funny and smile-wryly funny. The first time you saw it, you laughed the second the line came out of the character's mouth, and then several hours later after you thought about it. And years later, it's still a classic."

Film critic Richard Roeper says it's just one of those movies that, if you stumble across it, you feel compelled to watch it. "There's a repeatability factor, I guess," he says, "in movies that have great scripts." He acknowledges that the hockey depicted may be somewhat foreign to younger viewers today — few players wore helmets, the tube skates were soon to be out of style, much of the rest of the equipment was rudimentary and the off-ice fashions were heinous at best. "But funny is funny. There are certain things that, if they're funny, they're funny. There's a lot of politically incorrect humor in that movie . . . and Paul Newman is one of the few actors that could have pulled off that character and made him so likable."

But the main reason *Slap Shot* works and has worked, Roeper feels, is because it doesn't focus just on what's happening on the ice. "Like most great sports films, and I really do put it in the category of one of the best sports films ever, it has to be about more than the sport or it just won't be elevated. You need to have more. You need to have characters you care about. Sports is just the vehicle that carries you on the journey with these characters."

Maxim magazine, in March 1998, summed up *Slap Shot* in more basic terms in selecting it as not only the top sports film of all time, but choosing it to top its list of the 100 Greatest Guy Movies Ever Made. According to the magazine, it's because the Chiefs are living every "real" man's dream life:

"They drink beer, get laid, play sports, gamble, watch TV, avoid relationships, and successfully put off adulthood. And at the end of the film, their immaturity is rewarded with a Main Street parade in their honor! What's not to love?"

———— ● ————

Leslie Tenesi remembers the first real inkling she had that *Slap Shot* not only was not going away, it was growing in popularity. It was around the time of the film's 25th anniversary in 2002, when a special-edition DVD was released by Universal. The Tenesi family was attending a family reunion near Allentown, Pa., when the reality hit Leslie. "I couldn't believe it," she says. "My young cousins, who are 10 and 15 years younger than me, were quoting lines from this movie. And they didn't play hockey, but they knew it word for word. I thought, this is odd. This is like *Rocky Horror Picture Show* or *Monty Python* — it's almost the same thing."

Tag Mendillo, the son of Steve Mendillo, was attending UCLA and playing club hockey there when it occurred to him that his dad wasn't just an actor — he was a Charlestown Chief, something which would go on forever. He recalls sitting in the locker room and listening as his teammates threw lines from the film back and forth. "That's where I really realized it wasn't just this little regional thing," he says. "Everybody knew it, and they were all stunned and shocked and amazed to realize that my old man was in the film, to which I had never given a second thought. I think at that point I realized it was actually iconic. And that was kind of cool."

Not only did the new DVD include a commentary by the Hanson Brothers, it also highlighted the original soundtrack. Or most of it, with Maxine Nightingale's "Right Back Where We Started From" achieving even more prominence than before, replacing a Fleetwood Mac song in an early scene. Of course, none of the original songs had made it into the earlier VHS releases or in the edited-for-TV broadcasts, because Universal did not have the necessary rights from the copyright owners. Vincent Edwards, co-writer of the film's main theme, was thrilled that his song was back, saying *Slap Shot* hadn't been the same without it.

"I was very happy the way "Right Back" was used in this great movie," he says. "It made me feel like buying some skates and getting out there on the ice — better left to the Canadians."

Edwards says he thinks *Slap Shot* is the most honest movie of the 1970s because of its depiction of a declining industrial community and a declining hockey team, both being cast aside by those who no longer require their services. "The politics of the rich not giving a shit about the workers and communities and small towns that need an identity," he says, comparing the situation in Charlestown to what many communities in his native England would later go through in the mid 1980s when the government of Margaret Thatcher decided to close numerous coal mines in that country. "This town needed the team and the steel mills like those towns in the UK needed the coal mines. The profit was not just in the money, it went much deeper."

Brad Sullivan went for years without seeing the film, reluctant to be identified with it and his role in it. He gave up playing hockey in 1977 because of an injury that cost him an acting job. "I remember one guy said, 'Are you getting paid to play hockey or to be an actor?'" Sullivan said. "I also had back problems and shoulder problems, and I just didn't play any more after that."

He bought the DVD in 2006 and, as a devout Christian, wasn't keen on the language. "It's rather frivolous, blasphemy," he said. "I've done it in plays when it's come out in spite of you, but frivolity, no." That said, Sullivan also took pride in one aspect of his portrayal of Mo Wanchuk, pointing to the scene where Reggie Dunlop tells the Chiefs that he had lied and that the team was going to fold, but he wanted the team to go out and play a clean game to win the championship. While the rest of the players begin to get pepped up for the game, Mo remains downcast, slumped back against the wall of the locker room.

"He just was absolutely deflated. That's just the human-ness of it. We're not perfect and we have all kinds of problems, no matter what," Sullivan said of Mo. "These guys, for all their bravado and all that, are very vulnerable. It's a vulnerable situ-ation, and I wanted to show that in this character. For all his bullshit, you might say, this hit him hard.

"I was glad that that stuck out. You want to look for some kind of value that you might get out it."

It wasn't all that stuck out about Mo, of course. Sullivan knew it and, after years of trying to avoid it, had come to terms with it.

"Mo Wanchuk, he was in a fantasy world," he said, laughing. "People remember those lines of Wanchuk's, and I almost blanch when I think about it. But, you know, what the heck."

In addition to two sequels and a planned remake, other film projects have touched on *Slap Shot*. NHL Productions, in

2000–01, presented a TV series called *Chasing the Dream* which focused on members of the Johnstown Chiefs. Jerry Houser was enlisted to narrate the series. A documentary film called *The Chiefs* was released in 2004, telling the stories of members of the Laval Chiefs, a club in what is now called the North American Hockey League despite all of its member teams being based in Quebec. It's reputedly the toughest hockey league in the world and its stats back up that contention — in 2003–04, for instance, Jason Clarke of the Verdun Dragons racked up 657 penalty minutes in 66 regular season and playoff games, numbers that would make even Goldie Goldthorpe turn his head. At any rate, the Laval Chiefs had been named in homage to the Charlestown Chiefs and they certainly did their forebearers proud, winning playoff championships in 2002 and 2003 with five and seven players, respectively, topping the 200 penalty minutes plateau.

An even more bizarre yet hilarious *Slap Shot* project is an unproduced "mockumentary" called *'Cause My Family Has Money*, written by Boston humorist Chris Zell. It takes its title from a line in the original film's script, spoken by Lily Braden to Reggie Dunlop when he asks her why she talks dirty. In Zell's work, the line explains how a well-to-do family can buy everything desired by the heart of a man who becomes fanatically obsessed with a particular film.

"I've always wanted to write something *Slap Shot*-related yet not a sequel or rewrite. Something that captured the spirit of the thing but stood on its own," Zell says. "I didn't have rights to use the characters anyway so if I was going to spend time doing something on spec I'd rather do something I knew I could get away with."

Chapter 13

Zell became friends with Ken Blake, which took him into the realm of what he calls "the world of extreme *Slap Shot* fans." And they're out there, of course, the ones who ask the Hansons obscure questions about the time on the score clock. They're the ones who compile treasure troves filled with logical fan items like jerseys and baffling items such as tickets held by extras who sat in the War Memorial seats during Chiefs games. "Pucks and posters and trading cards that weren't a twinkle in the eye of the Universal marketing department were now sought after by fans, many of whom weren't even born when the film was released," says Zell, who was both appalled and fascinated by what he observed. His fascination turned to inspiration and, over a single weekend, he created the character of Fred Henderson.

"Fred, from childhood, was very bright and obsessive. One year he decided to watch every movie released in 1977. That all changed on February 25th when he watched *Slap Shot*. From that moment on his life was focused on this movie. I'm not talking about just watching it every day, that's a given. He needed to collect everything, know everything and know everyone connected to the movie. I'm not talking about the tidbits and trinkets someone like Ken collects, that would never be enough for Fred. He needed, and would get, everything. The locker room, Joe McGrath's office, the Hanson Brothers parade float. I thought about what every collector would covet and gave it to Fred."

Fred tried to date and live a normal life but gave up when the one girl he liked not only drank root beer, her name was Anita. His wardrobe consisted not only of Chiefs jerseys but also of the clothes of both Reggie Dunlop and Joe McGrath, as well as each item of clothing from the infamous fashion show. Fred's other possessions include, among many other items, the Federal League trophy, Jim Carr's wig, Dickie Dunn's typewriter, Reggie's boxer shorts, Ned Braden's jock strap, the opera glasses used by the old lady who wanted a better look at Ned and, disgustingly, the needle and thread that Chiefs trainer Charlie was using to sew "Killer" Carlson's lip back together before he went after Barclay Donaldson the second time. As Zell puts it, his work is something even casual fans would find funny, but it's full of "inside jokes that . . . people in Ken's tribe would eat up."

The real-life quest for memorabilia from the film forms a significant portion of a business operated by Mathieu and Alex Paquette of Vercheres, Quebec, near Montreal. Their business is called MadBrothers and they have established themselves as the leading retailers of official, licensed *Slap Shot* merchandise — jerseys, T-shirts, caps, patches, pictures and more. Alex says the business started when Mathieu created some T-shirts for his hockey team. Other people saw the shirts and asked about them, which prompted Mathieu to create more and start selling them. After someone asked Mathieu if his products were licensed, he located a man who at the time was managing the Hanson Brothers. He obtained a licence from the manager and asked Alex to come on board and help him with the enterprise. Eventually the Paquettes secured a licence from Universal Pictures directly.

"It's a niche product and not many people are supplying them," says Alex, who is such a fan of *Slap Shot* that he can recite the entire script in French. "We have the opportunity to reach lots of people around the world and have conversations with them. It's really fun."

Chapter 13

And when he says around the world, he means it. MadBrothers have shipped their merchandise as far away as Ukraine, Finland and Australia. They sell via their own website, www.madbrothers.com, as well as on eBay and also through physical stores which operate under the Paquettes' licence. They sell and have sold other apparel and products but the goods inspired by their favorite film remain their mainstay. "*Slap Shot* has always been on cruise control, always constant. It never drops," Alex says. "At first I was expecting a break or a fall but, the more and more we sell, the more and more I think we could sell. It's like a snowball effect."

Not only can one buy a Chiefs jersey from MadBrothers, they can also get a Syracuse Bulldogs sweater or a Long Island Ducks uniform or a Hyannisport Presidents jersey. "People are coming back and so we want to offer them more reasons to come back."

Of course, no uniform at all is also a *Slap Shot* hallmark. Eric Nystrom, now of the Calgary Flames, paid tribute to Ned Braden in February 2008 by copying his striptease during a fan appreciation and jersey auction event staged by the Quad City Flames, the AHL team for which he was playing at the time. He didn't get down to the altogether but he did raise $600 for charity.

"I was taking it from memory. I've seen the movie so many times, it was easy just to go out there," Nystrom said in an interview on the After Hours segment of *Hockey Night in Canada*. "I didn't even rehearse it. I just, kind of, was going to wing it. I did my best Ned Braden impression and it turned out pretty good."

Fittingly, Nystrom has a *Slap Shot* connection of sorts — his father, New York Islanders legend Bob Nystrom, played junior hockey in Calgary with Ross Smith, who was Barclay Donaldson in the movie.

———— ● ————

The popularity of *Slap Shot* has continually been enhanced by Paul Newman's noted fondness for it. Although he was reluctant to publicly declare it or any other as his single favorite movie, people who knew him have said *Slap Shot* was it.

Jennifer Warren met Newman at a function several years after they worked together as Reggie and Francine Dunlop. "He pulled me aside and said, 'Was that film as important to you as it was to me?' That was his favorite film," she says, also remembering the day she saw him on a TV program where he was being interviewed by a woman who asked which of his many projects had been closest to his heart. "I thought to myself, he's going to say *Slap Shot*, and she's going to be astonished. And he said, *Slap Shot*, and she *was* astonished. 'But, you've done *The Sting, Butch Cassidy and the Sundance Kid*.' He said, 'Yes, I know.'"

"Paul Newman told me the most fun he ever had making a movie was *Slap Shot*," adds Johnstown Jets captain-turned-president Don Hall.

Susan Wloszczyna, a film reporter with *USA Today*, had the occasion to meet Newman in 2002 when he was promoting his latest project, *Road to Perdition*. A native of Buffalo, NY, and a longtime hockey fan, she broke the ice by telling Newman that her favorite film of his was *Slap Shot*. As she describes it, he clapped his hands and laughed as though he were a child with a Christmas present.

Chapter 13

"I almost sabotaged my interview," she laughs, "because he went on and on about that instead of *Road to Perdition*." Newman's longtime publicist, the late Warren Cowan, finally broke up the party by telling Wloszczyna to start asking questions about his client's current picture. If not for that, Newman might have gone on indefinitely.

"He'd said in the past that of all the characters he'd played, he felt this one really was him. I think he liked swearing and he liked being dirty and he liked getting kind of beat up," Wloszczyna says. "He had so much fun making it and I think he felt that it got a side of him that never got shown. You watch it and he's having such a good time, and it's just a damned funny movie.

"It captures a sense of sports that I think people know about but when they make movies they try to sweep it under something. It's down and dirty and it's Paul Newman — how can you resist?"

That's just it — fans can't. That's why stories about the film are almost as popular as the film itself. Every so often, a newspaper will publish a story about a local native or resident who had a bit part in the film, and readers will eat it up. The article will be posted online, and re-posted, and will live forever as a testament to the local hero's fame. Other stories may not get published in the newspaper, but they're gems just the same. Like the time Frank Hamill, No. 12 of the Broome County Blades, visited his daughter while she was attending university in Sudbury, Ontario.

"She was going out with this guy and she mentioned that I was in *Slap Shot*. This guy was just beside himself — he had to meet me. Forget my daughter, he had to meet me, like it was some big deal," Hamill laughs. "We went out for dinner and he ignored her and was asking me about *Slap Shot*."

"It's incredible how that happens," Hall says. "If I'm traveling someplace and some guy will say, where are you from? I say Johnstown. I say *Slap Shot*. Right away they know what we're talking about. It's crazy, you know? At the time I didn't think the movie had a chance of doing anything dramatic. It's a local joke, the local people are going to get it, but how is it going to spread? And now it's become a cult thing of some sort, right across North America."

Ron Docken was a goaltending coach at the University of Minnesota in the 1990s. "Every time I'd walk in the locker room, one of the players would say a line from the movie. I'd always have to have a comeback for it. And I'm kind of going, does this thing ever end?" he says, laughing.

Dan Belisle laughs too. "I was coach of the year in the minor leagues four times and general manager of the year once. I won three Stanley Cups. And when I talk to certain people, they say, 'Yeah, but you were in *Slap Shot*!' That's what they know. I get more credit for that than for all the other stuff."

Producer Bob Wunsch was on a river trip in northern California with his grandchildren several years ago. He met a guide and chatted with him, learning that the man had lived and worked in Vermont and had also played minor league hockey.

"I said, 'I wouldn't normally say this on a vacation trip, but you might like to know that I produced *Slap Shot*. And he started quoting whole scenes to me," Wunsch says. "Then I met a kid at a funeral for a mutual friend maybe eight or 10 years ago. He was a senior in high school and he was headed off to Duke. We got to talking and he found out I produced *Slap Shot* and he went crazy. It's very gratifying for me to see that people are consistently attracted to this movie."

Wunsch has a right to brag about his involvement in the film, because for years he has stewed over false reports about how *Slap Shot* came to the attention of George Roy Hill. Various accounts have claimed that Nancy Dowd approached Hill directly with the screenplay or with the idea for the film. Daniel O'Brien's 2004 biography of Paul Newman is an example of this; it also included the usual nonsense about Reggie Dunlop being based on John Brophy. Wunsch suggests it was Hill's vindictiveness toward the producers that led to the stories being accepted as fact.

"George Roy Hill had never heard of Nancy Dowd and had never heard of me and had never heard of the Johnstown Jets until I took that screenplay to Pat Kelley, who took it to George Roy Hill, who said, in essence, I will do it," Wunsch says. "This is a classic Hollywood ploy to cut out the actual people who figured it out and made it work, which in this case was Stephen Friedman, who was very courageous and who came up with the money, and me, who was prescient enough to know there was a great project here.

"It's perfectly typical of the kinds of things that happen with creative people. I'm sure George let it be known that he had somehow found this project."

Hill's longtime associate, Bob Crawford, acknowledges that Wunsch brought the script to Kelley and understands why Wunsch holds some bitterness over being banned from the shoot in Johnstown.

"He's right to be burned by that. I can't blame him for a second for having a hard feeling about it," Crawford says. "It was a cruel thing to do to somebody who developed something and brought it to us. It's a kick in the pants and it's unkind.

"I wouldn't have the nerve to do it, but I was a facilitator in allowing it to happen. I was in a position to counsel for more participation (from the producers). I benefited from them not being there and being the person that George would turn to first. It's a sad commentary on both of our characters that we would do it at somebody else's expense. I could play more innocent than my youthful days, but I'm guilty as charged and I have some regret about that. That's the cruelty of the business, that you can't have, sometimes, the grace to treat people with a common decency."

The producer's hard feelings don't extend to the project itself, which still makes money for "profit participants," those people who had it written into their contracts that they would receive portions of the film's proceeds. "People buy the DVDs and they show it all over the world," Wunsch says. "In July of 2006, the cumulative accountable gross, which is just a Hollywood figure, was about $40 million. It continues to spin off small amounts of actual net profits as they're defined by Hollywood standards. It's a few thousand dollars a year for everybody."

"Our success was incremental," Crawford adds, "but it was successful enough." He says it's generally accepted in the industry that the break-even point for a film is an amount of money that is two-and-a-half times the production budget. In the case of *Slap Shot*, which had a production budget of about $6.3 million, it would therefore have broken even at approximately $15.75 million. Of course, it nearly doubled that amount in its original theatrical release, topping the

$28 million mark. "That's pretty damned successful in Hollywood," Crawford says.

"I think we've created something that has an infinite life to it, and it only took a year of our lives to do it. It was just a terrific time — it was really like going to camp. We're not killing anybody, we're only pretending that we're maiming them all. It's all just a movie. But what a wonderful day at Disneyland, the fantasy factory, and then to be able to sit back in your chair and say, look at that machine. It still goes."

"I'm delighted to talk about it. It was a great time. I loved it. That was one of my more fun pictures," said film editor Dede Allen, whose long and acclaimed career continued well into her 80s. She died in April 2010 at age 86 after suffering a stroke.

Cinematographer Victor Kemper also remains active in the industry in his 80s, serving most recently as the cinematographer-in-residence at the UCLA School of Film, Theater and Television. He remains proud of *Slap Shot* and watches it every now and again, generally when his grandchildren visit. "I think it's a good movie. It never got accolades or any of that stuff, but I thought it was a great amount of fun. It still is, when I watch it."

———— ● ————

In recent years, interest in *Slap Shot* has turned toward NCAA Division I men's hockey. No, not because Princeton had decided to retroactively nominate Ned Braden for all-Eastern status. It was because of a University of Notre Dame Fighting Irish player named Christian Hanson — as in the son of Dave Hanson. Or, as he's also become known, "Son of Slap Shot."

Born in 1986, Christian always knew his dad had played pro hockey but initially had little if any knowledge of Dave's film career, because Dave and his wife Sue would not allow him to watch *Slap Shot*. But neither parent was with him one day when Christian was about 11 years and on his way to a hockey game.

"We were on the bus and one of the dads just popped it in," Christian told writer Allison Hayes for www.blueandgold. com, a news website devoted to Notre Dame athletics. "I was actually shocked because my dad is such a mellow man at home. I heard stuff about him . . . but I really had no idea what it was. It was just a culture shock to me."

Christian played minor hockey in Pittsburgh and was good enough to play in the United States Hockey League, the top junior loop in the nation, at age 17. He was a member of the Tri-City Storm, the lineal descendants of his dad's old junior club, the St. Paul Vulcans. In his second season with the Storm, the USHL awarded him the Curt Hammer Award for gentlemanly play. "How ironic is that?" his dad asks, laughing.

But Christian developed a more physical game as he grew, both physically and mentally. By the start of his senior season at Notre Dame, where he majored in finance, he was 6'4" and weighed almost 230 pounds, and had learned how to use his size while not forgetting how to put the puck in the net. He became a highly touted NHL prospect and, following Notre Dame's elimination from the 2009 NCAA tournament, he signed as a free agent with the Toronto Maple Leafs. Christian was given No. 20 — the same number his father had worn with the Johnstown Jets — and placed on a line with Jason Blake and John Mitchell, apparently no relation to the longtime Jets GM of the same name.

The well-spoken young man has expressed a love and pride in *Slap Shot* and in his father and is clearly comfortable talking about the film and his family connection to it. Certainly he would also like to be known for his own career, and he's gotten off to a good start in that regard. On April 7, 2009, while playing in his third NHL game, Christian Hanson scored his first NHL goal against Martin Brodeur and the New Jersey Devils, helping the Leafs to a 4–1 win.

Chapter 14

Defending the Honor of Charlestown

———— ● ————

Once their work in Charlestown was complete, its defenders spread out to the four corners of the world.

Ron Docken, Jean Tetreault, John Gofton, Ross Smith and Guido Tenesi continued with their hockey careers, as did Dave Hanson and Jeff and Steve Carlson and most of the other players who worked on *Slap Shot*. Tenesi played until 1987 in an Italian league and now lives near Toronto with his family. Gofton's final season of pro hockey was 1975–76, after which he played two years of Senior A in his native Ontario. Smith also left pro hockey in 1976 and retired to the family farm in Alberta. Tetreault retired in 1978 and returned to Quebec. Docken called it quits in 1979 and eventually went home to Minnesota.

Lindsay Crouse and Melinda Dillon have both compiled respected bodies of work on stage, on TV and in feature films.

Dillon's next film was 1977's *Close Encounters of the Third Kind*, for which she received an Academy Award nomination for best supporting actress. Four years later, Dillon again acted alongside Paul Newman, in *Absence of Malice*, and was rewarded with another Oscar nomination. She's also well known for playing Ralphie's mom in the 1983 holiday classic *A Christmas Story* — "You'll shoot your eye out!"

Crouse's second appearance in a Newman film was *The Verdict*. She was nominated for an Academy Award for best supporting actress for her role in the 1984 film *Places in the Heart*, which starred Sally Field in an Oscar-winning portrayal. Crouse was married for 13 years to writer-director David Mamet, who developed an interest in her while watching her in *Slap Shot*. After seeing the movie, he was told that Crouse was appearing in his play "Reunion" at the Yale Repertory Theater; Mamet immediately announced he was "going to New Haven to marry Lindsay Crouse," and they were in fact wed two months later (although they divorced in 1990).

Michael Ontkean returned to acting permanently after *Slap Shot*, working in films and on TV. He earned notoriety for the 1982 feature film *Making Love*, in which he played a married man who fell in love with another man, played by Harry Hamlin. His later notable projects included the quirky David Lynch TV series *Twin Peaks*, bringing himself renewed fame as Sheriff Harry S. Truman. He lives in Hawaii and spends much of his time traveling, working less frequently.

Stephen Mendillo worked twice more on Newman projects, the play "Our Town" and the HBO mini-series *Empire Falls*. He's a prolific actor who frequently appears on stage with his wife, Lisa Richards, and has also done a great deal of feature film work, including two more sports movies, *Eight Men Out* and *Cobb*. "I always thought it'd be fun to be in a sports movie," he says. "I never hit a big jackpot but I earned my way as I went."

Allan Nicholls collaborated numerous times over the years with friend Robert Altman, working as an actor, director, producer and musician. He now lives and works in Singapore, where he teaches a graduate course in screenwriting. Several years ago he donated his Chiefs sweater, along with his skates, gloves and pants, to a charity auction. It brought in $500.

"Most of the actors were doing it for the joy of playing hockey. Most of the hockey players were doing it for the joy of being in a movie," he says. "Nobody thought it was going to have any legs. I don't even think people thought about those things in those days."

Jerry Houser has carved out an impressive niche for himself as a character actor and voice-over performer — his memorable roles include Wally Logan, the husband of Marcia Brady, in several *Brady Bunch* sequels, and one of the Keebler Elves in a number of animated TV commercials.

"The movie strikes a chord in people. It's still something that's watched and talked about. It's one of those movies that captured a moment and captured a feeling," he says of *Slap Shot*. "It's special to be part of something that's so unique, that people remember."

Ned Dowd used *Slap Shot* as a springboard to a long and distinguished film career, a move that his sister all but predicted. In a 1977 interview with freelance writer Carol Mithers, Nancy Dowd talked about the difference between herself and her more gregarious brother. "The thing that's been so agonizing the last month is that I haven't been able to write — I've just been going out promoting this movie. But I feel a certain responsibility as a writer, an artist and, I guess, as a woman, to go out and be visible, even though there's a side of that that's very distasteful to me. My brother loves all this — he's very friendly and people like him. I seem to arouse people's hostilities."

Although Ned had a handful of acting roles over the years, much of his work has been as an assistant director, producer and executive producer. He worked for years as head of production with Caravan Pictures, which was responsible for hit films like *While You Were Sleeping* and *Grosse Point Blank*. He now works independently and has served as an executive producer on such films as *Wonder Boys*, *Veronica Guerin*, *King Arthur* and *Apocalypto*. "Life takes you in different directions for odd reasons," Dowd says.

"I think, to a man, anybody who worked on (*Slap Shot*) can say it was probably the most fun they've ever had on a picture. It was a good party and nobody took it too seriously. In those days there wasn't so much on the line and so you could enjoy yourself. These days there's so much money out there and there's so much at stake every day. The business has gotten, well, you're not allowed to have fun, I'll put it that way."

Nancy Dowd, unlike Ned, had a comparatively brief career in the film business. In 1973 she wrote a screenplay called *Buffalo Ghost* that eventually was rewritten and turned into the Oscar-winning film *Coming Home*, but the experience was not at all pleasant for her. Dowd had lost control of the script and had to fight to ensure she received a credit, which ensured she shared in the Academy Award the movie won for best original screenplay. It soured her on the business, although she continued to write for a number of years afterward. Subsequent negative encounters compelled Dowd to choose to be credited under pseudonyms on some projects, when she opted to be credited at all. She is now retired.

"She was such a fabulous writer who didn't get treated that way. I think we really screwed ourselves and lost one of our major original talents," says Jennifer Warren. "She felt that everybody was against her and I'm so sorry. Everybody that I knew and I certainly felt just terrible that this fabulous talent was just being kind of squandered."

Warren's next major acting role after *Slap Shot* was 1979's *Ice Castles*, in which she played figure skating coach Deborah Machland. Eventually she moved behind the camera, working as a director and a producer. Now a senior lecturer at the University of Southern California School of Cinematic Arts, she served as an executive producer on the 1988 film *You Don't Have to Die*, about a young boy who successfully battled a brain tumor. It won the Academy Award for best documentary short subject — a prize, strangely enough, won the following year by *The Johnstown Flood*.

"I just loved it," Warren says of her *Slap Shot* experience. "I can't say too much about how everybody connected with it. We connected with it not because it was Paul Newman — it was because of the script."

Andrew Duncan has retired from show business but M. Emmet Walsh and Paul Dooley remain active character actors. Yvon Barrette, Paul D'Amato, Chris Murney and Yvan Ponton have also continued with their careers. D'Amato made a second hockey film, the made-for-TV movie *The Deadliest Season*, in 1977. Murney, like Houser, has done a great deal of voice-over work — Chester Cheetah, from the Cheetos commercials, is perhaps his best-known character. Ponton has become a hockey actor of great note in his native Quebec, starring in the highly successful *Les Boys* movies and in the long-running TV series *Lance et Compte*, known in English Canada as *He Shoots, He Scores*.

Slap Shot was Swoosie Kurtz's first movie, but she quickly established herself as one of the most prolific, versatile and honored actresses in the business. By the time she worked again with George Roy Hill on *The World According to Garp* in 1982, Kurtz was co-starring on the TV series *Love, Sidney* and had earned the first of 10 Emmy Award nominations. She has since starred on two subsequent series — *Sisters* and *Pushing Daisies* — and has held recurring roles on a number of other shows. The winner of one Emmy, Kurtz has also been nominated for five Tony Awards, winning two.

Her first film remains very close to her heart. She laughs when she thinks of the assistant directors on *Pushing Daisies* who, whenever there was a lull, encouraged Kurtz to liven up the proceedings with one of her Shirley Upton *Slap Shot* one-liners. "They would say, 'Okay, give us one,' and I would try to remember another one — 'Johnny always says, you can just screw so much and drink so much.' And they remembered all of them," she says proudly.

Interestingly, her portrayal of Shirley almost landed Kurtz another job in the months following *Slap Shot*. It had been a distinctive look for her, requiring hours each day to have her hair back-combed and sprayed into place, then washed clean each night, but it made a significant impression on someone.

Chapter 14

"I get this call from my agent, who says, 'You've finally made it!' I said, 'What do you mean?' He said, 'I just got a break-down that describes this character in this film, and it says, 'a Swoosie Kurtz type." I said, 'Wow, how cool!'"

Her agent got her an audition with the director, whose name she doesn't recall. The director was polite but Kurtz could tell something was wrong. Her agent called her later to tell her she didn't get the job. She was dumbfounded. "He doesn't think I'm right for it? It's a Swoosie Kurtz type! But we figured out later that he had seen *Slap Shot* and *that* was what he wanted, that person." She laughs, "You hear about these stories, but this really happened to me."

Strother Martin continued with his varied career and remained in high demand up until his sudden death from a heart attack on August 1, 1980. He was 61 years old. He played the father of Tommy Chong's character Man in the first Cheech and Chong feature film, 1978's *Up in Smoke*, and made one of his final screen appearances on April 19, 1980, as the host of *Saturday Night Live*.

John Mitchell, the inspiration for Martin's best-loved character, Joe McGrath in *Slap Shot*, died in 1986 at age 85.

——— ● ———

George Roy Hill directed only four more films. His next film, *A Little Romance* (1979), gave him a chance to work with Sir Laurence Olivier and provided 14-year-old Diane Lane with her first firm role. *The World According to Garp* (1982), mean-while, introduced movie audiences to Glenn Close.

Hill taught at Yale in the latter years of his filmmaking career and pursued the vocation full time after retiring from behind the camera. He cooperated on a biography written by Andrew Horton, his nephew by marriage, which examined Hill's career on a film-by-film basis. First published in 1984 with a foreword by Paul Newman, the book was revised in 2005.

Horton is a screenwriter and author with 15 books to his credit, and since 1998 he has worked at the University of Oklahoma as the Jeanne H. Smith Professor of Film and Video Studies. He remembers that Hill, taking note of the writing Horton was already doing, suggested the project. The idea surprised Horton, who knew of his uncle's reluctance to seek publicity. Feeling a problem may have arisen if the ground rules weren't agreed upon in advance, Horton said he would do it only if Hill pledged to cooperate fully, which meant lengthy interviews and access to Hill's papers. It was a demand to which Hill readily acceded.

"What is George Roy Hill's legacy? There is no easy answer as those who knew him well exemplify," Horton wrote. "He was an American director unaligned with any particular movement or trend who worked within the Hollywood commercial framework, drawing from a richly diverse background to make an equally diverse series of films that are surprisingly consistent in characterization, theme, and tone."

Hill loved classical music and playing the piano. He was a voracious reader of history and solver of crossword puzzles. He enjoyed flying his plane and gave himself a cameo in *Garp* as a pilot who crashes into Garp's house. Above all else, he remained a very private man who shunned the spotlight, although he maintained a group of friends and associates with whom he remained very close.

It likewise surprised John Hill when his father cooperated with Horton on the latter's book, and it came as an even bigger surprise to learn years later that the senior Hill had actually solicited the project. John is still employed in the film industry, having worked as an editor on movies like *Moonstruck*, *In & Out*, *The First Wives Club*, *Get Shorty* and *Nobody's Fool*. He worked with his father again on *Garp* and *Funny Farm* and is gratified to have had those experiences.

"He's a giant," John says. "I don't know if that's daunting to me or what, but it certainly was a pleasure to see his movies and be involved with them."

John is a keeper of sorts of his father's legacy. He retains some of George's personal items, such as an annotated copy of *Slap Shot*. The vast majority of his film-related materials — scripts, correspondence, production notes and more — reside today in Beverly Hills, in a special collection at the Margaret Herrick Library, operated by the Academy of Motion Picture Arts and Sciences. Hill donated these materials to the library in 1991 and 1992.

He retained a soft spot for *Slap Shot* and would be delighted to know that "the boys," as he called the Hanson Brothers, are still doing their thing today. The Hansons may not be happy to know this, but their first director owned their McFarlane figures and proudly displayed them.

"He loved them," Bob Crawford says of Hill and the Hansons. "He would be so thrilled that they were doing it, tickled by it.

"You always worry about, what's going to happen to those guys? They may not make their killing in their chosen profession, and what will they do after that? Will they find a life for themselves? Will they find a *good* life for themselves? God knows they put themselves way out there on a limb as players, as gunslingers, and George admired them. He admired their skill and their guts and their nerve and their toughness and their performances and their giving of themselves to act in the film. He was really inspired by them, and he liked them greatly.

"It's great that they've found a life for themselves. They are legends in their own time."

The film's cult status in general also pleased Hill, who told his son he had heard about an establishment in Canada that had the movie on a loop on a television. It was all *Slap Shot*, all the time. "It was a bar somewhere that he'd heard about where they'd play it constantly. That made him very happy," John says.

"He appreciated his successes, and was always probably a little surprised that he succeeded," adds Crawford, who also continues to work in the entertainment business. "Like all really great artists and geniuses, he was very self-critical but also a little bit shocked at his gift, and appreciative of having it.

"It would be a pleasure to him to know that he created something that still stood up to time. He would take it as an honor and embrace it."

In the spring of 2001, John Hill took his father to see the play *Judgment at Nuremberg* at the Longacre Theatre on West 48th Street in New York. It was the third time around for the story, which George Roy Hill had first brought to American audiences in an episode of *Playhouse 90* on CBS, broadcast live on April 16, 1959. Writer Abby Mann turned it into a 1961 film directed by Stanley Kramer that won two Oscars.

Mann adapted the story again for the Broadway stage. Maximilian Schell, who played defence attorney Hans Rolfe in the teleplay and won an Oscar for reprising the role in the film, starred this time as defendant Ernst Manning, a part created on TV by Paul Lukas and recreated on the big screen by Burt Lancaster. The elder Hill by this time was suffering from Parkinson's disease and his son wondered at first if the play would be a worthwhile experience. Louisa Horton Hill, who had divorced George but had remained very close to her former husband, encouraged their son to go through with it and to be sure they went backstage.

"He was sort of in and out at that point and he really couldn't say that much," says John, who reintroduced his father to Schell after the play. "And yet you knew how much it meant to him. He knew this was something he had done on TV. He knew Maximilian Schell. It didn't matter whether or not he could talk a blue streak. He was there.

"I mentioned this at his memorial service because it was the most amazing thing. Maximilian Schell shook his hand. Not a lot was said but my father was just beaming. He just got up and walked across the street and walked partly to 8th Avenue" — which is about 300 feet away from the theater — "and back. He just wanted to get up and show what he could still do — he was on top of the world."

George Roy Hill died a year-and-a-half later, on December 27, 2002, exactly one week after his 81st birthday. He was survived by two sons, two daughters and 12 grandchildren.

"He was the best friend that anyone could have: friend, mentor, enemy," Paul Newman said in a statement. "He gave everyone a hell of a ride. Himself included."

"Nancy Dowd and I used to call him the smartest man alive. George was a very intelligent guy," says Steve Mendillo. "He was a tough guy but he was a very nice man. I liked him very much. He was fun to work for."

Louisa was with George right up until the end. "It was the best divorce anybody could have hoped for," John Hill says of his parents' parting. "She was his guardian. When he got sick, she was the one who was always there. A lot of people dropped by the wayside but she got everybody to call and come by and she was always coming by. They just had a great relationship, and she was really good to him."

———— ● ————

Brad Sullivan, who played Mo Wanchuk, succumbed to a battle with cancer on the final day of 2008. He was 77 years old.

He had continued with a much-respected acting career after *Slap Shot*, immediately following up by making his Broadway debut alongside Al Pacino in 1977's *The Basic Training of Pavlo Hummel*. A year later, he received a Drama Desk Award nomination for the Stephen Schwartz musical *Working*.

Sullivan compiled several more credits on and off Broadway and in films and TV; his notable roles on the big screen were in films like *The Untouchables* and *The Prince of Tides*. On TV, he had recurring roles in *NYPD Blue* and *I'll Fly Away* and was a regular cast member on the series *Nothing Sacred* in 1997–98. He retired from acting in 2000 and thereafter devoted much of his time to Christian ministry, particularly at Columbia University, where he was very active in International Christian Fellowship. He also involved himself with Manhattan's Asian community, particularly Chinese, mentoring students at a middle school and tutoring people who wanted to learn to speak English.

"He had a special attachment for the people he loved and appreciated them without reservation," read Sullivan's obituary in the January 15, 2009, edition of the *Cape Cod Times*. "He will always be remembered by those who loved him for the richness of his life, the care he gave to others, and the integrity of his values."

While Sullivan preferred to downplay the role of Mo, he will always be remembered by *Slap Shot* fans for his unforgettable performance as the biggest lecher Charlestown ever saw. Need proof? When *Calgary Sun* columnist Eric Francis reported Sullivan's death, he said the news was "as hard as little rocks to swallow.

"While cancer was the official cause of death, we'd like to believe the *Slap Shot* soap junkie quietly passed away poolside while amidst underwater specialists in F-L-A."

——— ● ———

Only six days after Sullivan's passing, on January 5, 2009, former Universal Pictures president Ned Tanen died at his home in Santa Monica. Like Sullivan, he was 77 years old.

His career in the entertainment industry spanned five decades. After leaving the top job at Universal Pictures, he headed Paramount Pictures and also worked as an independent producer. Along with *Slap Shot*, he was responsible for developing and/or giving the go-ahead to such classic films as *National Lampoon's Animal House*, *Smokey and the Bandit*, *The Deer Hunter*, *Coal Miner's Daughter*, *Sixteen Candles*, *The Breakfast Club*, *St. Elmo's Fire*, *Top Gun*, *The Accused* and *Fatal Attraction*, among many, many others. And Tanen's cultural impact went far beyond the development and production of films — for instance, his surname was borrowed and given to the antagonist in the *Back to the Future* trilogy, Biff Tannen. Sloane, the female lead in *Ferris Bueller's Day Off*, was named after Sloane Tanen, the executive's daughter.

"I got a hand in a lot of incredible movies," Tanen said in February 2007. "I had a good instinct and that's all I had — believe me, I'm not that smart, nor do I pretend to be. And I had the position and ability to at least get them made without 55 people from Wall Street who have never been near the movie business and don't know anything about it second-guessing me.

"Everybody's an authority. I never considered myself any authority. I always thought I should be pumping gas. I'm sure a lot of other people thought I should be pumping gas."

Tanen held a special place in his heart for *Slap Shot* and took a lot of pride in his involvement.

"If this is not a cult classic, and I did a lot of movies or caused them to happen, I don't know what a cult classic is," he said. "And it's moment after moment . . . every time you sit down you think of another scene. It's one after another.

"When I think of *Slap Shot*, every time I think of it, I just smile."

He wasn't the only one.

———— ● ————

The legacy of *Slap Shot* had long been solidified when Reggie Dunlop, aka Paul Newman, died of lung cancer on September 26, 2008, at his home in Westport, Connecticut.

The years after the film's release were initially not kind to Newman. His son Scott died of a drug overdose in 1978. His next two films, *Quintet* and *When Time Ran Out* both disappointed, critically and commercially. But he bounced back, turning in two consecutive performances that earned him Oscar nominations — *Absence of Malice* and *The Verdict*. Although he didn't win either time, they were his first nominations for acting since *Cool Hand Luke* and proved that he still had the talent as well as a knack for choosing good material.

In 1986, the Academy of Motion Picture Arts and Sciences gave Newman an honorary Oscar in recognition of his career. One year later, he finally got the prize he had long deserved, an Oscar for best actor for *The Color of Money*. He would later gain two more Oscar nominations for his acting and another honorary Oscar for his humanitarian efforts; his last nomination, for best supporting actor in 2002's *Road to Perdition*, marked his final big-screen appearance.

After a voice-only performance in the 2006 animated film *Cars* and a job as narrator of the 2007 documentary *Dale*, about NASCAR legend Dale Earnhardt, Newman stunned the entertainment world when, on May 27, 2007, he announced his retirement on ABC's *Good Morning America*, saying his advancing age and declining memory and confidence meant he could no longer work "at the level that I would want to."

But Newman ensured his charitable efforts would continue through the Newman's Own Foundation, named after his food enterprise of the same name, which has expanded from salad dressing and popcorn to include such items as pasta and steak sauces, cereal and even beverages. Newman's Own has donated more than $250 million to worthy causes, including the Hole in the Wall Camps.

"My brother is an incredible human being," Arthur Newman said in February 2007.

Of course, his lasting legacy as far as hockey is concerned will always be *Slap Shot*. Tributes to the film and to Newman's portrayal of Reggie Dunlop poured in after his death and continued through the 2008–09 hockey season.

Newman looked like he was having a party inhabiting schlubby con man Reggie Dunlop. Your leading lights of cinema don't often break tradition in the middle of their careers and do a goofy comedy, but then Paul Newman wasn't usual." — Leslie Gray Streeter, *Palm Beach Post*, September 27, 2008.

"(He) cursed, caroused and shocked moviegoers as the hard-drinking reprobate coach and player for a ragtag hockey team in 1977's *Slap Shot*, one of the rowdiest, crudest, funniest and most scathingly honest sports comedies ever." — Susan Wloszczyna, *USA Today*, September 27, 2008.

"It's the best sports movie ever, in part because it didn't try to have it both ways, as so many sports films do now — claiming to be a true story, but going far beyond dramatic license in distorting what really happened. The irony is that as a broad satire, *Slap Shot* was far closer to the truth than many 'true' movies." — Terry Frei, *Denver Post*, September 29, 2008.

"I can't even type the name of this film without smiling. I watched *Slap Shot* around the same time I watched *North Dallas Forty* and *The Longest Yard*, two other classic sports films of the 1970s; *Slap Shot* is by far the goofiest." — Sara Foss, *Schenectady Daily Gazette*, September 29, 2008.

"A key contender for Newman's best movie of the decade . . . It's probably Newman's funniest performance — especially in scenes with the Hanson Brothers." — Mike Clark, ABC News, September 30, 2008.

"Since *Slap Shot*, almost every comic actor, from Bill Murray to Will Ferrell, has tried to duplicate the Dunlop role, yet none of them brought what Newman did to the table." — Lynn Crosbie, *Globe and Mail*, September 30, 2008.

"(T)he battered, spectacularly profane and intensely likable hockey player-coach of *Slap Shot* . . . " — Joe Morgenstern, *Wall Street Journal*, September 30, 2008.

Newman's *Slap Shot* castmates joined in the tributes. "I raised a drink to his memory," Jennifer Warren said, calling Newman a "very special man. I was lucky to know him."

"My last mentor is gone," said Mike Ontkean. "That's the shape of life and we must accept. But there's a profusion of beautiful memories.

"He was a giant. As good and deep and soulful as any to walk this planet."

The Johnstown Chiefs immediately placed No. 7 patches on their sweaters. The Syracuse Crunch of the AHL went even further. The Crunch play in the Onondaga County War Memorial and, noting part of *Slap Shot* was filmed in the arena, took No. 7 out of circulation for the 2008–09 campaign and raised a banner to the building's rafters on the season's opening night. Taking part in the ceremony were two brothers and a sister who have, while dressed as the Hanson Brothers, attended every Crunch home game since the team was founded in 1994.

The Anaheim Ducks didn't forget Newman either. Joe Trotta, the team's video coordinator who had compared his club, on the day of its greatest triumph, to the Charlestown Chiefs, created a video tribute. During a stoppage in the first period of the Ducks' game against the Vancouver Canucks, on September 28, 2008, a clip from *Slap Shot* was shown on the scoreboard at the Honda Center in Anaheim. It was followed by a still picture of Newman and the words, "Paul Newman (a.k.a. Reggie Dunlop) 1925–2008."

The tributes were still coming when Universal released a new print of *Slap Shot*, something Kori Bernards, the company's senior vice president of media relations, says was already in the works prior to the actor's death. "We've gotten lots of requests," she says. "It certainly is a favorite of people who remember it and like the story."

Many theaters showed the film as part of Newman retrospectives, like the Brooklyn Academy of Music's BAMcinematek repertory film program, which slated it alongside *The Hustler*, *The Effect of Gamma Rays on Man-in-the-Moon Marigolds* (which Newman directed but did not appear in) and *Torn Curtain*, directed by Alfred Hitchcock.

"It is a film I like very much," says BAM programming associate Jake Perlin, "and my colleagues and I thought it important to include to give a representation of Newman's range. Aside from an iconic role (*Hustler*), a directorial effort (*Gamma Rays*) and a collaboration with a classic Hollywood figure (*Torn Curtain*), *Slap Shot* seemed the must-have '70s film. Plus it seems a great film to see with a crowd."

The film was originally scheduled to be shown in December but was postponed after only half the print arrived. When it was finally shown in March, it again filled the same slot in a retrospective — with *The Long, Hot Summer* serving as the iconic role, *Sometimes a Great Notion* an example of Newman as director and *Quintet* representing a collaboration with a legendary director, in this case Robert Altman.

Slap Shot was chosen to conclude the Overcoat Film Series at the public library in Westport, CT. The Vancouver International Film Centre selected it as the centerpiece of its Hockey Nights in Film series in March, calling it, "for most sports and movie fans, the *ne plus ultra* of hockey films."

In April, the Full Frame Documentary Film Festival in Durham, NC, staged a thematic program called This Sporting

Chapter 14

Life and asked Steve James, director of the acclaimed basketball documentary *Hoop Dreams*, to curate the program. He picked *Slap Shot* as one of 10 titles, described collectively in a news release as "work that has contributed to the evolution of the contemporary sports film as well as more recent titles that continue to push the genre in new directions."

"They demonstrate the range and vibrancy of filmmaking that's going on within the genre of sports," James said in the release. "And it was particularly fun to put together a program that includes films from the worlds of documentary and fiction. I mean, what could be better than having a special Full Frame screening of *Slap Shot?*"

Pittsburgh Filmmakers staged the film entirely on its own, not as part of a retrospective — seven well-attended showings of the film at the Regent Square Theater in the borough of Edgewood. "Unrepentantly crude, *Slap Shot* showcases Newman's prodigious comedic talents," said a news release announcing the showings, which took place between January 1 and 4, 2009.

"Why would you not show it?" asks Richard Engel, the media arts center's director of marketing and public relations. "It's brilliant. It's the only good hockey movie that's ever been made."

Dave Hanson introduced the final showing of the film and, unsurprisingly, drew the largest attendance of the run. He took questions from the audience and signed copies of his book. Hanson also asked a question of the gathering — how many people had *not* already seen the movie? Engel says perhaps nine of the 200 or so people raised their hands.

"He was really giving, a warm individual," Engel says, noting many fans showed up wearing Chiefs jerseys with Hanson numbers and nameplates on the back.

The American Film Institute, which celebrates and promotes film history, has largely ignored *Slap Shot*, the film not making the grade in any of its various commemorative lists — not even the Top 10 sports films list. But the institute did include it in a Paul Newman Remembered tribute in the spring of 2009 at the AFI Silver Theater and Cultural Center in Silver Spring, Maryland, just outside Washington, DC.

———— ● ————

There's an old saying that imitation is the sincerest form of flattery. That might explain film sequels and remakes, if you can get past the notion that, rather than flattery, they're often little more than crass cash grabs.

Such was obviously the case with Universal's 2002 release, *Slap Shot 2: Breaking the Ice*. While it's somewhat true to say a sequel was long-awaited, the hope was that it would find some way to better incorporate the original characters and storyline, or at least some believable connection to the Charlestown Chiefs. Fans of *Slap Shot* certainly didn't expect to see the Chiefs turned into the Washington Generals of hockey, a team set up to lose regularly in a Harlem Globetrotters-style circus overseen by Gary Busey.

It's a situation you couldn't see Reggie Dunlop tolerating. In fact, with rumors swirling around for years that a sequel would be made, Newman tried to dissuade Dave Hanson from taking part. He himself had only ever played the same character twice — Lew Harper and Eddie Felson — and he argued that the lack of a sequel preserved an original film's legacy. "He said, '*Slap Shot* is such a great, great film. There's no way you could do it justice in a sequel,'" Hanson remembers.

Chapter 14

Newman was right. Not only did fans find the premise of *Slap Shot 2* ridiculous, they could not empathize with the sad-sack captain portrayed by Stephen Baldwin. As the film was made in Vancouver, giving his character the surname "Linden" may have been an attempt to capture some of the goodwill afforded to popular Vancouver Canucks stalwart Trevor Linden. It didn't work. Thankfully, at least it didn't sully the real Linden or his reputation.

Throwing in the Hanson Brothers for what amounted to cameo appearances that book-ended the film was perhaps the biggest insult to fans, because it was only a cynical appeal to fans of the original movie who were rewarded by nothing once they hit "Play" on their DVD players. Although it was first thought *Slap Shot 2* might have a theatrical release, it was instead distributed straight to video and deservedly sank out of sight — watched once by many, watched more than once by few, remembered fondly by no one.

"It's unwatchable. It's a total piece of shit," says Bob Wunsch. "It was just beyond belief how stupid it was. I literally could not watch it to the end, it was so bad."

"Don't even use it as a drink coaster," uber-fan Ken Blake says of the DVD. "They could have done way better with a sequel. There are so many things they could have done . . . there are so many ways they could have brought the other guys into the film instead of just the Hanson Brothers with this Harlem Globetrotters BS."

Fans weren't clamoring for another sequel but they got one anyway. Universal did sort of learn from the debacle, waiting several years before trying again, perhaps waiting for the bad taste of *Slap Shot 2* to dissipate into memory. Patti Jackson, a senior vice-president of live-action production in

Universal's Home Entertainment division, was responsible for spearheading the creation of the second sequel. A devotee of the original film, she was interested in something that wouldn't embarrass its legacy.

"She's a big fan and she's been trying to push this through for a long, long time," says Brad Riddell, who was enlisted to write *Slap Shot: The Junior League*. "She thought of me and I came in with an idea. They liked my take on it and I began developing a story and working on a script."

Riddell teaches courses in screenwriting at the USC School of Cinematic Arts, where his colleagues include Jennifer Warren. He had become a hockey fan while attending the University of Kentucky in Lexington, and he later worked with the Kentucky Thoroughblades, a now-defunct AHL team also based in Lexington. Along the way he saw *Slap Shot* at the urging of his Nova Scotia-born roommate and fell in love with the film, saying he recognized immediately that it was very different from anything he had ever seen before.

"It had a bawdiness and a raucousness and a grungy, dirty, seedy atmosphere and it wasn't focused on the big leagues, which I think was interesting and which I've always found appealing," he says. "Even the supporting characters were all so rich and vibrant. I felt it stood apart, especially as a sports movie. There's a handful of sports movies that people love, and I put *Slap Shot* in my top five instantly after seeing it."

Riddell watched *Slap Shot* "two or three times" before starting to write his script, then would watch it again after each draft, taking notes to aid him in piecing his own story together. "I wanted to pay homage where I could. I wanted it to feel like a *Slap Shot* movie even though it's kids. I wanted to keep the script in that legend and that myth and that sort of vibe that everyone loves about the original. I did draw a lot from the film and I studied it very closely."

Conscious efforts were made to give the Hansons more priority and screen time and to reconnect the Chiefs with their roots, beginning with a montage of clips from the first movie. Although it was filmed in British Columbia, the setting of *The Junior League* was said to be Charlestown, where the Hansons and their sons, Dit, Toe and Gordie, were enlisted in helping to save an orphanage called the "Newman Home for Boys." The plot was filled with similarities and direct references to the original storyline, including a variation on the "let 'em know you're there" locker room speech.

The Chiefs' main rivals now were from Binghamton, home of the old NAHL Dusters, although it was depicted as a neighboring, affluent community across the river, as compared with the still-dying Charlestown. Canadian comic legend Leslie Nielsen was cast as David Kenneth, the mayor of Charlestown, and cameos by retired hockey superstars Mark Messier and Doug Gilmour were intended to further appease fans, as was a rendition of "Right Back Where We Started From" by punk rock band The Hanson Brothers. The new sequel was released directly to video in late 2008; it was an inoffensively entertaining movie that promised nothing it didn't deliver and, ultimately, was hardly the embarrassment its predecessor had been.

"I'm aware of the critical response it got," Riddell says of *Slap Shot 2*. "I think you're always worried when you take on a project that has a huge following, that people really cherish.

It's a little bit nerve-wracking. But everybody has tried to create something new and fresh but also with that sense of respect and homage to the original. They've done a great job making it look and feel of that world. Charlestown feels very much alive, like it did in the original."

Universal hasn't stopped going to the well. Even as *Slap Shot 3* was in development, plans were underway to remake the original movie. Stuart Blumberg was slated to write the screenplay but at some point he was replaced by Peter Steinfeld, the writer of the casino caper movie *21*. Steinfeld visited Johnstown as part of his research and has said he wanted to adhere to the original wherever possible.

"It's been an interesting ride so far. I wrote a brand new script. It was a little more along the lines of what Nancy Dowd had done," he told Mike Mastovich of the *Johnstown Tribune-Democrat* in June 2008. "I referred back to her script and kind of used that as a jumping off point."

In a later interview with the internet site YourMovieMaven. com, Steinfeld acknowledged there has been public resistance to the idea of a remake. "I've never had so many people hate me for writing something they haven't seen yet," he said. "It's such a classic film and fans of the original feel like I'm grave-robbing or something. But I think the movie will be really fun and will capture what it's like to play minor league hockey in 2008."

It was announced in February 2009 that Dean Parisot, who directed the Jim Carrey-led remake of *Fun with Dick and Jane*, would helm the new *Slap Shot*. It has yet to go into production, there has been no word on who will star in the film and it is not expected to be released until 2012 at the earliest.

———— ● ————

Chapter 14

As for Nancy Dowd, she is no longer active in the entertainment business and she lives a private life away from the spotlight. Occasionally she surfaces to speak about *Slap Shot* but
only when she chooses to do so. Several unsuccessful attempts
were made to contact her regarding this book; she responded
only once, telling an intermediary that she did not wish to
participate but offered her best wishes.

Epilogue

Remember when Reggie Dunlop told his team that the Chiefs were history, that there wasn't no Florida deal?

Well, the Chiefs are indeed history, gone not to Florida but to South Carolina — coincidentally, the state where Johnstown Jets legend Dick Roberge now makes his home.

Yet Johnstown remains a preferred hockey destination of sorts. Within a day of the announcement that the ECHL's Chiefs would depart for, um, greener pastures in Greenville, S.C., a new league made it known that it would like to place a team in the Cambria County War Memorial.

"We have ownership and we're ready to go in," says Don Kirnan, commissioner of — are you ready for this? — the Federal Hockey League.

The league, which hoped to begin play in the fall of 2010, sees itself as a class A circuit, a step below the ECHL and perhaps on the same footing as the Southern Professional Hockey League in the southeastern United States. Less travel, fewer games and lower payroll costs are among the factors that would permit teams to operate with annual budgets of around $500,000, Kirnan says.

By comparison, the Chiefs were operating with a budget of about $1.2 million. That's a shoestring in the ECHL, where most other teams' budgets start at $1.6 million. "We could definitely be very solvent there," Kirnan says of Johnstown. "There would be no problems as far as keeping the team there. They could count on that team being there, basically, forever."

Epilogue

The caliber of player sought by the FHL is the guy who is coming out of NCAA Division I or Canadian major junior but may not yet be ready for the ECHL or the AHL. "It's going to be a very good feeder system," Kirnan says of his operation.

He says that although the league is not necessarily named after the fictional loop of movie renown, it's obviously a recognizable brand. And Johnstown is a natural fit for the Federal league.

"We'd love to make it work there. Semi-pro hockey in that town is perfect," he says. "It'd be terrible if it wasn't there. It's what people want."

———— ● ————

February 2010 was not a kind month to Johnstown. News of the Chiefs' departure came less than a week after the death of John Murtha, the longtime congressman who was widely credited with bringing much needed stimulus funding — or pork, depending on who you ask — to the area.

"You have no idea what a blow that is," says Denny Grenell, noting that former president Bill Clinton, Speaker of the House of Representatives Nancy Pelosi, Secretary of Defense Robert Gates, Central Intelligence Agency Director Leon Panetta, National Security Advisor Gen. Jim Jones and Adm. Mike Mullen, Chairman of the Joint Chiefs of Staff, all attended Murtha's funeral in Johnstown. "That speaks volumes about this guy's power and influence. In fact, Pittsburgh Magazine called him the most powerful man in America."

A special election to replace Murtha was scheduled for May 18, 2010. The 12th Congressional District of Pennsylvania will again come up for grabs in a regularly scheduled election in November. There is no guarantee that someone from Johnstown, which is only a part of a huge geographic district, will prevail. The city and region may no longer be the recipient of the same kind of federal funding as in the past.

That's bad news considering the local economy was already struggling, a huge factor in the demise of the Johnstown Chiefs.

Grenell helped bring the Chiefs to life in the winter of 1987-88 and their loss is undoubtedly a personal one. But he understands why it happened. The business community found it difficult to commit money for sponsorships, he says.

"Everybody had to see this coming, quite frankly. They've been struggling for years, financially. And it was tough in this economic environment for businesses to step up and give money like they used to."

It's "somewhat accurate" to say ECHL outgrew Johnstown, Grenell says, but the team's play has also been a concern. In 2008-09, the Chiefs lost 26 of their final 41 games, going winless in their last five contests, and missed the playoffs by a single point.

Their final season in Johnstown was awful, with only 14 wins in 51 contests when the move to Greenville was announced. Attendance had dropped to an average of 1,975 fans per home game at the War Memorial, where the Chiefs won only five times in their first 24 tries.

"The fact that they didn't win many games this year is disheartening," Grenell says. "When you lose 13 straight home games, people aren't going to go and support you."

But youth and high school hockey are still thriving. And Grenell expects that minor-pro hockey will be back in Johnstown soon, if it's not there in the fall of 2010.

Epilogue

"We're used to adversity in this town, because we've lived through it for many, many years. We have a history of resiliency."

———— ● ————

It's unclear if Johnstown will be the site of the filming of the remake of *Slap Shot*. Little has been heard of the project since it was announced in February 2009 that Dean Parisot would direct it. But the original film's spirit lives on in other new works; Will Ferrell's comedy *Semi-Pro*, about a man's desperate attempt to save his fictional American Basketball Association franchise from extinction in 1976, was widely seen as a derivation. Ferrell himself commented on the similarities to *Slap Shot*.

"Our director, Kent Alterman, he really wanted to get a flavor of that," Ferrell told Amy Orndorff of the *Washington Post* at the time of his movie's release in February 2008. "When you think back to that film, it is obviously broad and funny, but it was really gritty and real at times, and it went in and out of the very serious relationship story."

Drew Barrymore cited it numerous times as an influence and inspiration for her 2009 roller derby film *Whip It*, for which she was the star, director and an executive producer. "I love the movie *Slap Shot*, and Paul Newman was an icon for me," she said to Sam Alipour for his Media Blitz column on ESPN.com's Page 2.

"Ellen and I talked a lot about Paul Newman in *Slap Shot*," Barrymore elaborated to Michael Almereyda of the *New York Times*, referring to co-star Ellen Page. "I was like, 'I want you to be Paul Newman.' Paul Newman allowed himself to be flawed, and he seems all the more charming for those flaws."

Epilogue

Mike Ontkean was pleasantly surprised to learn that George Clooney reflected on *Slap Shot* while co-producing and directing his 2008 football comedy *Leatherheads*. The two men worked together in 2010 on the film *The Descendants*, and director Alexander Payne screened *Slap Shot* one day for the company. That's when Clooney told Ontkean that he was a big fan of the Charlestown Chiefs. "He gathered very specific inspiration for the direction of *Leatherheads* from multiple viewings of *Slap Shot*," Ontkean says. "He had seen it many times."

According to the Internet Movie Database, the remake of *Slap Shot* remains "in development." So do other Parisot projects like a retelling of the 1951 caper comedy *The Lavender Hill Mob*, which has been in the works for several years; Parisot's participation in that remake was first announced in 2004.

Which makes it all the more incredible that the story of the 1975 Johnstown Jets got on the big screen at all, much less within two years of the legendary hockey team's greatest triumph.

ACKNOWLEDGMENTS

This book actually began more than 30 years ago with another book, little known and, I suspect, not well regarded.

When I was eight or nine years old, before I was really aware that there was a film called *Slap Shot*, I discovered a novelization of the screenplay, written by Richard Woodley. It was published at the time of the movie's release; such tie-ins were common back then. It looked interesting to me if for no other reason than I was a huge hockey fan and also an avid reader who couldn't get enough of my favorite subject.

But this was unlike any other hockey book I had ever read. The vivid descriptions of the Charlestown Chiefs and of the world they inhabited were accompanied by every swear word you could imagine. Between the bloody brawls and the two sex scenes — one more than the film showed — it was a real eye-opener for a pre-pubescent boy. There was nothing in *A Boy at the Leafs' Camp* that ever suggested hockey, great as it was, could be like *this*.

I consider the book to have been a gift from my older brother Randy, although it wasn't so much a gift as it was a realization on his part that he just wasn't going to get it back once I got my grubby little hands on it. He had bought it after seeing the film in Honolulu, Hawaii, of all places, while vacationing there with our parents in the spring of 1977. And so it is he who deserves the credit for indirectly sparking my first interest in *Slap Shot*. Thanks, Jake.

I wish I could cite every individual who made an impact on this book. The majority of people with whom I spoke are

Acknowledgments

quoted by name in these pages. There are others whose contributions will not be evident in the final cut, but that certainly is no reflection on what they meant to this process. Many thanks to everyone for their time, their patience and their love for this film.

Certain people must be mentioned for going above and beyond. John Hill and Andrew Horton never tired of my seemingly endless questions about George Roy Hill and his work, and their insight into his life and work is much appreciated. Thanks to Reg and Barb Kent for the place to stay in Johnstown, as well as for the great conversations. While I was in California, Jennifer Warren, Stephen Mendillo and Bob Wunsch and their respective spouses also very graciously welcomed me into their homes and gave me all the time I needed. Bob Crawford took me on a wonderful tour of the Warner Brothers lot in Burbank, CA and bought me lunch in the famous studio commissary while we chatted. Speaking of food, it was fun to be introduced to the culinary delights of In-N-Out Burger as I talked and hung out with Ken Blake. I also want to thank Jenny Romero and the rest of the staff at the Margaret Herrick Library in Beverly Hills for their invaluable assistance.

My friends Gare Joyce, Terry Koshan and John Richardson saw early the merit in this project and deserve thanks for their encouragement. Damien Cox not only recognized the value in it, he took it to his editor at John Wiley & Sons, and I doubt I can ever fully repay him that kindness.

That editor, Karen Milner, has been incredibly supportive throughout this process. She took a flyer on a writer and a proposal, both of which must have seemed like a good idea at the time, and I'm eternally grateful that she hung in there. I hope the finished product affirms her initial thoughts.

Acknowledgments

Production editor Pauline Ricablanca, publicity manager Erin Kelly and marketing manager Robin Dutta-Roy have all shown a great deal of enthusiasm for this project. I am very thankful, and very fortunate, to be able to work with such a solid team.

My team includes my literary agent, Shari Wenk, who realized right away that this was a labor of love that deserved to see the light of day, and then worked hard to help make it happen. It's been a marvelous experience.

Last but certainly not least, many thanks are owed to the people who brought *Slap Shot* to life — the cast, the crew, the executives, the people of Johnstown, PA — and to those who keep the film alive today. I can say in all honesty and sincerity that you've really captured the spirit of the thing; my hope is that this book will do the same.

Jonathon Jackson
April 2010

Index

Index

Index

Index

Index

Index

Index

Index